Culture Moves

Culture Moves

IDEAS, ACTIVISM, AND CHANGING VALUES

Thomas R. Rochon

PRINCETON UNIVERSITY PRESS

PRINCETON, NEW JERSEY

Copyright © 1998 by Princeton University Press
Published by Princeton University Press, 41 William Street,
Princeton, New Jersey 08540
In the United Kingdom: Princeton University Press, Chichester, West Sussex

Library of Congress Cataloging-in-Publication Data

Rochon, Thomas R., 1952–
Culture moves : ideas, activism, and changing
values / Thomas R. Rochon.
p.   cm.
Includes bibliographical references and index.
1. Culture.   2. Social change.   3. Social values.
4. Social movements.   I. Title.
HM101.R56   1998   306—dc21   97-27020

ISBN 0-691-01157-5 (cl : alk. paper)

This book has been composed in Times Roman

Princeton University Press books are printed on acid-free paper
and meet the guidelines for permanence and durability of the
Committee on Production Guidelines for Book Longevity of the
Council on Library Resources

http://pup.princeton.edu

Printed in the United States of America

1 3 5 7 9 10 8 6 4 2

For Lorraine, Deb, Lynn, and Tim

Super siblings, one and all

CONTENTS

FIGURES

TABLES

PREFACE

We're not sure where we *want* to be. And we're not sure
where we're *going* to be. But we sure are a
long way from where we *were*!
—Martin Luther King, Jr.

THIS IS a book whose moment of origin can be identified with precision.
While rummaging around in an antique store a few years ago, I came across
a copy of *Life* magazine from the week of my birth. Despite an initial feeling
of umbrage that something my age could be labeled "antique," it was striking how ancient the America portrayed in *Life* in July 1952 actually seemed.
Among the feature articles was one titled "Reds Kidnap Enemy in West
Berlin," a reminder of the cold war fear and hatred that are now a fading
memory. Another article previewed a movie about a justice of the peace who
inadvertently "married" five couples one week before his appointment went
into effect. Two years later the couples were informed that they were not
legally married and each was presented with the opportunity to reaffirm or
repudiate their wedding vows. Since divorce and cohabitation outside of
marriage were both taboo subjects in Hollywood in the 1950s, this plot de-
vice was necessary to make possible an exploration of the circumstances
under which couples might choose not to stay married after two years together.

The advertisements in *Life* in 1952 appear even more antiquated to the
contemporary eye. Ads for cigarettes are prominent, with celebrity and ath-
lete endorsements. We learn on the back cover that more doctors smoke
Camels than any other brand. In consumer goods ranging from automobiles
to appliances the message is that bigger is better, and the trait of efficiency is
never mentioned as a selling point.

Still more remarkable than what was portrayed in this magazine is what
was *not* portrayed: of the over three hundred people depicted in this issue of
Life, only one was African American (Gordon Parks, a staff photographer),
and none was Asian American or Hispanic. The all-white America portrayed
in the pages of *Life* extended to photographs of military units in ads meant to
encourage enlistments, group shots of people on golf courses, and the Du-
Pont Company's sesquicentennial party for employees.[1]

[1] For a more systematic analysis of trends in the portrayal of African Americans in magazine
advertisements, see Humphrey and Schuman 1984.

The ultimate impression from reading these pages is of a United States that is white, middle class, and suburban, with an unlimited potential for increasing wealth, comfortable in the knowledge that it is without peer among nations. It is a Norman Rockwell image of America, but an image that is represented as reality rather than as a kitsch or nostalgic look at a largely fictional past.

Our image of America today is not the same as it was in 1952. We now have a different image of what we are as a country and a different image of what we ought to be. Some of the changes in our preoccupations are a direct response to historical events such as the collapse of communism, or to increased knowledge of the adverse health consequences of smoking. But much of the change is strictly a conceptual reevaluation of an unchanging reality. We are far more aware today of being a multiracial and multicultural society, and of the limits of the melting pot image that long dominated our perception of the American immigrant experience. Americans have learned to discuss openly the strains within marriages that lead to divorce. Energy efficiency has come to play a role in the purchase of most consumer durables, even though energy costs now take a far smaller portion of the household budget than they did in 1952.

It does not go too far to say that the United States is no longer the same country it was in 1952. The differences lie in our perception of reality as much as they do in the reality itself. Despite enormous objective gains during the past two generations in social equality and civil rights for a variety of minority groups, we are subjectively more conscious of the flaws in the American dream of equal freedom and opportunities. Despite historically unparalleled opportunities for women to participate in economic and political life, our awareness of limits to gender-blind equality is heightened rather than blunted. Despite equally impressive gains in the range of technologies available to us, we are subjectively more conscious of the ethical and environmental dilemmas of a high-technology society. American culture has developed a language for talking about these and other problems, and the policy implications of these concerns are among the most important issues being debated today.

When we think about current political issues such as abortion, affirmative action, endangered species, and toxic wastes, we are likely to be struck by the political stalemate that often prolongs such issues without any clear resolution. Yet that sense of stasis conceals the fact that these are all issues of recent vintage. Nearly all educated people today have an awareness of the relationship between human activity and the natural environment that employs ideas familiar only to biologists forty years ago. Although the goal of completely erasing distinctive gender roles is contentious, no one today assumes without reflection that a woman's place is with her family, as was usually the case a generation ago. Issues of equity between majority and minority groups now play a major role in public and private decision making. In 1952, however, America was still one year away from the path-breaking Baton Rouge bus boycott, two years from the Supreme Court decision in *Brown v. Board of Education*, and twelve years from the 1964 Civil Rights Act. It appeared then that segregation and exclusion would be the enduring form of American race relations. Contemporary debates about affirmative action may challenge some civil rights era legislation, but they also underscore the extent to which the language of integration and equal opportunity has become the only culturally acceptable language for discussing race relations.

These are all instances of cultural change, changes that are individually and collectively so fundamental as to constitute a remaking of American society in the span of a single generation. The specific changes that have occurred, particularly the reformation of race relations and the rise of feminism and environmentalism, are familiar to all of us. This book is a probe into the origins of these cultural changes, and the process by which new cultural values are diffused into the society. We will examine instances of cultural change drawn from the last 150 years of American history in order to develop a better understanding of the factors that aid the development of new value perspectives, that encourage broad social and political movements to champion these new ideas, and that ultimately lead to a reorientation of culture.

The investigation is divided into three sections. In the first section we will develop a picture of the process of cultural change. Chapter 1 will examine the nature of cultural change and its significance in producing fundamental shifts in public policy and everyday behavior. Chapter 2 will define the role of critical communities and movements in creating and spreading new cultural perspectives. In chapter 3 we will distinguish three variations on the process of cultural change and examine in some detail one instance of each type. The first three chapters provide an overview of how cultural values come to be transformed and of the role of critical communities and movements as agents of that transformation.

The second section of the book develops a microlevel theory to account for the question of why individuals devote themselves to movements for social and political change. In order to mobilize activists for collective purposes, movements must rely on a strong sense of group solidarity. And in order to turn mobilized activists into effective agents of change, movements must imbue them with a high degree of political skill and engagement. There can be no cultural change without group solidarity and political engagement; these are the subjects of chapters 4 and 5 respectively.

The third section of the book moves to the macrolevel of analysis. Chapter 6 examines structural changes in American society over the past fifty years that have made it increasingly easy for critical communities to develop and for movements to organize. Chapter 7 shows that both the enduring principles of the American political system and recent changes within that system make possible the ready translation of new public concerns into altered governmental policies.

Our current state of knowledge about social and political movements is on a par with our understanding of earthquakes. Both are sudden events, variable in size but potentially massive, and predictable only in the loose sense that we can identify the conditions that make an upheaval highly probable at some unspecified future date. One goal of this book is to bring the study of movements up to speed with the study of earthquakes by improving our understanding of outcomes. The effects of an earthquake are immediately obvious, but movement impacts remain in many cases obscure and controversial. Particularly when movements are evaluated by their ability to change political laws and institutions, they often appear to have created a great deal of noise with a very small result. By shifting our gaze from changes in the law to changes in cultures, the impact of movement activity snaps into focus. Rather than the weak track record of most movement organizations in rewriting laws, we see instead their uniquely powerful ability to mobilize activists and create controversy about ideas that were once consensus values in the culture. The final chapter of this book explores the link between movements and cultural change, drawing conclusions about movements and about the process of cultural change itself. The final chapter also connects this theory of cultural change to theories of agenda setting in the policy process.

Acknowledgments

Writing this book has caused me to delve into an unusually eclectic range of scholarly work. I have relied heavily on the research and data collections of others, and in so doing I have been struck by the range and quality of contemporary scholarship on American politics and society. To those scholars who have left their datasets in public archives, particularly the Interuniversity Consortium for Political and Social Research (ICPSR), I owe a special debt of gratitude: Donald Matthews and James Prothro for their "Negro Political Participation Study"; M. Kent Jennings and Richard Niemi for their three-wave Youth-Parent Socialization Study; William Gamson for his survey of challenging groups; and Warren Miller and the team of scholars behind the series of American National Election Studies. To these social scientists and to all those whose names appear in small print in the footnotes I offer my deepest respect and appreciation.

I have also had in the past few years a large number of fascinating conversations with scholars from a variety of disciplines on the subject of movements, critical communities, and cultural change. For their insightful suggestions and commentaries on particular chapters or sections of the book, I thank particularly Delwin Brown, Harry Eckstein, Susan Imbarrato, Barbette Knight, David Meyer, and Bruce Snyder. Russell Dalton, John Geer, Daniel Press, Robert Putnam, and Sidney Tarrow read entire drafts with the blend of criticism and encouragement that you only get from a scholar-friend. An anonymous reviewer of the manuscript for Princeton University Press opened my eyes to a number of important issues and set a standard for constructive criticism. Kim Lane Scheppele brought fresh insights and solutions to knotty organizational problems in the manuscript at a late stage, helped me overcome the inertia needed to drag the project across the finish line, and gave me an improved title to boot. None of this advice would have helped me had I not also enjoyed the skilled research assistance of Jason Abbott, Mimi Constantinou, Chris Hoene, Dietlind Stolle, and Stephen Wood, all of whom sometimes knew what I was looking for better than I did.

Academics are fortunate in the guildlike system that provides intellectual homes on the road, wherever you might happen to be. Many of the ideas here were first put to paper during a year spent on a teaching Fulbright at the Kobe University School of Law, while I was musing on the institutional features that encourage movements and cultural change in the United States but discourage them in Japan. I am particularly grateful to Professor Ichiro Miyake for inviting me to Kobe in 1992–1993 and for allowing me to present my preliminary ideas and findings at a conference there. A first draft of this book was completed during a five-month term as Visiting Fellow in the Board of Environmental Studies at the University of California Santa Cruz. The significance of critical communities for the process of cultural change became apparent to me while admiring the work of the interdisciplinary Board of Environmental Studies. I owe an enormous debt of gratitude particularly to Daniel Press for arranging that visit, for his unflagging enthusiasm about the project, for introducing me to the scones at the College Eight Café, and for allowing me to be honorary *tonton* to his daughter Isobel. I am also grateful to the John Randolph and Dora Haynes Foundation, whose funding of a related project on successive generations of environmentalist thought enabled me to pull together many of the environmental examples in this book.

In between the genesis in Kobe and the final push in Santa Cruz was a long middle period of writing and revising during which I relied constantly on the critiques and encouragement of John Geer. Geer was a pit bull during two long weekends in his home, at which we took turns shredding each other's work-in-progress. John's book came out before mine, a fact I can only attribute to his having been a more thorough and critical reader than I was. I owe John a major debt of gratitude, dwarfed only by my debt to Marie, Megan, and James Geer for their willingness to have two political scientists in the house at the same time.

I dedicate this book to my brothers and sisters, who grew up with me in an America different from the one we know today. Our testament to the significance of cultural change is that we are all living lives that would have been highly unusual in our parents' generation. The ties of family affection between us have been the one constant on which we can rely.

DATA SOURCES

Data used in this book, when not derived from content analyses generated by the author, come from one of the following five sources:

American National Election Study series. Use is made here of the surveys from presidential election years between 1952 and 1992. These data are made available through the Interuniversity Consortium for Political and Social Research.

Gallup poll data. These data are available through a variety of publications by the Gallup Poll, including most prominently the annual volume titled *The Gallup Poll—Public Opinion* (Wilmington, DE: Scholarly Resources).

Gamson data on challenging groups. These data were collected by William Gamson. Information about this dataset, and the data themselves, are published in Appendixes B through E in Gamson (1990).

Negro Political Participation Study, 1961–1962. Donald Matthews and James Prothro are the principal investigators for this study. These data are made available through the Interuniversity Consortium for Political and Social Research (ICPSR #7255).

Youth-Parent Socialization Study. M. Kent Jennings and Richard Niemi are the principal investigators for this study. These data are made available through the Interuniversity Consortium for Political and Social Research (ICPSR #9553).

PART ONE

Theoretical Perspective

Chapter 1

ADAPTATION IN HUMAN COMMUNITIES

A state without the means of some change is without the
means of its conservation.
—Edmund Burke, *Reflections on the
Revolution in France*

One who is late to reform will be punished by history.
—Mikhail Gorbachev, at the fortieth and final anniversary
celebration of the German Democratic Republic,
October 1989

THERE ARE times in the life of any human community when change is the
only course of action that will permit continuity. Abraham Lincoln said that
a house divided against itself cannot stand. Karl Marx wrote of the class
contradictions that would bring down capitalism. Betty Friedan referred to
"the problem with no name" that made life unbearable for the American
housewife. Authors of *The Limits to Growth* wrote of the "overshoot and
crash" pattern that would result from continued resource depletion. Each of
these perspectives is an assertion that the existing social and political order
must at times be adapted, if it is not to be overthrown. We must change in
order to survive. Edmund Burke (the conservative's conservative) and Mikhail Gorbachev (the reforming Communist) agree that if you try to preserve
everything, you end by saving nothing.

Consider the condition of race relations in 1950. The United States of
America, the world's first mass democracy and the recently anointed leader
of the free world, had a domestic social order that placed its African-de-
scended citizens in a marginalized social, economic, and political status not
readily distinguishable from the conditions of serfdom in medieval Europe.
Nonwhite citizens averaged three years less education than whites.[1] Among
those under thirty the gap was closer to four years, and even these figures do
not take into account differences in expenditure and quality found between
schools for white children and schools for black children. Average income

[1] Statistics on the effects of segregation and environmental exploitation presented in the next
pages are from the *Historical Statistics of the United States: Colonial Times to 1970* (Washington, DC: U.S. Department of Commerce, Bureau of the Census, 1975), except where other
sources are noted in the text.

among nonwhites in the labor force was 50 percent that of whites. Inequality pervaded every sector of the economy: while 22 percent of white farmers were tenants rather than owners of their land, this was true of 64 percent of nonwhite farmers. Whites lived to the age of sixty-nine, on average; nonwhites did not quite live to the age of sixty-one. There were two nations in America: one was white and the other was not.

Already in 1950 a careful observer would have noted a number of strains in this system of race relations. African Americans were moving to cities in the north and west, escaping rural poverty with factory jobs and slowly increasing the number of black professionals trained as doctors, lawyers, and ministers. These trends contributed to a growing demand for racial equality.

The price of racial discrimination to American society was also growing. The postwar wave of industrialization and the shift toward a service economy required a skilled labor force that could little afford to exclude a large segment of the population. Regional politicians could still get elected by playing the race card, but any leader with national aspirations was aware of the power that would come from attracting black voters if it could be done without alienating other supporters. And, as the number of independent third world states began to mushroom, American diplomats realized that their influence was hobbled by the state of race relations back home.

The end of Jim Crow was morally desirable, it was ever more strongly demanded, it was economically functional, it was strategic good sense for political parties in competition for black voters, and it would assist the American democracy in its global competition against Soviet socialism. Yet, racial segregation and exclusion were woven throughout the social and political fabric of the nation. Efforts to enact effective civil rights bills went nowhere in the Congresses that gathered during the 1950s (Sundquist 1968: 221–286). To many observers at the time, change seemed both necessary and impossible.

Much the same story could be told with respect to environmental protection in the year 1965. Over the previous twenty years, the population of the United States had increased by 46 percent and the per capita standard of living had grown by 85 percent. In unprecedented numbers and with unprecedented affluence, Americans were consuming resources as never before. But the environmental costs of intensified production can be severe. In 1910 farmers used 6 short tons of fertilizer per 1,000 cultivated acres. In 1965 the use of fertilizers was up to 29 short tons per 1,000 acres. Pesticide production grew sixfold, from 50,000 tons to 300,000 tons, between 1945 and 1960 (Bosso 1987: 63). Although some air pollutants such as soot and smoke appeared to be under control, the period 1940 to 1970 saw an increase of over 60 percent in the amount of volatile organic compounds (one of the principle components of ozone) and sulfur oxides released into the air. In that same period, nitrogen oxide levels in the atmosphere nearly tripled

(Bryner 1993: 47–61). These trends are disturbing enough, but to a biologist the ultimate indicator of environmental health is the maintenance of biological diversity. The twentieth century has seen a dramatically increasing tempo of extinctions, recently estimated at between forty and one hundred species per day (Owen and Chiras 1995: 340).

The warning signs of unsustainability in the exploitation of resources and the destruction of natural habitats were unmistakable to anyone who cared to look in 1965. The outlines of what needed to be done were becoming known, but it was far from clear whether the necessary steps in environmental protection and restoration could be taken. An ecologist surveying in 1965 the heedless and even joyful destruction of the environment by the impressive American economic growth machine would be forgiven for concluding that "You can't get there from here."

In short, there are times when human communities face the need to adapt, and to do so quickly. But adaptation does not occur automatically just because it is needed. The institutions of human society are constructed in the first instance for continuity. As Fernand Braudel put it, a cultural mentality is a "prison de longue durée" (cited in Tarrow 1992: 179). Families and schools pass on cultural values between generations. Social and economic institutions teach entering members appropriate roles and then enforce them. Bureaucracies generate standardized rules and then apply them. Politicians seek the stance of the median voter and cluster tightly around that position. Negotiations between legislative committees, regulatory agencies, and interest groups are structured in policy networks that typically remain undisturbed for long periods of time.

This is not only a tolerable state of affairs but a necessary one, for routinization is an essential element of any highly organized social system. And yet, the more extensive the interdependencies among humans become, the more substantial the need to maintain adaptive capabilities. In order to prosper, in order even to survive, we must constantly remake our society by refashioning the roles and behaviors of the people who compose it.

When we think of the sources of adaptation in human communities, we are likely to think in the first instance of government. In doing so, we view politics as the locus of what Karl Deutsch (1963) has called the steering capacity of society. Political change is the result of a constant process of learning, and policies evolve in response to a continual monitoring of social conditions and demands.

Political processes can indeed identify the need for change, translate these needs into new policies, and enforce compliance with those policies. Certainly in the examples of race and the environment, looming crises led to bursts of legislation. Modern civil rights legislation made its tentative beginnings in 1957 and culminated with the Civil Rights Acts of 1964 and 1965. Environmental laws in the late 1950s and the early 1960s mandated study of the problems of air and water pollution, leading to the flood of legislation that began with the National Environmental Policy Act of 1969–1970. In both the civil rights and environmental areas, new governmental agencies were created. These extensions of the bureaucracy were given broad mandates involving significant additions to governmental power.

For example, the Environmental Protection Agency (EPA) is among the youngest of governmental regulatory agencies, having commenced operations in 1972. Today it employs the greatest number of lawyers of any regulatory agency, whose job is to write and enforce the largest single body of federal regulation. Twenty years after the inception of the EPA the United States spent 2.4 percent of its GDP, $140 billion, on environmental protection and cleanup (Hahn 1994). The translation of environmental concern into a massive body of regulation shows that change in cultural values can effectively reshape political institutions and the allocation of resources.

These departures in political organization and activity are instances of what Baumgartner and Jones (1993) have identified as punctuated equilibrium in policy making: periodic bursts of rapid change when all previous bets are off, when authority is taken from some and given to others, when policy networks are broken up and reconstituted with new participants, when policy making comes to be based on a new set of premises and purposes.

The proximate conditions of political innovation have come to be increasingly understood. Based on a wide variety of case studies, Kingdon (1984), Polsby (1984), and Baumgartner and Jones (1993) identify circumstances in which innovations reach the political agenda. These involve new currents of thought within communities of policy experts, political leaders looking for new issues, and shifting patterns of media attention. Because of the stickiness of institutional routines, policy adaptation often proceeds only by changing the participants in the process. This can occur by importing existing solutions to fit new problems (Kingdon 1984), by bringing in new experts with different ideas (Polsby 1984), by expanding the types of interest groups involved in policy consultation (Walker 1991), or by shifting the political jurisdictions within which a policy issue is handled (Baumgartner and Jones 1993). Incremental change is the norm, but the political process has means of circumventing the normal barriers to rapid adaptation.

These understandings of the potential for innovation within political institutions leave untouched the question of where the impulse for rapid change comes from. All of the scholars just cited refer to the incentives for innovation built into a political system that features regularly scheduled electoral contests between rival leaders. But this answer begs the question of when and why voters will provide politicians with the incentive to make new issues central to their campaigns. Stokes (1992) has pointed out that electoral campaigns are conducted in terms of valence (consensus) issues whenever possible. And Geer (1996) has observed that leaders seeking an issue to

differentiate themselves from rivals will publicly back major policy innovation only if they are persuaded that the public is prepared to support the new
initiative. In other words, a burst of political innovation to address some
basic issue will occur only if there are clear signals from the electorate
demanding those changes.

The puzzle of political innovation, then, is to understand the root impulse
that sets into motion the adaptive potential of the political system. In their
insightful account of innovation in policy agendas, Baumgartner and Jones
(1993: 237) recognize that

> there are powerful forces of change that sweep through the entire system. These
> are not controlled or created by any single group or individual, but are the result
> of multiple interactions among groups seeking to propose new understandings of
> issues.
>
> . . . Leaders can influence the ways in which the broad tides of politics are
> channeled, but they cannot reverse the tides themselves.

The same imagery of irresistible forces is often used in connection with
social change as well as political change. Four black college students sat in
at a segregated lunch counter in Greensboro, North Carolina, in February
1960. Their protest spread quickly and permutated to such forms as "sleep-
ins" in the lobbies of segregated motels, "wade-ins" at restricted beaches,
and "kneel-ins" at segregated churches. By the time the protest wave sub-
sided in the spring of 1961, more than 3,500 young people had been arrested
during sit-ins held in seventy-five towns and cities across the South and in
the border states (Fishman and Solomon 1970: 144). Segregationist practices
that in January 1960 appeared to be firmly entrenched were being abandoned
six months later. Desegregation occurred first in a trickle of public facilities
in twenty-seven Southern cities and counties, and then in a flood of chain
store lunch counters across the South (Oppenheimer 1989: 179).

Both the audacity of the sit-ins and—paradoxically—the sense they created of being an irresistible force for change are best conveyed by the then
president of North Carolina A&T, whose students began the sit-in movement. Looking back on the events, Dr. Warmoth Gibbs felt a sense of relief
at his passive response to the sit-in demonstrations, of which he did not
personally approve. "I could just as easily have done something foolish. I
could have tried to stop it. I could also have jumped in front of an oncoming
freight train with about the same result" (cited in James 1993: 126).

This book is a study of irreversible tides and oncoming freight trains.
What causes tidal forces to sweep periodically through the political system,
disrupting long-standing policy networks and widely accepted understandings of policy issues? What are the circumstances that enable public demands for reform to gain the momentum of a runaway freight train?

The one-word explanation for these events is "crisis." Public recognition of a crisis generates demand for a political response; it represents an opportunity for bureaucratic agencies and policy advocates to put forward their cherished proposals. Crisis divides old allies and makes possible new coalitions. For political leaders, crisis loosens the normal constraints on action by creating expectations of the kind of leadership that is normally hemmed in by institutional routines.

Crisis is the one word answer, but crisis is not an adequate answer. Crises are not simply exogenous events, and sometimes they are not events at all. Crises are rooted in interpretations of events, imputations of causality that carry with them claims that the events will be recurrent. The breakup of an oil tanker off some pristine coastline is a disaster. The disaster becomes a crisis only when connected to the idea that oil dependence, ship construction, the choice of sea lanes, and the training of crews will lead to repeated spills. Crises are a matter of interpretation. As Nelson Polsby (1984: 168) has succinctly stated, crises are a social product.

In pointing to crises as the source of "irreversible tides of political change," we are simply pushing our questions one step back. If we are to understand the primitive energy that moves the political process into the mode of innovation, we must know how crises come about. Specifically, we must understand where the ideas and interpretations that turn disasters into crises come from. We must understand how some interpretations rather than others come to be the center of widespread public attention and debate. We must know something about the circumstances under which citizens mobilize behind demands that the crisis be resolved. Finally, we must understand how political institutions are prodded to respond to new demands, translating the public perception of crisis into a set of proposals for policy reform.

This book will attempt to answer these questions. We will have occasion to consider such diverse issues as how claims of crisis get formulated and publicized, why people become involved in movements for change, and what makes powerful social and political institutions receptive to new ideas and demands. Fortunately, many of these issues converge on a single overarching question: How do cultural values change? Under what circumstances do people come to adopt a new set of beliefs and expectations with regard to some topic? If we can trace the origins and spread of new ideas that create or reshape public concerns, then we will have understood the source of the tidal waves that remade American social and political life on so many fronts in the second half of the twentieth century.

The argument of this book, in a nutshell, is that political and social transformation both occur in response to rapid cultural change. The creation of new values begins with the generation of new ideas or perspectives among small groups of critical thinkers: people whose experiences, reading, and interaction with each other help them to develop a set of cultural values that is out of step with the larger society. The dissemination of those values occurs through social and political movements in which the critical thinkers may participate, but whose success is determined to a far greater degree by the course of collective action in support of the new values. Together, critical communities and movements are sometimes able to initiate changes in cultural values that represent a truly original break from past ways of thinking about a subject.

Civil rights offers a clear illustration of the process. The civil rights movement is today remembered primarily as a dramatic series of protests against segregation linked to a leader whose birth is now celebrated as a national holiday. But if we think of the outcome of the movement as having ended racial segregation, we are getting at best only half of the story. The process of cultural change involves a change of mentalities as well as a change of laws. Prior to the civil rights movement, the language of minority group rights was not part of the vocabulary of politics. The cultural impact of the civil rights movement was to foster widespread acceptance of a language of rights that has since been applied (with varying success) to other ethnic minorities, to women, to gays, to people with handicaps, to endangered species, and to animals in research laboratories. The spread of a group rights discourse, for all the political controversy connected to it, is testimony to the rapidity of changing values. These were not matters of public debate at the end of World War II. They are central and highly contested matters of public debate at the end of the twentieth century.

In short, America today is fundamentally different from America fifty years ago, and the root of that difference lies in changed cultural values. It is the goal of this book to offer some ideas on how and why this extraordinary burst of cultural change has come to pass. For that reason, the best place to begin is with an examination of the nature of cultural values themselves.

CULTURAL VALUES

Culture consists of the linked stock of ideas that define a set of commonsense beliefs about what is right, what is natural, what works. These commonsense beliefs are not universal, but are instead typically bounded by time as well as by space. Today's orthodoxy may be the heterodoxy of yesterday and tomorrow. Although cultural change is not usually perceptible from day to day, when we look over a longer time span it becomes apparent that even the most fundamental assumptions about morality and the standards by which quality of life should be evaluated are subject to change. Anthony Downs (1972: 45) offers a vivid illustration of the extent of cultural change with his observation that "One hundred years ago, white Americans were eliminating whole Indian tribes without a qualm. Today, many serious-minded citizens seek to make important issues out of the potential disappearance of the whooping crane, the timber wolf, and other exotic creatures."

How does a society move from indifference about the fate of human beings to concern about the timber wolf? How did child labor, poverty among the elderly, disenfranchisement of women, and racial segregation undergo a transformation from conditions viewed as natural or inevitable to being considered tragedies that society could and should remedy? How has the current of individualism in American culture come to be modified by a pervasive concern for group rights, as manifested in the civil rights movement, the women's movement, the gay rights movement, and others?

Much cultural change occurs during explosive upheavals, followed by a lengthier period in which new concepts are diffused through the society and assimilated into patterns of individual and institutional behavior. Karl-Werner Brand (1990) cites periods of "general cultural crisis," such as the 1830s, the end of the nineteenth century, and the 1960s. These are times of widespread rejection of mainstream culture and experimentation with alternative values and ways of living. Aristide Zolberg refers to "moments of madness," those occasions when people come together and demand a transformation of society. Such change occurs in a "torrent of words [involving] a sort of intensive learning experience whereby new ideas, formulated originally in coteries, sects, etc., emerge as widely shared beliefs among much larger publics" (Zolberg 1972: 206).

Brand and Zolberg each evoke an image of explosive rapidity in cultural change. In fact, cultural change seems to occur at two speeds, slow and fast, with relatively little in between. Rapid cultural change occurs during periods of social unrest and protest. Sidney Tarrow (1995: 94) has developed the concept of protest cycles as periods that "produce new or transformed symbols, frames of meaning and ideologies that justify and dignify collective action." These cycles of protest lead to the development of new cultural symbols, give prominence to new issues, and mobilize new social groups. They are also the occasion for innovation of new forms of protest.

The phases of rapid and slow change are both illustrated in figure 1-1, using the cases of support for Prohibition and willingness to vote for a woman as president of the United States. The "normal" condition of slow cultural change is found in support for Prohibition, which has ebbed gently away since the mid 1930s ($b = -.44$). Similarly, readiness to vote for a qualified woman for president increased at a gradual rate for most of the period from the mid 1930s to 1970 ($b = .76$).[2]

Gradual changes in beliefs may be modeled as the product of Bayesian updating and generational replacement. For Bayesians, the evolution of

---

[2] Ferree (1974) points out that responses to the question of whether one would be willing to vote for a qualified woman for president cannot be taken as a literal statement of voting intentions. It is instead a measure of willingness to admit prejudice (generally to a female interviewer). This makes the question valuable as a measure of cultural change precisely because it taps the strength of the cultural norm that any (native-born) citizen who is qualified can become president.

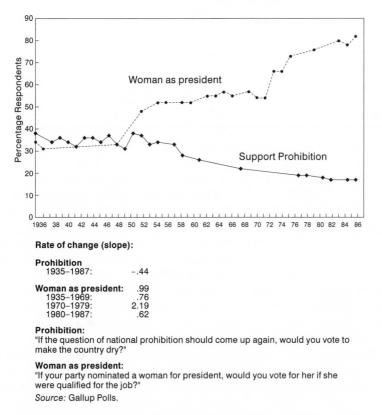

Rate of change (slope):

Prohibition
1935–1987:   −.44

Woman as president: .99
1935–1969:   .76
1970–1979:   2.19
1980–1987:   .62

Prohibition:
"If the question of national prohibition should come up again, would you vote to make the country dry?"

Woman as president:
"If your party nominated a woman for president, would you vote for her if she were qualified for the job?"
Source: Gallup Polls.

Figure 1-1   Rates of change in support of Prohibition and for a woman as president, 1935–1987

values occurs with the accumulation of experience or exposure to new ideas. This is an orderly process of cultural change, marked by slow but consistent adaptation. As Denzau and North (1994: 22) point out, "Bayesian learners are never surprised, or forced within the updating process to completely change the dimensions of the model space." The way in which the problem is viewed remains consistent; one simply evolves in a particular direction by adding new information to the existing base of experience.

Gradual change may also be accounted for by generational replacement of the population.[3] Younger people are most likely to feel favorably toward the idea of a woman as president, so generational turnover has led to a gradual increase in this attitude. Because Prohibition sentiment is found most often

[3] Technically, one must add a provision for partial replacement of people sharing the disappearing value, analogous to the transmission of a recessive gene. Thus, the children of parents who support Prohibition may also support laws against alcohol use, but intergenerational transmission of this value is sufficiently imperfect that Prohibitionists are unable fully to replace themselves in the population.

among older people and those living in rural areas, generational turnover and continuing urbanization of the population have contributed to its gradual decline. These demographic relationships have remained almost perfectly constant since the 1930s, as we would expect in a process of evolutionary change stemming from Bayesian updating and population replacement.

There is a second, more rapid, and potentially discontinuous form of learning that appears at times to substitute for the gradual inclines of Bayesian process. During rapid changes in cultural values the very categories of observation are called into question. Uncertainty about relevant values replaces the stability of assumptions that Denzau and North (1994) call "shared mental models." Accumulated experience is instead thrown overboard along with the whole Bayesian approach, as large numbers of people are induced to rethink the basis of their earlier opinions on a subject. Rapid change is, in other words, not just an accelerated version of gradual change. Rapid cultural change relies uniquely on large-scale conversions to a new way of thinking about a subject. As a result, rapid change affects everybody because it alters the very standards of cultural evaluation. As Mayer (1992: 300) concludes in his study of rapid changes in public opinion, "when major shifts in public opinion have occurred, they have not been confined to a single region or educational class or gender. . . . Such changes tend, instead, to reverberate through the entire society."

Figure 1-1 shows two periods of rapid, non-Bayesian change in support for a woman as president. In both periods, prior assumptions about the public roles of women were being questioned. The first upward lurch in support for a woman as president occurred just after World War II, during which women's involvement in the war effort was widely accepted.[4] The second period of rapid change in support for a woman as president occurred from 1970 to 1980 ($b = 2.19$). By the time this period of change came to a close in 1980, there had been a 25 percent increase in popular support for a woman president—exactly equal to the total growth of support during the prior thirty-five-year history of measuring that attitude.

Generational turnover is too gradual to explain periods of rapid change. During the 1970s people in all age cohorts changed their attitudes toward the idea of voting for a qualified woman as president. Mayer (1992: 152) found that 85 percent of the 25-point change in support for a woman as president was due to intracohort conversion rather than population replacement. Such conversions, on a large scale and predominantly in one direction, are among the phenomena that must be explained by any theory of cultural adaptation.

A strictly evolutionary theory, whereby cultural principles are altered incrementally through Bayesian updating and population turnover, cannot ac-

---

[4] There are not enough observation points in this period to make a reliable calculation of the rate of change for the 1940s.

count for rapid change of this kind. There must instead be active agents of cultural change somewhere in the social environment. Figure 1-1 tells us that these change agents fluctuate in intensity over time. They also affect some portions of the population more strongly than others. Prior to 1970, men were slightly more supportive of the idea of voting for a woman for president. Though the rate of change in support among men accelerated during the 1970s, women changed even more quickly, so that by 1972 women were more supportive than men of a woman for president. Whatever caused this rapid change to occur in the 1970s, it was a force that affected men and women both, but that affected women most strongly.

What are these agents of cultural change? The sources of cultural change most commonly identified are alterations in social or economic conditions, and in technological capabilities. Cultures change in response to urbanization, increasing levels of wealth, and exposure to mass media. The growth of material security has had a particularly important impact on culture over the past half century. As Ronald Inglehart has pointed out, the spread of affluence has led to a revised political agenda in which the quality of life has become more prominent and securing material welfare less so. These changes have altered the very structure of political debate. Inglehart (1990: 46–47) observes that "the core meaning of 'Left' is no longer simply state ownership of the means of production and related issues focusing on social class conflict. Increasingly, it refers to a cluster of issues concerning the quality of the physical and social environment, the role of women, of nuclear power and nuclear weapons."

It is certainly the case that changes in the physical environment have an impact on behavioral constraints, resulting in the reformulation of culture. One cannot conceive of working-class consciousness, an AFL-CIO, or a National Labor Relations Board in an agrarian society. As E. P. Thompson (1967: 97) put the matter, "there is no such thing as economic growth which is not, at the same time, growth or change of a culture."

But the causal link between material conditions and cultural beliefs is not fully specified. Economic or technological changes have no inherent meaning for values; they cannot be the direct agents of cultural change. Karl Marx is overly deterministic with his claim that "it is not the consciousness of men that determines their being, but, on the contrary, their social being that determines their consciousness."[5] One's "social being" is, according to Marx, defined by class position. And yet, differences between (for example) the United States, Germany, Italy, and Japan in working-class consciousness, the organization of labor, and the process by which labor demands are negotiated with employers cannot be laid to material differences in their lives. There are other agents of cultural formation and change at work in each of these settings.

---

[5] "Preface to a Contribution to the Critique of Political Economy," cited in Tucker 1978: 4.

Much the same point could be made of the cultural changes that have resulted from the development of postindustrial society. That the economic conditions of advanced industrial societies have led to a change in culture is incontestable. But these economic changes need not have generated the precise forms of cultural change that actually emerged. It takes no great stretch of the imagination to picture a postmaterialist value system that embraces rather than rejects nuclear energy as a substitute for the burning of fossil fuels. It is easy enough to picture a postmaterialist opposition to abortion as an inhumane practice, provided that other social institutions make possible a high quality of life for mothers and for babies brought to term. Such innovations as the electronic mass media, birth control pills, networked computers, and genetic screening create opportunities to reexamine existing cultural attitudes and ethical prescriptions. None, however, mandates that particular cultural values be adopted, or even that values must change at all. Environmentalism, feminism, and other bundles of new cultural values are responsive to changes in the material and social conditions of life, but the specific elements of these new values cannot be deduced from those conditions alone. That postmaterialist values are in fact associated with rejection of nuclear energy and insistence on the right to choose abortion cannot be understood without consideration of past cultural values, the institutions that grew up around those values, and the ways in which demands for change have been linked to new values and new behaviors.

In summary, cultural changes are responsive to changes in the economic and social environment, but they are not simply a function of them. The agents of cultural change work in the context of an institutional and technological environment, but they are not passive mirrors of that environment. To see how contingency enters into the process of cultural innovation, we must take a step back and ask just what it is that is being altered when cultures change.

Societal Sources of Cultural Change

Culture is a meaningful concept only because the social and political worlds are constituted conceptually. The boundaries of a political community, the legitimacy of social structures and political institutions, and the nature of justice all exist as ideas rather than as immutable, knowable facts. Our political and social worlds are constructed from a "Moral language [that] maps political possibilities and impossibilities; it enables us to do certain things even as it discourages or disables us from doing others" (Ball, Farr, and Hanson 1989: 3). This moral language is, of course, grounded in tangible facts. Such facts are what Charles Taylor (1971: 8) calls the "brute data" of social reality, data whose validity cannot be questioned by offering another interpretation of them. Brute data are the reality Philip K. Dick refers to when he writes "Reality is that which refuses to go away when I stop believing in it."

Reality may refuse to go away, but its meaning, and even whether we choose to give it any meaning at all, is a matter for the culture to decide. For example, artificial additions to the air, water, and soil are labeled pollutants only when the effects judged to be harmful become a concern significant enough to outweigh our perception of benefits that stem from the polluting activities. Heavy metals are water pollutants but fluoride is not. Human beings and cars both emit carbon dioxide, but only the latter is considered a source of pollution. Similarly, recognition of income disparities rests on conceptual agreement about the traits that define relevant social groupings, and on agreement concerning appropriate ratios of income between groups. Income differentials between ethnic groups and between men and women are matters of contemporary public concern, but they were not fifty years ago. Comparable differentials between age groups and between people with different skills or education levels do not arouse the same concern because they are seen as legitimate. Differentials between left- and right-handed people do not arouse any concern at all because we do not view these as income-relevant social groupings. The contrast between a front-page newspaper story about gender differences in income and a brief squib on handedness differentials filling some corner of an inside page is a reminder of the importance of our conceptual categories for sorting and filtering information.

If we don't have a conceptual category for some phenomenon, we are less likely even to become aware of it. As Rubin (1994: 14) put it, "Problems do not announce themselves." Gamson and Modigliani (1989) offer the example of a serious nuclear accident in 1966 at the Fermi reactor near Detroit, in which the fuel core underwent a partial meltdown and the automatic shutdown system failed. The accident went unreported for five weeks and was never the subject of a public protest, demands that the plant be mothballed, or even calls for external oversight of the power company's inspection and repair procedure. With no organized critics of nuclear energy in 1966, and with no culturally accepted language for talking about nuclear energy other than as the energy of the future, the accident at Fermi was viewed as an anomaly, a temporary problem that the experts would take care of.

Cultural change occurs when we alter the conceptual categories with which we give meaning to reality. It is a matter of *how* we think, not simply *what* we think. As Gusfield (1981: 326) put it, "what was unthinkable is now seen as thinkable. What was taken for granted as an item of consensus can no longer be so taken." Or, as Laitin (1988: 589) put it, "Culture instills not values to be upheld but rather points of concern to be debated." Reaction to the Three Mile Island nuclear accident in 1979 took the form of angry questions being raised about plant safety, the adequacy of precautions taken by the utility, and the inherent dangers of nuclear power (Walsh 1988). The contrast with the noncontroversy over the Fermi accident just thirteen years earlier offers a striking illustration of the practical consequences of change in Laitin's "points of concern to be debated."

The process of cultural change involves the introduction of contention into how events should be viewed. The turmoil in Los Angeles after acquittal of the police officers who beat Rodney King reflected disagreement over whether the police in minority communities are guardians of public order or an army of occupation. This cultural conflict becomes visible in the use of different terms to describe the same events. In this instance, the outbreak of civil violence was referred to as a riot, a rebellion, or an uprising. Each term contains a distinctive interpretation of the same brute data of arson and looting. The reality of broken glass and merchandise missing from stores would not go away even if you refused to believe in it. But that reality can be given any of several meanings. And each possible meaning is reflected in an alternate language used to describe the events. As Murray Edelman (1964: 131) concludes, "the terms in which we name or speak of anything do more than designate it, they place it in a class of objects, thereby suggest with what it is to be judged and compared, and define the perspective from which it will be viewed and evaluated." Or, as Oliver Wendell Holmes observed, "A word is not a symbol, transparent and unchanged, it is the skin of a living thought" (cited in Rodgers 1987: 16).

The connection between language and culture is so close that changing use of language is one of our primary signals that culture is being re-formed. Cultural change is invariably accompanied by innovations in the language used to describe a particular subject, or in the meanings assigned to existing linguistic usage. Quentin Skinner (1978: 352) observes that "The surest sign that a society has entered into the secure possession of a new concept is that a new vocabulary will be developed, in terms of which the concept can then be publicly articulated and discussed." Giving names to phenomena is indicative of cultural change, but such change is seen even more clearly in the development of a new system of thought, a Gestalt, or a way of making connections between events. The linguistic expression of a system of thought is called a discourse: a shared set of concepts, vocabulary, terms of reference, evaluations, associations, polarities, and standards of argument connected to some coherent perspective on the world (Ricoeur 1971).

Cultural change can be mapped by examining changes in discourse. Thus, substitution of the phrase "biological diversity" for "species preservation" highlights new aspects of the same phenomenon by shifting our attention away from a museum-collecting orientation toward species and replacing it with the idea of maintaining ecological wholeness in natural habitats. Renaming "rape" as "sexual assault" and rape "victims" as "survivors" highlights the crime as an act of violence (Estrich 1987). When female circumcision is referred to as genital mutilation, when jungles become rainforests and swamps become wetlands, the same subject is placed into an entirely different evaluative frame.

The need to alter language in order to change cultural values has been especially appreciated within the women's movement, which in English has given us new terms like sexism, glass ceilings, and Ms. That there is a symbolic order at stake in the use of language and naming is apparent from the fact that language innovators generally face ridicule for their proposed usages. To poke fun at efforts to retitle occupational and status titles in gender-neutral terms was the sport of a generation. Sometimes the very ability to speak about a topic in public signals a significant change in cultural values. Staggenborg (1991: 29) observes that "the word 'abortion' could barely be mentioned in public when the [pro-choice] movement began."

The survival of laws limiting the right of medical professionals to offer abortion counseling is a reminder that language innovators may face sanctions for their defiance of cultural values. In the mid-1970s, married women in New Jersey were removed from the voting rolls if they would not register under their husbands' names. Such episodes suggest that struggles to rename reality are more than empty symbols.[6]

Cultural change is difficult to study because it takes place in a highly decentralized way, largely in the invisible settings in which individuals go about their daily lives. But because of the link between values and public discourse, cultural change leaves a readily observable imprint in the form of new ideas that are widely discussed. We can observe the transformation of new ideas into cultural—that is, shared—values by examining the diffusion of new concepts in the mass media, in political speeches and judicial decisions, and in the writings of academicians.

Much of the study to follow is centered on the ways in which new cultural values enter public debate. We will examine the genesis of controversies, especially political controversies, over new values. To raise a value to the status of controversy is a necessary first step in the process of cultural change, but it is just a first step. Cultural change is completed only when the new values are no longer highly controversial, when they have been accepted as a "normal" part of thinking. As this point, there will still be specific controversies about the way in which cultural values should be articulated in social behavior and public policy. The shared value need not include a consensus on specific policy beliefs, but instead reflects agreement only about the underlying principles on which policy claims in that area must be justified. Thus, it is no longer possible to develop a major construction project without making reference to its environmental impact. It is no longer

---

[6] On the power that lies in controlling symbols by naming objects, see also Bourdieu 1991.

possible to defend some employment practice on the basis of its benefits for male heads of households. That said, there are still controversies about specific construction projects and specific employment practices.

The end point of cultural change with respect to some value occurs when the value is diffused into the wider society to such a degree that it is no longer a matter of contention, or even necessarily of conscious awareness. At this point the new value has been generalized to realms that are not overtly political. As new values become rooted in people's thinking and behavior, they have implications in areas of social life far removed from the primary concerns of the critical community and movement. The best indication of value change may be precisely the extent to which the new values leave trace residues in places where they are likely to show up only after having been widely accepted in the society. Forms of popular culture such as novels, movies, and leisure activities are a good place to look for value diffusion; they are a kind of lagging indicator of the absorption of the values into social thought.

Advertisements are a particularly good channel for studying values because advertisers frequently attempt to position their product in relation to cultural symbols and values. This is particularly the case when new cultural values have clear implications for product consumption. Thus beer advertisers were quick to support campaigns against drinking and driving by incorporating messages to "drink responsibly" in their ads. This became a means of channeling public concern about alcohol-related auto fatalities into ideas (such as designated drivers) that are not threatening to the alcohol industry.

Because of the power of women as consumers, the phenomenon that Stuart Ewen (1976: 160) calls "commercialized feminism" has a long history. In 1929 the American Tobacco Company attempted to associate women's demands for greater freedom with the right to smoke in public. The company sponsored a march of ten women down New York's Fifth Avenue, lighting their "torches of freedom" as they went. Ewen reports that the march achieved front-page coverage in many newspapers.

Commercialized feminism continues today. Marilyn DeLong and Elizabeth Bye (1990) have studied trends in the images conveyed in fragrance ads between 1955 and 1985 in *Harper's Bazaar*, an authoritative and traditionally oriented source of information on fashion. Examining every aspect of the pictures and text in each advertisement, DeLong and Bye found that the fragrance ads use one of five different images in their effort to appeal to women. Their results are summarized in table 1-1.

DeLong and Bye's study of fragrance ads shows a clear shift away from the traditional role, in which women used scents exclusively to project an image of femininity and elegance. The decade between 1955 and 1965 saw movement in several directions, with increasing emphasis on the romantic

TABLE 1-1
Images of Women in Fragrance Ads, 1955–1985 (in percent)

Image	1955	1965	1975	1985
Traditional: femininity, elegance, charm	91	58	76	41
Romantic	1	13	4	17
Seductive, sensuous	7	19	5	30
Intellectual, independent, powerful, strong	0	0	4	10
Casual, outdoors, active, informal	1	10	11	2
Total	100	100	100	100
Number of cases	79	98	55	146

Source: Calculated from DeLong and Bye 1990.

and the sensuous as well as on a more casual, active, natural image. Despite some recovery of the traditional image in 1975, by 1985 the diversity of images conveyed in fragrance ads was greater than ever, with the traditional image found in fewer than half of all advertisements.

The actual degree of change in the images projected by these advertisements is even greater than that shown in table 1-1, for there was also evolution *within* the category of traditional ads. DeLong and Bye (1990: 84) find that:

> In the eighties women continue to be featured with males, but not in the usual manner of the male looking down upon the female who is wearing her best come-hither look. More often the men and women pictured together appear on the same level as equals. Overall, there appear to be fewer pedestals and less pedestal-dressing for the female [even] in more recent *traditional advertisements*. (emphasis in the original)

It is worth stressing that changing the focus of fragrance advertisements was never a goal of the women's movement. If any of the types of image found by DeLong and Bye correspond to a "feminist" approach to fragrances, it would be the intellectual/independent and the outdoors/active categories, the two least common types of images. But there is nonetheless a clear imprint of the women's movement on the evolution of fragrance ads. That imprint is found less in the content of the advertising images than in their sheer diversity. Diversity of roles, even in the choice of scents, is a value that has come from the women's movement; and the idea that women should be able to express different aspects of their character through multiple fragrances is both a reflection and a reinforcement of broader cultural changes in the role of women.

The extent of cultural spillover stemming from a particular movement will vary depending upon the degree to which ideas of the movement have direct implications for daily life. The women's movement and the environmental movement are two whose values, when diffused into the culture, alter daily patterns of behavior. Other movements, such as movements against nuclear weapons, have fewer implications for daily life. Such movements may still be able to spread their messages to a number of venues of political communication. Thus the impact of peace movements has been traced in presidential speeches (Meyer 1995), in articles in leading journals of foreign affairs (Meyer 1995), and in political cartoons (Gamson and Stuart 1992). But the values of peace movements are less likely to diffuse from themes directly associated with nuclear weapons to everyday patterns of thought and behavior.

Conclusion

Rapid cultural change occurs when the social and political discourse in a particular subject area is altered. It is not simply a matter of changing opinions about an existing topic, but rather involves an alteration in the basis on which opinion is formed. Such change rests on the development of an entirely new framework for thinking about the topic. This new discourse brings with it a change in the concepts, vocabulary, and mental associations that are connected to a particular subject.

Existing understandings of political action and public policy rest on the idea that if you want to understand a policy outcome you must look at the interests of the various groups and institutions mobilized to affect that policy. When policies change dramatically, as happens on rare but important occasions, we generally find that new groups have been mobilized into the policy process while some established groups have been marginalized and others have changed their ideas about where their interests lie. After the fact, connecting interests to particular groups may seem unproblematic. Leaders in the civil rights movements wanted integration, the feminists who founded the National Organization for Women (NOW) wanted "to bring women into full participation in the mainstream of American Society,"[7] environmentalists want the preservation of biodiversity. But these interests could have come to be specified in different ways. Instead of seeking integration, African Americans could seek separation and compensation (as some do). Instead of seeking equal access to jobs and equitable conditions of employment, women could instead seek to alter the social institutions that distinguish so sharply between paid employment and unpaid work in the home. Among environ-

---

[7] NOW Statement of Purpose 1966. The full text is available at http://www.now.org/history/purpos66.html.

mentalists the priorities for preserving biodiversity remain unsettled between those who seek primarily to limit the effects of industrial activity on the planet and those who argue that the top priority is to reclaim large areas of territory from any human activity at all.

It has long been appreciated that the mobilization of a group sharing common interests cannot be taken for granted, and that mobilization will in fact occur only under fairly special conditions. To that important insight we can add that group interests are themselves problematic, and that for any given group one can readily imagine a range of interests being defined as "the group interest."[8]

We began this chapter with the question of what causes the irresistible tides that periodically sweep aside established patterns of social thought and political action. We can now answer that these tides are caused by rapid changes in the political and social discourse in a problem area. People begin not just to think differently about the issue, but to think in a different way.

These reflections on the nature and impact of cultural change help us understand more precisely the conditions that create profound movements in social behavior and political priorities. But they do not tell us the factors that cause transformations in the way in which we view social and political issues. For that, we must introduce the two lead actors in this theory of cultural change: critical communities and movements.

---

[8] Each of those group interests might of course also rest on a different specification of the boundaries of the group.

Chapter 2

CRITICAL COMMUNITIES AND MOVEMENTS

CONCEIVING of cultural change as the adoption of altered language to express a newly developed discourse suggests a two-step process in which concepts are first created and then spread through the society. In practice, these two steps are not always neatly separable, either in timing or in agency. Even so, it is useful to think of the creation and diffusion of new ideas as two distinct stages in the process of cultural change.

We will examine in the course of this book a number of social and political institutions, such as the mass media and political parties, that play a key role in developing and publicizing new ways of thinking about problem areas. But our primary focus will be on critical communities as the originators of new value perspectives and on movements as the source of pressure that brings these ideas to the attention of social and political institutions. In this chapter we will examine critical communities and movements; in the next chapter we will look at a number of case studies to see how they work together to produce cultural change.

CRITICAL COMMUNITIES AND VALUE INNOVATION

The creation of new ideas occurs initially within a relatively small community of critical thinkers who have developed a sensitivity to some problem, an analysis of the sources of the problem, and a prescription for what should be done about the problem. These critical thinkers do not necessarily belong to a formally constituted organization, but they are part of a self-aware, mutually interacting group.[1] I shall label these groups "critical communities."

In saying that critical communities develop around problem identification, analysis, and prescriptions, it is important to understand that these are not simply specifications of a group's interests. Interests can be articulated using existing policy concepts, and interest groups invoke established cultural values to promote the welfare of their members. Critical communities seek

---

[1] Ties between members of critical communities are analogous to those between members of an "invisible college": a circle of scientists working on a particular problem, who are connected to each other by informal means of communication that overlap with institutional affiliations but are not limited to them. See Crane 1972.

acceptance of a new conceptualization of a problem—they want to make sure that other people "get it."[2] Critical communities do not seek specific outcomes so much as they attempt to influence the conceptual framework used to think about a cluster of issues.

As a critical community coalesces, it rapidly develops its own channels of communication. Kielbowicz and Scherer (1986) report that 560 feminist publications were founded between 1968 and 1973, creating in a short time a dense network of shared discourse. Although members of a critical community are united by an overriding concern about a particular issue area, they need not be united by much else. Particularly in the early stages of identifying a social problem there are likely to be substantial differences within the critical community over the scope of the problem and the relative weight to be assigned to its various causes. As Rubin (1994: 14) put it, "agreement that there are problems does not mean there is agreement on what those problems are, or on what makes them problems, or on what to do about them." In their analysis of over three thousand articles on the environment published by specialist and general interest magazines between 1959 and 1979, Strodthoff, Hawkins, and Schoenfeld (1985) found that many of the earliest articles dealt with such basic themes as how the natural environment should be viewed, appropriate criteria of a healthy environment, and the kinds of policies that should be adopted on environmental issues. Between 1959 and 1966, articles in the specialist magazines reflected rival schools of thought on these issues.

Over time, a critical community may or may not be able to resolve these internal differences. The case studies presented throughout this book suggest that a relatively high degree of unity within the critical community is helpful, and perhaps even necessary, to foster wider social acceptance of a critical perspective. Unity may be produced through debate and mutual persuasion within the critical community, or it may be imposed from outside the community if one problem formulation becomes more prestigious than others. Rival interpretations may, for example, be vanquished if a particular critical perspective reaches the best-seller list, such as Rachel Carson's *Silent Spring* (1962) or Jonathan Schell's *Fate of the Earth* (1982). Or, one critical interpretation of the issue may come to predominate if the media or political authorities give it preference over others. This occurred when the White House entered periodic negotiations with Martin Luther King Jr. (rather than other civil rights leaders), and when the Equal Employment Opportunity Commission (EEOC) adopted an approach to sexual harassment associated with the ideas of Catherine MacKinnon.

---

[2] "You just don't get it" was a phrase often used during the portion of Clarence Thomas's confirmation hearings devoted to sexual harassment. This is an example of critical community influence on cultural change that will be further developed in chapter 3.

No matter how the critical community reaches a common perspective, exerting influence over culture requires that its members develop a relatively coherent, unified discourse on the issue area. In the case of the critical community concerned with the environment, unity of basic perspectives was developed in the specialist magazines by 1966 (Strodthoff et al. 1985).[3] This critical community agreement made it easier for general interest magazines to increase their attention to environmental issues such as pollution, toxic wastes, and nuclear proliferation. General interest magazines not only picked up these issues from the specialist magazines, but employed the critical community's underlying perspective on environmental protection as well.

John Zaller (1992: 316–317) offers the example of a group of psychiatric researchers who began in the late 1940s to examine homosexuals for evidence of psychological disorder. As their studies turned up consistently negative results, pressure grew within the American Psychiatric Association to remove homosexuality from the association's list of diseases, an action that was taken in 1974. This authoritative declaration, in turn, contributed to a shift in media coverage of homosexuality, from a context centered on vice to a context emphasizing the civil rights of gays. This example illustrates the importance of achieving substantive agreement within the critical community before those outside the critical community take the new viewpoint as authoritative.

Critical communities bear some resemblance to the networks of establishment-oriented experts named epistemic communities by Haas (1992).[4] Epistemic communities are particularly powerful in the policy process when the complexity of an issue prevents political leaders from addressing it with established policy routines. Moore (1988: 72) comments that expert ideas "define conventional wisdom in the area, set out questions for which evidence is necessary, suggest the alternative policies that are plausibly effective, and (most important), keep alternative formulations off the public agenda." Bradford (1994: 86) refers in a similar vein to the role of networks of experts in assisting with "crystallization of certain ideas and interests into operational discourses that clarify policy goals and map political alliances." By presenting an authoritative understanding of the problem and its policy implications, then, epistemic communities reduce the uncertainty surrounding new legislation. Routinely consulted in policy formation, networked experts become part of an advocacy coalition that champions a particular way of looking at the issue (Sabatier 1988; Sabatier and Jenkins-Smith 1993). This is the source of their power.

Critical communities are, like epistemic communities, networks of people

---

[3] For a succinct account of the basic doctrinal themes of environmentalism as developed in this period, see Strodthoff et al. 1985.

[4] See also Brooks and Gagnon 1994.

who think intensively about a particular problem and who develop over time a shared understanding of how to view that problem. There are, however, a number of significant differences between epistemic communities and critical communities. First, critical communities are *critical*. They develop alternative, challenging ways of looking at an issue, and their perspectives are critical of the policy establishment rather than being oriented toward helping it function better. Second, critical communities increase policy uncertainty by offering new perspectives on established issue areas. This contrasts with the function of epistemic communities, which is to reduce policy uncertainty in new issue areas. Finally, the power of critical communities does not come from a web of formal and informal ties to established political institutions, as is the case with epistemic communities. Members of critical communities may have such ties but they are more likely to be without establishment connections. Epistemic communities are linked directly into the political system as policy advisers. Critical communities have (at best) indirect influence. As we will see, critical communities are powerful only to the extent that their ideas are taken up by wider social and political movements.

Ron Eyerman (1990) has pointed out that belief in the critical role of the intellectual has ancient roots, but was articulated most forcefully in the eighteenth-century Enlightenment, a remarkable cultural transformation that developed in France at the end of the age of absolutism. The critical community that nurtured these new ideas was composed of a group of literary, philosophical, and scientific intellectuals known as the philosophes. Collectively, they developed the view that human reason should be the source of all political and social authority. The human mind was held to be capable of improving the material and moral conditions of life, if only reason, observation, open-mindedness, and experimentation would be permitted to triumph over traditional and dogmatic sources of authority. As the philosophe Condorcet put it, "Superstition, which covers despotism with an impenetrable shield, must be the first victim [of the new age], the first link in the chain of bondage to be broken" (cited in Lough 1960: 319).

The philosophes were a foundational critical community in the sense that their conceptual innovation was the justification of critical communities themselves. Under the French *ancien régime* neither political organization nor the advocacy of reform existed in the sense that they are known today. The philosophes could not petition the king for reform, for they had no vocabulary other than their own emerging philosophy with which to claim authority for their ideas.

Communication within the critical community took the form of works in philosophy, literary criticism, novels, plays, essays, music theory, art criticism, letters, pamphlets, and, above all, the *Encyclopédie*, an international best seller (twenty thousand copies in print by the mid 1770s) that appeared in twenty-eight folio volumes of text and illustrations between 1751 and

1772 under the editorship of Diderot and d'Alembert. In the absence of electronic mass media and even of widespread literacy, the philosophes hoped to use these vehicles to spread their ideas among the nobility and clergy.[5] The idea of changing cultural values in the wider society was too farfetched for even the most freethinking of eighteenth-century intellectuals. The revolution that the philosophes had in mind, then, was an intellectual revolution limited to the social strata comprising those who were literate and able to engage in the kind of rational discourse on which the philosophes pinned their hopes for social progress.

Despite these markedly premodern elements of the Enlightenment movement, the philosophes were conscious of their role as a critical community. They wrote to each other extensively, critiquing each others' ideas and seeking to develop through their debates a common ground on issues ranging from the best systems of political administration, social stratification, law, and criminal justice, to the proper roles of church and state in the society. There was little agreement at first in philosophic circles even about such basic issues as the best form of government. Gradually, though, there emerged a widely shared view that large democratic republics were inevitably corrupt, and that the best form of government was a reformed monarchy advised by an aristocracy selected on the basis of intellect and achievement rather than of birth. As Voltaire explained, "Despite my strong taste for liberty, I would rather live under the paw of a lion than be gnawed at continually by the teeth of a thousand rats who are my peers" (Lough 1982: 21).

A critical community under absolutism pays a price for expressing its views. Most of the leading philosophes, and often their publishers, spent time in the Bastille. Voltaire spent part of his life in exile in Prussia and England, Rousseau in England and Switzerland, Diderot in Russia. Publication in France required a prior license from the king, and licenses were often denied for the work of the philosophes. Even books that received a royal license could be suppressed after the fact by the church, the nobility of the First Estate, or by the courts of law (Lough 1960: 305–319). Chartier (1991: 79) comments on the frequent confiscation of philosophic works by observing that "Although only seven prisoners were inmates in the state prison on 14 July 1789, all the classics of the Enlightenment were there, victims of censorship and the king's police."

Equally pernicious were the problems of earning a living in a country where positions of scholarship were at least nominally under the patronage

---

[5] Literacy rates were between 25 and 30 percent in eighteenth-century France, as measured by the generous standard of the number of people who could sign their own name in a marriage registry. Literacy expanded significantly during the century, leading by century's end to the development of lending libraries. As late as the Revolution of 1789, though, the elevated forms of philosophy, literature, and criticism written by most of the philosophes had an audience limited primarily to the aristocratic classes.

of either king or church. Royalties from book sales were not large, and they were still smaller if one had to publish abroad and then have the book smuggled into France.[6] Favored writers of the period were given a sinecure in the court or were sponsored by a member of the aristocracy. Although some philosophes were at times supported by court officials, their writings inevitably got them into trouble and their sources of patronage never endured for long. Some of the philosophes were themselves of the nobility and so were of independent means, such as the Baron d'Holbach and the Marquis de Condorcet. A few, such as Voltaire, managed to turn their celebrity into a wealth sufficient to dispense with the need for patronage. Most, however, lived a hand-to-mouth existence on the sale of their works. A constant theme of their letters to each other was the sharing of information about available sources of patronage income, the royalties paid by different publishers, the opportunities for writing more freely and more lucratively abroad, and other aspects of simply maintaining one's material existence.

Despite being in official disfavor, the philosophes were never the object of a systematic proscription or repression—the organizational techniques of totalitarianism would not be invented till the twentieth century. Lack of a royal license to publish made publication riskier, but hardly impossible. And the philosophes were advantaged by the fact that they were the intellectual stars of the Parisian *salons*. Voltaire, who in the 1720s had been beaten up by hired thugs after offending the Chevalier de Rohan and then sent to the Bastille for seeking revenge, was fêted on his return from exile in 1778. That April the future American president John Adams reported attending a performance of one of Voltaire's tragedies at the Comédie Française, a performance also attended by Voltaire himself. Adams reports that he "happened to be placed in the Front Box very near to Voltaire. . . . The Audience between the several Acts, called out, Voltaire! Voltaire! Voltaire! and clapped and applauded him during all the intervals. The Aged Poet on Occasion of some extraordinary Applause rose and bowed respectfully to the Spectators" (Adams 1961: 77–78).

The social position of the philosophes in these later years is also indicated by a wax museum tableau described in the journal of an English visitor, Mrs. Cradock. "We entered to see the wax figures. One of the groupings depicted the king, the queen and the crown prince, seated beneath a canopy, and a bit in front of them, leaning on a table, three people. They were Mr. Voltaire, Mr. Rousseau and Dr. Franklin" (Lough 1987: 216).

A visiting Scot, John Moore, concluded after his tour of the Parisian *salons* that "You can scarcely believe the influence which this body of men

---

[6] Rousseau received two thousand francs, enough to live modestly for a year, from the initial publication of the enormously successful *La nouvelle Heloïse*. Subsequent editions earned him nothing (Lough 1960: 243).

have in the gay and dissipated city of Paris. Their opinions not only determine the merit of works of taste and science, but they have considerable
weight on the manners and sentiments of people of rank, of the public in
general, and consequently are not without effect on the measures of government" (Lough 1960: 266–267).[7]

This burgeoning influence of the philosophes cannot be attributed solely
to the intellectual force of their ideas, but has to do as well with the changing social structure of eighteenth-century France. By championing the possibility of material and moral progress in a society that embraces human
reason, the philosophes questioned the legitimacy of authority based on tradition and inheritance. As time went on they wrote with increasing force and
specificity of the rights of man. Such ideas could not but appeal to the ambi-
tions of the growing class of urban dwellers in the upper-middle classes,
whose aspirations went unrecognized by the entrenched powers of the mon-
arch, the nobility, and the church. The philosophes might have remained a
small sect in the absence of social and economic change. Their influence on
cultural values and ultimately on political revolution was substantially aided
by the correspondence between their ideas and the interests of powerful
emerging classes in society. But the philosophic critique was not a predeter-
mined by-product of the change in French society; the philosophes instead
gave a specific focus and direction to the growing discontent with the opu-
lence and isolation of the monarchy and church. Chartier (1991: 68) answers
the question posed in his chapter title "Do Books Make Revolutions?" by
observing that "the new [philosophic] ideas conquered people's minds,
molded their ways of being, and elicited questions. If the French of the late
eighteenth century fashioned the Revolution, it is because they had in turn
been fashioned by books."

This is not to say that there was a straight road from the Enlightenment to
the storming of the Bastille. The mass uprising that ignited the French Revolution occurred almost completely in ignorance of the writings of the philosophes, and indeed was accomplished largely by people who were illiterate.
Though Condorcet became chairman of the Legislative Assembly in 1791,
most of the philosophes would have been horrified by the violence and the
mass passions unleashed by the Revolution.[8]

---

[7] The ideas of the philosophes also spread to the infant United States by virtue of the fact that
many early American leaders held diplomatic posts in Paris at some point in their careers.
Thomas Jefferson, who referred to Voltaire and "the constellation of Encyclopedists" as living
proof that France "can produce her full quota of genius," wrote in 1799 to William Green
Munford that "I am among those who think well of the human character generally. I consider
man as formed for society, and endowed by nature with those dispositions which fit him for
society. I believe also, with Condorcet, . . . that his mind is perfectible to a degree of which we
cannot as yet form any conception" (1984: 1064).

[8] Even Condorcet was associated with the most moderate of revolutionary factions, the Gi-

Even so, the philosophes laid the conceptual groundwork for the central principles of the Revolution, particularly its secularism, its language of citizenship rights, and its commitment to the abolition of inherited privilege. The French Revolution gave currency to the philosophic term "ideology," used to refer to a science that would expose the propagation of religious illusions to the public (Goldie 1989). The concepts of citizen, nation, general will, and social contract were also adapted from the philosophes in order to legitimize the revolution. The language of citizenship rights created by the philosophic critical community was a necessary prologue to the cultural changes that ended absolutism and eventually gave birth to republican democracy (Baker 1990).

The example of the French philosophes demonstrates key features of critical community formation and influence, even across the chasm that divides the age of absolutist monarchy from the age of liberal democracy. The philosophes were a critical community in much the sense that environmentalists, feminists, and advocates of group rights have today formed critical communities. They developed heterodox ideas, extended the reach and implications of those ideas, related them more and more systematically to shortcomings in the social and political structure, and found their popularity growing among groups on the fringes of social and political power.

We will examine a number of contemporary critical communities in the course of this study. The cultural transformations that have occurred in the areas of the environment, consumer rights, relations between the sexes, and the rights of various minority groups have all been preceded by the development of a critical community in which a new discourse has gradually evolved. Public concern about the environment is often dated from the publication of Rachel Carson's *Silent Spring* (1962); histories of feminism refer to Betty Friedan's *The Feminine Mystique* (1963) and to Kate Millett's *Sexual Politics* (1969). Every account of the consumer movement begins with Ralph Nader's *Unsafe at Any Speed* (1965). These books are landmarks in the development of their respective critical communities, but behind these best sellers can be found literally thousands of other books, scholarly articles, newsletters, and—increasingly—Internet bulletin boards. For every Voltaire and Rousseau, there are hundreds of lesser-knowns who contribute to the gradual development of a new perspective on some problem area.

Of course, contemporary critical communities do not mirror the experience of the philosophes in every respect. Differences between then and now are related chiefly to the limits on action imposed by the form of the regime, the technologies of mass communication, and the extent of public exposure to the mass media. The process of cultural change has itself been trans-

---

rondists. When the Revolution radicalized, he was arrested by the Jacobins and ultimately died in jail.

formed between the eighteenth century and today, primarily in the rate at which new values are spread throughout society. The philosophes spanned several generations, and they only began to have important influence on upper-class society fifty years after the basic elements of their ideas had been articulated. Voltaire developed his vitriolic attacks on the church, particularly on the monastic orders, more than half a century before church lands were seized, the orders abolished, and their wealth taken or taxed. It was twenty-seven years before the Revolution that Rousseau first connected the words "liberty, equality, fraternity" in a succinct summary of the necessary conditions of a happy life. At about the same time, Rousseau and a number of fellow philosophes were elaborating the principles of a secular and national system of education that would be freed from church control, and in which the modern subjects of science and math would be taught alongside the classical disciplines. D'Holbach began to enumerate the rights of man twenty years before the leaders of the French Revolution drew up their Universal Declaration. Condorcet drew up his electoral systems and his plan for social security long before these ideas ever reached the public agenda. Abolition of feudal dues and tithes, adoption of a uniform system of weights and measures on the metric principle, development of a uniform and integrated legal code, secularization of marriage and divorce procedures, the freedom to organize and to publish—these are among the social reform projects that were already on paper when Louis XVI was crowned, but that came to fruition only after he was beheaded.

Differences in audiences, channels of communication and influence, and above all differences in speed of diffusion separate the eighteenth-century Enlightenment from the critical communities with which we are familiar at the end of the twentieth century. These differences are explicable in terms of changes in the technologies and institutions of communication, decision making, and power. But critical communities of the eighteenth century and today are united in their ability to elaborate a discourse that names new problems and identifies their contexts, causes, and consequences.

Without critical communities we would not have the incubation of new ideas. But without collective action and protest, critical communities would remain on the margins of cultural awareness. It falls to social and political movements to carry the ideas of the critical community to a wider audience, to provoke a reexamination of existing values, and to create social and political pressure for change. Movements are, then, the second key element in the process of cultural change.

MOVEMENTS AND VALUE DIFFUSION

The role of movements in the process of cultural change is to bring the new ideas of critical communities to a wide audience. Movements coalesce around the perspectives developed in the critical community, and they reformulate those perspectives into terms that will be effective in mobilizing activists and winning social and political allies. In the hands of movement leaders, the ideas of critical communities become ideological frames, orientations to an issue. As Diani (1995: 13) points out, "Frames provide social movement actors with definitions of the issues at stake, of their potential allies and opponents, with evaluations of appropriate strategies, and a rationale for action."

The critical community is interested primarily in the development of new values; the movement is interested in winning social and political acceptance for those values. While the critical community operates mainly through communication within a network of people engaged in conceptual clarification and empirical analysis of a problem, the primary tools of the movement lie in collective action. These differences mean that there can be no one-to-one relationship between critical communities and movements, and movements are not simply an extension of the critical community. As an abortion rights activist put it, "If you are going to have the strategy of appealing to the broad middle-class . . . it just doesn't help to say 'get your laws off my body'" (cited in Staggenborg 1991: 121). Rather, movement leaders take an active role in choosing, bundling together, and shaping the ideas of one or more critical communities, in such a way as to maximize the chances of movement success. Movements seek social and political influence by "rais[ing] cultural challenges to the dominant language, to the codes that organize information and shape social practices" (Melucci 1995: 41). But not all cultural innovations developed in critical communities are equally suited to motivating collective action. As a result, there are many more critical communities than there are movements.

It is conventional both in scholarship and in everyday speech to distinguish between social and political movements. There are important differences between the two. Social movements seek to spread the values of the critical community throughout the society. Political movements seek authoritative sanctioning of new values in the form of binding laws and regulations. When we label a movement as being political or social, we are saying that one or the other strategy of cultural change takes precedence within that movement. Although movements may choose to place greater stress on one arena or the other, however, social movements generally have a political agenda and political movements always require manifestations of societal support. Moreover, success in one arena has an impact on the other. Changing social values find political expression in altered policies, and these policies in turn speed the dissemination of new values through the society by articulating norms of behavior and by sanctioning deviance. The political and the social dimensions of movement activity each reinforce the other.

I propose to elevate the existence of dual goals in the society and the polity to the defining trait of movements:

Movements are formed by the melding of a critical discourse to collective action. Movement strategies and action are aimed at achieving change in both the political and social arenas.

Movements are commonly defined as any collective action that employs protest to further the goal of producing change. While protest is a distinctive strategy often associated with movements, protest can also occur outside of a movement context. Nor do all movement organizations engage in protest. The defining trait of movements, therefore, is not protest but rather the attempt to obtain change in both the political and social arenas. Based on his review of the range of definitions of movements in the scholarly literature, Diani (1992) concluded that the traits common to most definitions are that movements are *networks* of individuals and groups, based on *shared collective identities*, engaged in *political or social conflicts* (see chapter 4). Since all collective action involves networks and shared identities, I take the focus on political or social conflicts to be the truly distinctive traits of movements. And, as will be shown throughout this book, the collective actions that we conventionally identify as movements all share the trait of being engaged in *both* political *and* social conflict.[9] The distribution of activities between the political and social arenas may vary greatly, but both are required.

This two-front war can be found in all those phenomena we intuitively label as movements. The women's movement is interested both in affecting legislation concerning women (which Gelb, 1990, calls the equal rights sector) and in changing cultural values about the roles of women in society (which Gelb refers to as the women's liberation sector). The civil rights movement may be profitably analyzed as a coalition of organizations that prodded the government to create legal equality between the races, but it was at the same time a social movement that discredited segregation and spread a sense of pride and self-worth among African Americans. The environmental movement is concerned with legal changes that encourage conservation of resources and discourage pollution, but it is equally engaged in fostering heightened ecological awareness among people. These movements are both social and political.

Collective actors other than movements may also maintain some level of presence in the two arenas. An interest group may conduct a public advertising campaign on behalf of its goals, and a religious organization may lobby a legislature for favorable tax treatment. In these cases, however, action in one arena is simply a means of achieving the goals of the organization in the other arena. Movements are the unique form of collective action that seeks both to change social values and to influence policy makers, and for which neither arena is viewed merely as a means to exert leverage on the other.

Movements have distinctive characteristics in the two arenas, as shown in

---

[9] See also Calhoun 1995 and Tesh 1993.

TABLE 2-1
Two Arenas of Movement Activity

Traits	Social Arena	Political Arena
Seeks to influence	Cultural values	Government policies
Target of activity	Individuals	Institutions
Resources	Ideas and grass-roots activism	Votes, money, information, allies
Optimal organization	Decentralized, participatory	Centralized, hierarchical
Typical activities	Teach-in, street theater, door-to-door canvas	Referendum, electoral organizing, lobbying
Time horizon	Indefinite	Bounded campaigns

table 2-1. In the political arena, movements seek to change policies or to alter the behavior of political institutions. In the social arena, movements seek to change cultural values by raising new issues or by fostering a reconsideration of old issues in the light of new normative frameworks. Political arena objectives include passage of the Voting Rights Act for the civil rights movement, the Equal Rights Amendment for the women's movement, and the Clean Air Act for the environmental movement. Social arena objectives include changing cultural values on race relations, on the role of women in society, and on the proper relationship between man and nature. The political arena is the world of movement organizations, leaders, large-scale protests, and specific policy demands. The social arena is the world of changing values, identities, preoccupations, and daily behaviors.

In the social arena, movements "provide a challenge to the dominant assumptions of the social order" by spurring a debate about new ideas (Eyerman and Jamison 1991: 165). This debate is reflected in the mass media, but its true locus is in homes, schools, and workplaces. The movement in society is decentralized and without centrally controlled direction. Its prime activities are those that engage people in conversation or provoke them to new thoughts. Its optimal form of organization is one that maximizes participation, creating settings for interactions that serve to articulate, publicize, and disseminate critiques of existing institutions, practices and values.

National organizations are the vehicle by which movements operate in the political arena. Movement activity in the political arena draws chiefly on the centralized resources of leadership, political access, and the support of politically influential allies. A strong central organization is needed so that the movement can act swiftly and in a unified way to capitalize on opportunities for political influence. The rank-and-file members of this organization serve primarily as a source of funds and a reservoir of willingness to write letters or gather for a demonstration on occasions determined by the movement leadership.

This understanding of the dual nature of movements is not new. Herbert Blumer's classic essay, first published in 1939, makes a distinction between "general" and "specific" social movements. A general movement involves the emergence of new social values and is "episodic in its career, with very scattered manifestations and activity" (Blumer 1974: 5). Specific movements represent a crystallization of the "dissatisfaction, hope, and desire awakened by the general social movement and the focusing of this motivation on some specific objective" (Blumer 1974: 6). According to Blumer, this crystallization of objectives centers on a particular policy goal, and on the development of a well-defined movement organization and leadership. The general movement operates in the social arena, while the specific movement is active in the political arena. Blumer's hypothesis is that movements begin in the social arena and then shift to the political arena as their perspectives and grievances crystallize.

Joseph Gusfield (1981) has captured the distinction between movements acting in the social and political arenas in yet another way, contrasting the "linear" and the "fluid" dimensions of movements. Studies rooted in the linear image of movements stress their origins, organization, tactical choices, and ability to gain policy changes—in short, the movement in the political arena. The fluid image focuses on movements in society. In their fluid dimension, movements are found "not in the actions of this or that organization . . . but in the quickening of actions, the change in meanings, and the understanding that something new is happening in a wide variety of places and arenas" (Gusfield 1981: 322).

Whether we refer to the social arena and the political arena, the general movement and the specific movement, or the fluid dimension and the linear dimension, the central point is that movements are unique among the various forms of collective action in their striving to alter the everyday thoughts and behaviors of people in a society, even as they put pressure on government for political reform. When the power of a movement is harnessed to the ideas of a critical community, the conditions are created for rapid cultural change. And in the most successful of movements, these conditions include a blending of activity in the social and political arenas, in order to transform cultural values as well as to enact a political agenda. Consider Kirkpatrick Sale's (1993: 96) summary of the impact of the environmental movement:

> Within the space of a single generation, environmentalism has become embedded in American life, in law and custom, text and image, classroom and work-

place, practice and consciousness. . . . It is embedded in national legislative and administrative institutions. . . . It is embedded in the acts of individuals, from schoolchildren to CEOs, in the functions of communities, from villages to block organizations, in the performance of governments, from city water departments to national administrations. It is embedded in political life . . . in economic life . . . in cultural life . . . and in social life.

Sale's list of the impacts of environmentalism mingles the political and social arenas, the realm of legislation and the realm of everyday thought and behavior. The environmental movement would have had only a small fraction of its actual impact had it been successful in one arena but a failure in the other. In practice, the environmental movement is both a political movement and a social movement. Organization, action, and ultimate goals in the two arenas are intertwined.

RELATIONSHIP BETWEEN THE TWO ARENAS

When we view movements as operating in both the political and the social arenas, the question naturally arises of how political and social movements are related to each other. Does success in one arena contribute to success in the other? Success in the political arena may give a significant boost to the social influence of the movement's program. Community organizers have long known that the task of altering social values is made much easier when one can point to a recent victory in the political arena. As Aldon Morris (1984: 26) observed, "Whenever the NAACP won a legal contest, it served to delegitimize the white racist system in the eyes of blacks."

There is one notorious instance in which movement success in the political arena failed to generate the anticipated change in cultural values. The Prohibition amendment to the Constitution was a political arena victory of the Anti-Saloon League, but it is known today as "the failed experiment" because social behavior was insufficiently altered by a change in the law. Violations of the Prohibition law threatened to overwhelm the federal courts: there were more Prohibition convictions in 1926 (36,000) than there had been federal court cases of *any* type in 1920 (34,000). By 1929 federal courts were dealing with 75,000 Prohibition cases per year, with such predictable consequences as wholesale plea bargain arrangements. In 1930, fully one-third of the federal prison population was in jail for liquor law violations (Kyvig 1979: 30). The keenest observer of the consequences of Prohibition may have been Al Capone, who concluded "Prohibition is a business. All I do is supply a public demand" (Kyvig 1979: 26).

Clearly, the political victory of Prohibition did not lead to a transformation in cultural values. But even in this exceptional case, political success had a substantial effect on social behavior. Although violations were flagrant, there was a steep decline in alcohol consumption during Prohibition. Nor was this decline solely a result of the possibility of being apprehended for illegal sale or purchase. Even after repeal, per capita consumption of alcohol (especially of distilled liquor) remained far below pre-Prohibition levels. Kyvig notes that pre-Prohibition per capita consumption of alcohol was not reached again until 1970.

Changes stemming from either the political or the social arena do have some impact on the other. At times, though, the connections between the political and social arenas may be indirect or delayed. The relationship between the two arenas of movement activity may be illustrated by a comparison of two episodes from the contemporary American women's movement. For each episode, we will first consider the success of the movement from the perspective of its policy impact. We will then examine the events from the perspective of their social impact. Finally, we will show how the interactive perspective, taking into account both the political and social arenas, leads to different insights not accessible from the viewpoint of either arena when considered separately.

EEOC Enforcement of Title VII

The first episode concerns the addition of gender discrimination to the enforcement procedures set up by Title VII of the 1964 Civil Rights Act. Title VII created the Equal Employment Opportunity Commission (EEOC) to function as a board of appeal for claims of discrimination in employment. The Civil Rights Act, and Title VII in particular, proclaimed a policy of equal employment opportunities regardless of race, color, religion, sex, or national origin. The leadership of the EEOC, however, decided to focus its efforts on racial discrimination. Those within the EEOC who wanted sex discrimination to receive more attention let it be known that greater efforts were likely only if there was an external source of pressure on the agency in the form of "some sort of NAACP for women" (Freeman 1975: 54). Within weeks, on June 30, 1966, a group of twenty-eight women attending a conference of the State Commissions on the Status of Women resolved to form the National Organization for Women (NOW). Their first target was the refusal of the EEOC to deal with sex discrimination cases.

Since the 1964 Civil Rights Act had already authorized the EEOC to consider sex discrimination cases, the political goal of getting the agency to do so could be met without new legislation. All that was required was to obtain an executive order mandating the change in priorities. The first step was to write a letter to President Johnson in the fall of 1966, followed by meetings with a number of administration officials in the Justice Department and in the Civil Service Commission. The assistant secretary of labor (the department in which the EEOC falls), a woman sympathetic to the endeavor, was particularly helpful in this lobbying effort within the administration.

Over the course of the next year, the idea of adding sex discrimination to the purview of the EEOC was cleared by several agencies within the federal government as well as by the Office of Management of the Budget. At the end of these reviews in October 1967, Lyndon Johnson signed a one-page executive order that directed the EEOC to examine complaints of employment discrimination based on sex, and that further directed the Civil Service Commission to hear complaints about sex discrimination against federal employees. One year had elapsed between the initial letter to the president and the signing of the executive order (Freeman 1975: 53–55; Ferree and Hess 1985: 54–55). The total number of people involved in this effort was most likely no more than several hundred, and their activities were confined to the executive branch of government.

The action to bring sex discrimination under the purview of the EEOC was an unqualified success in the political arena. From the perspective of the social arena, however, the campaign was completely invisible and without impact. With no public involvement on the issue and minimal public awareness of it, the one-year effort to obtain the executive order had no resonance in the social arena.

This lack of visibility can be monitored in the *New York Times*'s coverage of gender discrimination in employment, as shown in figure 2-1.[10] Between 1961 and 1969 issues related to discrimination against women in the labor force were reported in an average of eleven articles per year. The campaign for the executive order in 1967 left no perceptible impact on press coverage. The signing of the executive order itself was reported in a single brief article on page 11 of the October 14, 1967, edition of the *New York Times*.

Although the campaign is sometimes described as part of the early women's movement, we can reasonably conclude that no women's movement yet existed at the time of the executive order in 1967. There was certainly no social movement on women's issues. Indeed, media interest in the topic remained minimal for several years following the signing of the executive order. Figure 2-1 shows that press coverage of gender discrimination began a sustained increase only in 1970, more than two years after the executive order. Data on sex discrimination prosecutions collected by Paul Burstein (1991) also show a delayed impact on EEOC behavior. Until 1971 complaints of sex discrimination were underrepresented among cases the EEOC chose to prosecute, compared with complaints of race discrimination. Sex discrimination cases were proportionately represented in EEOC litiga-

---

[10] The *New York Times* index category "Labor—US—women" is broadly phrased. Articles directly related to gender-based employment discrimination from this category have been selected for analysis in figure 2-1.

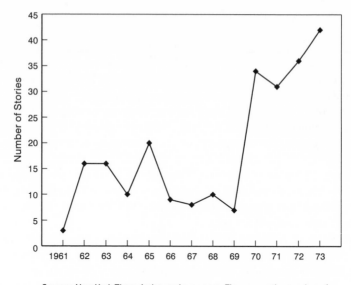

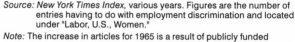

Source: *New York Times Index,* various years. Figures are the number of
entries having to do with employment discrimination and located
under "Labor, U.S., Women."

Note: The increase in articles for 1965 is a result of publicly funded
child care having become an issue in New York State in that year.

Figure 2-1   Press coverage of gender discrimination in employment,
1961–1973

tion between 1972 and 1976, and from 1977 onward sex discrimination
cases were substantially overrepresented in the EEOC docket. From 1977 to
1983, women filed 33 percent of all EEOC discrimination complaints, but
sex discrimination was the focus of 43 percent of prosecutions.

This reorientation of EEOC priorities yielded important policy success
for the nascent women's movement. Cases subsequently considered by the
EEOC led to the abolition of separate employment want ads for men and
women and the end of mandatory retirement for airline stewardesses (as
they were then known) when they married or reached the age of thirty-
two. But signing the executive order in 1967 was not sufficient to prod
the EEOC into vigorous action; something else happened in the course of
the 1970s to reorient the agency more heavily to the prosecution of sex
discrimination cases. That "something else" was, of course, the women's
movement, which had an impact on both the political and social arenas in
the 1970s. Figure 2-1 tells us that media interest in employment discrimination based on sex began to increase in 1970, the same year that saw the
startling increase in the rate of growth in public support for a woman as
president (see figure 1-1).

The Equal Rights Amendment

If the drive to get the executive order was a quick policy success with little immediate impact on society, then the campaign for the Equal Rights Amendment (ERA) may be characterized in exactly the opposite way. The ERA became the focus of a political movement that ultimately failed, but that triggered a social movement that has since transformed relations between men and women.[11] Among the many ways in which the ERA differed from the campaign for the executive order is in the length of the struggle. The Equal Rights Amendment was first proposed in the House of Representatives in 1923, and it continued to be proposed in the House every year after that. In March 1972 a confluence of powerful sponsors in the House and the Senate helped get the measure through both chambers. It was duly sent to the state legislatures for ratification. The ERA campaign was concluded ten years later, when the time for ratification by two-thirds of the states definitively expired.

Unlike the campaign for EEOC enforcement of Title VII, pressure for the ERA came not from a few hundred politically connected women, but from hundreds of thousands of women (and men) across the country, many of whom had never before been active in politics (Mansbridge 1986). In 1972, shortly before the ERA was passed by the House, Majority Leader "Tip" O'Neill said that the Equal Rights Amendment was generating more mail to Congress than the Vietnam War (Freeman 1975: 218). When the ratification process moved to the states, the level of involvement increased still further.

The design of the constitutional ratification process is ideal for fostering an inclusive political movement. It gives every interested person across the country a local target, his or her state legislator, to work on. It is possible to take action in whatever ways one is comfortable with: writing to a legislator or a newspaper, organizing local discussion groups, demonstrating at the state capital, and so forth. The ERA campaign thus provided the women's movement with an opportunity to marry local action to a nationwide cause. It served to unify a movement that had previously been quite diverse in purposes, ideas, and forms of action. It was the perfect vehicle for generating

[11] The extent of the policy arena failure of the ERA campaign was mitigated during the 1970s by Supreme Court decisions that used the Fourteenth Amendment to invalidate many of the laws that the ERA was designed to abolish (Mansbridge 1986). Moreover, Costain (1992: 86–87) reports that Congress passed an unprecedented number of gender-equity laws between 1972 and 1977. By 1996 Justice Ginsburg could write for the Supreme Court (in *U.S. v. Virginia*) that government must have "an exceedingly persuasive justification" for excluding women or otherwise discriminating against them, and that the burden for showing such justification "is demanding and rests entirely with the state." As significant as they are, these developments do not alter the fact that the ERA itself did not succeed in the political arena.

widespread mobilization, and the ERA campaign became identified in the minds of most people with the women's movement itself.

As an effort to change policy by passing a constitutional amendment, the campaign for the ERA was, of course, a failure. The time allotted for passage expired in June 1982, at which point the ERA had been endorsed by only thirty-five of the necessary thirty-eight state legislatures, and by no new legislatures since January 1977. As a by-product of this failed ratification campaign, however, the ideas of the women's movement were put in front of large numbers of people. Figure 2-2 provides evidence of the extensive publicity achieved by the ERA. There was a substantial and sustained level of *New York Times* coverage of the ERA from 1972 to 1982, followed by a sharp falloff in interest immediately after the defeat of the amendment.[12] Recall from figure 2-1 that *Times* coverage of gender-based employment discrimination reached only eight articles in 1967, the year the executive order was signed. By contrast, there was an average of seventy-nine articles per year on the ERA in the *New York Times* during the eleven years of the campaign. The ERA certainly achieved the level of attention one would expect of an issue connected to a social movement.

The second key trait that helped the ERA campaign foster a social movement is that the issue reached beyond government and movement organizations to be taken up by many in the population. A movement in the social arena rests on conversations and debates that cause people to think about new issues, or to reevaluate their positions on old issues. The existence of a social movement would best be measured by listening in on millions of conversations. That is not possible, certainly not after the fact. But some reasonable inferences can be made about the extent of the public debate by looking beyond the number of newspaper articles to the type of newspaper articles published by the *New York Times* during the ERA campaign.

Table 2-2 shows that the ERA was covered by the *New York Times* under a variety of rubrics during its decade in the state legislatures. In the first years of the campaign, 1972–1974, press coverage was dominated by accounts of official actions marking the road to passage. Because passage of the ERA was initially expected to occur quickly, half of all articles in these years described the measure's progress through the state legislatures.

As the campaign for the ERA began to stall, the struggle between organizations taking opposite sides on the amendment began to achieve more prominence. Despite the slowdown in official progress in passing the amendment, press coverage of the campaign doubled to almost two articles per week between 1975 and 1977. Most of this additional coverage was devoted

---

[12] The falloff in attention to the ERA after 1982 was so great that the *Times* index category "US—constitution—amendment—women" was in 1984 broadened to "US—constitution—women." In 1985 the category disappeared altogether.

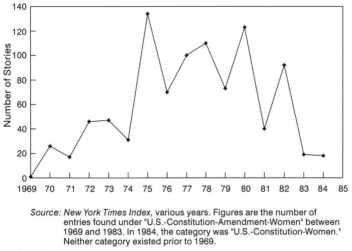

Source: New York Times Index, various years. Figures are the number of entries found under "U.S.-Constitution-Amendment-Women" between 1969 and 1983. In 1984, the category was "U.S.-Constitution-Women." Neither category existed prior to 1969.

Figure 2-2   Press coverage of the Equal Rights Amendment, 1969–1984

TABLE 2-2

Types of Press Coverage of the Equal Rights Amendment, 1972–1984 (in percent)

	1972–1974	1975–1977	1978–1982	1983–1984	All Years
Political arena					
Governmental actions and reports	49.2	33.2	38.6	56.8	39.0
Social arena					
Nongovernmental conferences, speeches, or demonstrations	24.2	28.3	30.8	18.9	28.6
Feature article on issues, individuals, or groups	13.7	22.4	12.8	8.1	6.0
Editorial, op-ed article, letter to editors	12.9	16.1	17.8	16.2	16.5
Total	100	100	100	99.9	100.1
Number of cases	124	304	438	37	903
Mean number per year	41.3	101.3	87.6	18.5	69.5

Source: Content analysis of all articles in the *New York Times* on the Equal Rights Amendment, 1972–1984.

to activities of NOW (which took the lead in the pro-ERA campaign) and to Phyllis Schlafly's STOP-ERA. Press coverage also broadened to include a monthly diet of feature articles reviewing the history of the amendment and its prospects for passage. In the absence of much official news concerning the progress of the amendment, the *Times* also offered increased coverage of the campaign in those states, such as Utah and Nevada, where the ERA became entangled with debates over the proper role of church officials in politics. Finally, the *New York Times* increased its editorial coverage of the issue in a series of editorials and op-ed pieces favoring the amendment, as well as letters from readers on both sides of the issue.

Shifts in type of press coverage represent not only an altered focus of attention (e.g., from governmental to nongovernmental actors), but also a change in the types of information presented. Articles centered on governmental decisions or reports tend to be legalistic in approach, concerned mainly to describe the channels by which a decision was reached and the procedures that must still be followed to complete ratification of the amendment. Thus, the typical report of a state decision on the ERA would give the voting division in the legislature, the partisan split of votes, and the role that had been played by the governor or other important officials.

As coverage of the ERA came to include more prominently the activities of NOW and STOP-ERA, the nature of the stories changed. The ERA was no longer treated as a disembodied piece of legislation going through a labyrinthine political process. It was presented instead as a hotly contested issue that served as a symbolic focus for a much broader debate about the place of women in society, current changes in their status, and what the role of federal legislation should be in promoting change. When presenting stories about NOW and STOP-ERA rallies, or feature articles on local activists and organizations working on the ERA, journalistic norms of balance come into play.[13] Reports of nongovernmental political activities were accompanied by acknowledgment that there is an opposing position and by a statement from a representative of that position. This meant that NOW and STOP-ERA came to be paired against each other in hundreds of news stories that contained contentious claims, angry quotations, and passionate pleas. While accounts of activities in the political arena focused on the institutional process, accounts of the movement in the social arena highlighted ideas and controversies. "The result," as Mansbridge (1986: 188) put it, "was both creeping feminism and creeping antifeminism."

In sum, the period 1975–1977 was marked by an increase in the amount of attention given to the ERA, a shift of focus from the governmental to the nongovernmental sphere, and a shift of theme from legislative process to the

---

[13] For an elaboration of the effect of the journalistic balance norm on media representations of movement activities, see chapter 6.

confrontation of opposing ideas about gender equality and social change. It is in this period that the ERA campaign can be said to have been the focus of a true social movement.

The third period shown in table 2-2, 1978–1982, encompasses the dying gasps of the ERA campaign. It is striking that the flow of news articles remained almost undiminished during these years despite the fact that the amendment made no further progress toward ratification. In this phase the political arena news was dominated by repeated "no" votes in the remaining states needed for ratification, and by attempted recisions of prior ratification in some other states. NOW organized a boycott of states that had not ratified the amendment, and there was considerable coverage of efforts in some states to have the boycott declared illegal.

But the greatest amount of ERA news in the period 1978–1982 continued to come directly from the NOW and STOP-ERA camps, both of which worked at a fever pitch as the original ratification deadline of 1979 approached. There was widespread coverage of the campaign to extend the deadline for ratification, and coverage picked up once again during the final ratification drive leading up to the new 1982 deadline. Editorials, op-ed pieces, and letters from readers reached their maximum volume between 1978 and 1982. The continued focus in *Times* coverage of movement organizations and the regular appearance of the amendment on the editorial page shows that the issue remained highly newsworthy even in the absence of progress toward ratification.

The final period, 1983–1984, represents the collapse of the ERA campaign. Articles related to the ERA appeared at the rate of one every three weeks, compared to one every four days between 1978 and 1982. Both NOW and STOP-ERA disappeared completely from the news, at least in the context of the ERA campaign. Even this reduced rate of coverage substantially overestimates the place of the ERA in the national media, since one half of the articles in the *New York Times* during these two years came from Governor Cuomo's effort to pass an equal rights amendment to New York's state constitution. Despite reintroduction of the ERA into Congress in 1983, coverage of the amendment came to a virtual halt after 1982.

The ERA campaign is suggestive of the ways in which a movement campaign in the political arena can spill over into the social arena. Unlike the more restricted political lobbying that led to the executive order on sex discrimination, large political arena campaigns such as the one to pass the ERA can become the focal point of a wider social debate. The ERA campaign was a launching pad for the women's movement in the social arena, as evidenced by the spread of coverage in the *New York Times* from initial accounts of governmental actions to later news of the activities of a wide variety of local organizations and activists.

The breadth of the social debate sparked by the ERA campaign is suggested by a Gallup poll question that asked participants in a national sample in 1976 whether they had heard of the equal rights amendment to the Constitution. Ninety percent said they had heard of the ERA.[14] Men were as likely as women to have heard of the issue, all age groups were equally likely to have heard of it, and the gradient based on level of education was remarkably mild, ranging from 96 percent of college graduates to 77 percent of those with a grade school education.

This level of ERA recognition can be put in perspective by a 1977 Gallup poll that asked respondents which of a long list of Republican Party leaders they knew anything about. Ninety-two percent said they had heard something about Gerald Ford, who had just been defeated for reelection as president. Eighty-nine percent had heard something about Ronald Reagan, who had the previous year given Ford a tough contest for the Republican nomination. The next politician on the list was recognized by only two-thirds of the public.[15] At the ninety percent public awareness level, the ERA was clearly a superstar among issues, in elite company when it comes to public recognition. Coverage patterns of the ERA in the *New York Times* are thus reflective of (and contributed to) broad awareness of the issue.

At first blush, we might expect a straightforward complementarity between movement efforts in the political and social arenas. Success in the political arena means redefining legally sanctioned behavior, which can ultimately change cultural values. Success in the social arena means changing perceptions of what the most important political problems are. Altered cultural values bring new problems from the private realm onto the public agenda.

And yet, there are also tensions between the conditions that generate progress in one arena and those that lead to success in the other. Indeed, the launch of a feminist social movement in the 1970s was an important factor in the failure of the ERA ratification effort. In 1972 the ERA was seen as a matter of guaranteeing equity between men and women. But the spread of feminist thinking through the women's movement raised new questions about the meaning of equity. Would women have to serve in combat roles in the armed forces? Would single-sex schools and colleges be outlawed? Would there be unisex public bathrooms? In their story of ERA politics in North Carolina, a state that did not ratify, Mathews and De Hart (1990: 210) conclude that the ERA stalled because "It became a feminist issue instead of a women's issue. As such it became controversial and generated intense conflict, an issue a majority of legislators came to view as dangerous to the political affability of the legislative culture of bargain and trade." Indeed, the

---

[14] In similar Gallup surveys between 1975 and 1980 the percentage of respondents saying they had not heard of the ERA ranged between 9 and 13 percent.

[15] Former Texas Governor John Connally was third with 67 percent recognition.

ERA became more emotionally and politically charged as the decade went on. This was a sure sign of the spread of a social movement, but it was devastating to ratification hopes.

If we are to understand movements, then, we must be attentive to the interaction between their manifestations in the social and political arenas. Success in either arena may be helpful to the movement in the other, but the relationship between arenas can take other forms as well. The allocation of resources and effort, the contrasting requirements of organizational structure and tactical choice, and the contradictions between building a broad political coalition and undertaking cultural reeducation all make for difficult relations within a movement between advocates of action in the two arenas.

In summary, the successful launch of a social movement based on the political arena ERA debate did not prevent the eventual failure of the ERA ratification drive, and it may have contributed to that failure. Success of a movement in one arena does not mandate success in the other. Yet, the development of a women's movement in the social arena during these years is inexplicable if we ignore the political arena. The ERA campaign brought the women's movement together, held it together for a decade, and kept the issue of women's roles in society before the public eye. It was, as Mathews and De Hart (1990: ix) put it, the most politicizing issue for women since suffrage.

THE CREATION OF A SOCIAL MOVEMENT

The importance of the ERA campaign to the women's movement should not tempt us to conclude that the social movement was created by the political movement. Instead, the campaign gave focus and media prominence to a social movement that had already begun. The evidence from figure 2-1 suggests that the women's movement was already gathering momentum between 1970 and 1972, when the issue of gender discrimination in employment took a sudden jump in visibility. This increased attention occurred as a result of a diverse and diffuse social movement, without any single organization, leader, issue, or event serving as a catalyst.[16]

Indeed, the ERA campaign was as much a consequence of the developing social movement as it was a cause. The spread of interest in the movement caught the attention of political leaders who were aware of the need to re-

---

[16] Coverage of gender-based employment discrimination in the *New York Times* follows the same pattern of spread from political arena to social arena news as did coverage of the ERA. While stories about official governmental actions related to sex discrimination increased by 250 percent, stories on the actions of nongovernmental organizations and leaders increased by 600 percent. There had been only two feature articles on the problem of gender-based job discrimination in 1968–1969, but between 1970 and 1973 there were six per year. Editorial comment and letters from readers increased by 800 percent between 1965–1969 and 1970–1973.

spond to shifting patterns of social concern. President Nixon echoed the thoughts of many savvy politicians when he told his secretary of health, education and welfare in September 1970 that "we need to do some things to see that women are properly recognized and that we get credit for things we do carry out with women" (Hoff 1994: 103).

What happens to cause a politician to want to do something for a particular group, and to receive credit for it? The creation of a social movement implies the expansion of public and media attention to a particular issue area. This generalized expansion of coverage means, among other things, that press attention was newly given to activities that the government had been carrying out without publicity for years. For example, information on differential unemployment rates and income levels among men and women have long been collected and reported by the Bureau of Labor Statistics. These reports were routinely printed in the *New York Times* beginning only in 1970. In 1971 *Times* articles appeared on decisions related to gender discrimination taken by the Allegheny (Pennsylvania) County Common Pleas Court, by the Federal District Court in Ohio, and by the city council of the District of Columbia. Each of these jurisdictions is far afield for a newspaper based in New York and none of them would have been covered in the absence of widespread public interest in the issue.

The appearance of such stories suggests that the spread of a women's movement in the social arena increased the level of press attention to related activities in the political arena. Judicial decisions, municipal laws, and executive branch reports related to gender-based job discrimination were now considered to be news. Increased media attention, in turn, forced political leaders to become more attentive to the issue. This change is reflected in the heightened level of governmental activity on gender-based job discrimination issues in the 1970s, an issue that came into its own only several years after the signing of the executive order. In 1970 the U.S. Labor Department, its statistics on gender-based job discrimination now subject to public scrutiny, gave employers new guidelines on hiring and promotion practices. Shortly thereafter the Justice Department filed a number of suits that were widely understood to be critical test cases of the new guidelines. In January 1971 the Supreme Court issued a ruling on one of these test cases (*Phillips v. Martin-Marietta*), finding that the refusal to hire mothers of young children was an impermissible form of sex discrimination. This ruling, and the many court cases that followed it, reflected a heightened level of interest in gender discrimination that spanned several agencies and branches of government. The circle was closed between the political and social arenas.

Monitoring press coverage of the ERA can be a bloodless way to observe the development of a social movement. We should therefore not lose sight of the most important characteristic of movements in the social arena, namely the deep passions that are stirred with the introduction of new identities and values into the culture. These passions are the reason that press coverage of issues connected to the ERA was so extensive, so sustained, and so varied in focus.

"Passions" is not too strong a word to use in this context. Consider the 1977 decision by the National Directors' Board of the Girl Scouts of America to endorse the ERA, an endorsement that was reported in the *New York Times*. This news led to an attempt by the STOP-ERA chapter in Chatham, Georgia, to organize a boycott of Girl Scout cookies. That boycott was also reported in the *Times*, as was the decision by the Chelsea, Michigan, chapter of the Girl Scouts to resign from the national organization in protest against the national board's stand.

In the larger scheme of cultural change, boycotts of Girl Scout cookies are a minor matter. But these events represent only the visible tip of a much larger social movement iceberg. Decisions by the national board of the Girl Scouts, much less by local chapters, would not have been given national media attention had they not been connected to a widespread debate on the role of women in society—a debate that came in the 1970s to be seen through the prism of the ERA. It is precisely the role of a movement in the social arena to generate controversy by provoking debate over new cultural values. When the Girl Scouts start arguing among themselves, we should suspect the presence of a social movement.

Movements and Cultural Change

Movements figure prominently in this account of cultural change, but they have not been analyzed in the manner customary among movement scholars. The unit of analysis used throughout this book is the specific element of value change, such as the belief that "separate but equal" is an unjust vision of race relations, or that maintenance of biodiversity is essential for human survival. Movements are generally active on behalf of a large cluster of related value changes that are pursued more or less simultaneously, often through different channels and via different organizations. Organizations within the women's movement have sought to achieve legal equality, to strengthen affirmative action efforts in occupations where women are underrepresented, to raise women's self-esteem, to maintain a vigilant lobbying effort in Washington, to publish information on women's health concerns, to obtain and then preserve abortion rights, to change the laws and the judicial process concerning rape, to criminalize sexual harassment, to get more women elected to political office, and to create shelters, co-ops, bookstores, counseling services, health centers, and a variety of other associations exclusively for women. This list, incomplete as it is, spans a diversity of goals in both the social and political arenas. These goals are not strictly consistent with each other: some assert equality between men and women and others claim for women both difference and privilege. Some goals have been realized in the form of political arena victories and some have seen political arena defeats. Some have made significant progress in the social arena and others have not. It is little wonder that attempts to analyze the goals, organization, strategy, and impact of "the" women's movement (or any other movement viewed as a unitary entity) are forced to choose between emphasizing one part of the movement or concluding that there are actually many distinct movements sharing a single label.

By choosing as our unit of analysis a single cultural value, we are able to trace the interaction between a critical community, a variety of movement organizations, and other social and political institutions. Movements, in other words, are disaggregated into a number of separable groups and organizations. None of these groups is the movement itself; the movement exists in the relationship between them. There can be no movement (but only anomic protest) in the absence of linkage between a critical community and movement organizations.

Assessing the impact of movements is a problem that has particularly vexed students of social and political movements. The most common criterion of success is change in policy, but there are problems with that formulation. It is usually difficult to tell if governmental policies conforming to movement demands were adopted as a result of movement pressures. Movement ideas are often translated into public policies only after the movement has faded away.

Gamson's (1990) study of challenging groups, first published in 1975, includes as a measure of success any policy changes that occurred up to fifteen years after the group ceased to function. By this definition, policy success was achieved by just under half of the groups Gamson studied, and the lag from formation of the group to the achievement of success ranged from one year to fifty-five years (with a mean of twenty-one years). Goldstone (1980) has disputed Gamson's assumption that policy changes conforming to group demands can always be attributed to group action. He shows that policy success fits a stochastic curve generated by a constant probability factor of $p = .05$. The implication is that a steady rate of policy innovation may result in the adoption of some movement proposals, without the activities of the movement organization having been influential. The fact that over 40 percent of Gamson's movement organizations were able to obtain policy reforms without political or social resources reinforces the suspicion that such reforms do not always result directly from movement pressure.[17]

Evaluating policy impacts becomes even more tangled when a delayed

---

[17] See chapter 7 for further discussion of social resources, political resources, and movement success.

governmental response takes the form of legislation that mimics movement reforms without producing the transforming effect hoped for within the movement. John Hicks (1961: 406–423), an important historian of the Populist movement, lists among its successes the direct election of senators, primary elections, women's suffrage, addition of the initiative and referendum to state constitutions, the secret ballot and improved registration laws to fight electoral fraud, establishment of the Federal Reserve Bank and of emergency currency reserves to make the money supply more elastic, federal farm loan programs, establishment of a federal farm board to purchase surplus farm products in order to maintain a target price, regulation of railroads and other carriers of interstate commerce, passage of antitrust laws, and establishment of national parks and forests to preserve "the people's land." These reforms were all adopted between 1900 and 1929, and it is not Hicks's contention that the Populists were directly responsible for any of them. However, Hicks points out that support for these reforms was often greatest in regions where the Populists had been strongest. His general conclusion is that these reforms vindicated the Populist effort.

The difficulty is that some of these same reforms have been looked upon by others as representing the definitive rejection of Populist principles. Lawrence Goodwyn (1978: 267–270) claims that the Federal Reserve Act and the farm loan acts were anathema to the spirit of Populism because they operated through the commercial banking system rather than undermining the power of private bankers, as the Populists intended. Much the same can be said of antitrust legislation and the establishment of the Interstate Commerce Commission, which proved to be less of an inconvenience to monopolists and railroad magnates than a palliative against public discontent. "Meanwhile," as Goodwyn (1978: 269) put it, "the idea of a substantial democratic influence over the structure of the nation's financial system, a principle that had been the operative political objective of greenbackers, quietly passed out of American political dialogue."[18]

A final problem with the attribution of particular outcomes to specific movements lies in the fact that movements occur in clusters, a phenomenon referred to by Tarrow (1989) as cycles of protest. Mobilization into many movements is facilitated by (some would say caused by) the success of the pioneer movement(s) in a given protest cycle. It is clear, for example, that the civil rights movement aided in the development of the 1960s protest cycle in a variety of ways: by developing a language of group rights that could be applied to other causes; by training a large cohort of movement

---

[18] Goodwyn believes that Progressivism succeeded where Populism failed. The Progressives called for many of the reforms previously demanded by the Populists, but their intention was to soften the impact of elite institutions rather than to democratize them. This makes the attribution of policy reform even markier, for some degree of Progressive success was surely due to the work of the Populists before them.

activists—both black and white—who later became involved in other movements; by piecing together political and social coalitions that later supported other movements; by innovating a number of protest tactics, most prominently the sit-in, that were adopted by follow-on movements; and by spreading in the American culture the idea that movements for change could break through political stalemates and help remedy significant social problems. As McAdam (1995) points out, movements following closely the trail blazed by a pioneer movement benefit the most; within a few years the new language of values may come to seem overextended and the social and political coalition in support of change may begin to fragment. Even so, the existence of a protest cycle means that a one-to-one mapping of movements and outcomes becomes even more problematic. Some significant portion of the gains in women's rights in the 1970s must be jointly attributed to the women's movement *and* to the civil rights movement before it.

In summary, there are four difficulties with using policy reforms as a measure of movement success. First, movement organizations concentrated on change in the social arena may not be inclined to seek policy reforms, at least until they have first accomplished their objective of altering social values. Second, it is often difficult to distinguish between policy reforms that result from movement activity and those which are the work of other forces. Third, although it is to be expected that movement demands will be narrowed to fit the requirements of legislation and implementation, there are times when the translation of movement idea into governmental action fails to have the effects desired by the movement, and times when the reform may even have adverse effects from the movement perspective. And, fourth, the existence of cycles of protest means that movement outcomes are contingent partially on the success of prior movements in fostering change in their own issue areas.

These problems raise difficult questions about movement influence on policy. Under what circumstances can we consider the movement to have been influential if its ideas are adopted after the movement has disappeared? Should we consider the movement to have been influential if its demands are not feasible until some circumstances have changed? Should we consider a movement to be influential if policy reforms, once adopted, fail to achieve the results expected within movement circles?

Evaluating movement impacts by their influence on cultural values avoids the problems of estimating policy impacts. Changing cultural values are essential to movement success in both the political and social arenas, so it is an appropriate yardstick for all movements. It requires a movement presence in both the political and social arenas to foster rapid change in cultural values. The extent of change in values is therefore the best criterion by which movement impacts can be judged. When movements achieve their policy objectives only after a lag, the relevant question is whether belated success is due to cultural change or to changes in circumstances that are unrelated to movement efforts. Changes in the political feasibility of movement demands often have less to do with the objective condition of the physical world than they do with innovations in the way people think about the physical world. Cultural change is the common denominator behind all movement goals.

By focusing on specific cultural changes rather than on entire movements, we are able to incorporate the diversity of means and ends that exists within any movement. We build on the observations of scholars like Blumer and Gusfield, who recognize the significant differences between movements in the two arenas. We resolve the linguistic confusion created by the terms political movement and social movement. We cast aside the less fruitful aspects of scholarly debates about whether movements are strategic or cultural, resource-based or identity-based, while utilizing the very substantial insights generated by each of these approaches. Finally, a focus on cultural change enables us to appreciate the interactions that exist between the political and social arenas of movement action. Since movements convey new cultural values to both arenas, we are led to examine the relationship between them, the tensions involved in simultaneous activity in them, and the means by which movements organizations try to cope with these tensions.

Through their actions in the social arena, movements help spread familiarity with a new discourse. Through their efforts in the political arena, movements generate pressure to undertake significant departures in policy. By acting simultaneously in both arenas, movements create the irreversible tides that periodically reform the landscape in a particular policy domain.

CONCLUSION

Critical communities and movements are the key actors in the two-stage process of value generation and value diffusion. Critical communities engage in the identification and elaboration of group interests. This is not only a matter of specifying the interest itself, but also of embedding that interest in a value structure, Gestalt, or discourse. "I have a dream" summarizes the view that racial integration reflects the noblest ideals of American culture and political institutions. "Fifty-nine cents" is a capsule version of the argument that equity in the workplace means equal pay for men and women.

Movements mobilize thousands of people behind the ideas of the critical community. In so doing, they cannot use the ideas developed in critical networks as off-the-shelf packages. Some critical ideas lend themselves better to mass mobilization than others; many critical ideas are destined never to be embraced beyond the restricted network of thinkers in which they originated. At a minimum, the ideas of a critical community must be repackaged in a way that connects them with mobilizable social groups. As we shall see in chapter 4, the people who join a movement generally do so through their affiliation with a preexisting social group or network. Such networks are not simply conjured out of the air; there are continuities and elements of conservatism even in the process of cultural change. The discourse of a critical community is useful to movement leaders only when it can be connected to existing group networks and to a plan for collective action.

Separating the two steps of idea generation and diffusion, while useful for analytical purposes, is a simplification of the actual process of cultural change. For one thing, there is often overlap in personnel. Martin Luther King was both a theorist linking racial integration to a campaign of non-violent civil disobedience and the preeminent leader of the movement that carried out that campaign. Participants in movements are also originators of cultural values, as they find their ideas evolving in the process of movement struggle.[19] As we shall see in chapter 5, movement activists frequently broaden their sense of what they are fighting for as they begin to think in more abstract ideological terms. Contact with activists in related movements may also broaden the sense of commitment from a narrowly defined cause to a more inclusive one. In short, those in the critical community also take action, while those active within the movement also contribute to the development of new value perspectives.

There is, additionally, overlap in timing between the critical community and the movement. As environmental organizations found that an emphasis on "limits to growth" had little resonance beyond college campuses, advocates of alternate ways of thinking about environmental protection generated other ideas, including an emphasis on the use of market incentives to clean up industry and to preserve lands from development. Similarly the 1960s student movement was founded on a critical discourse about the lack of participatory democracy in capitalist society. But the cultural message of the student movement changed radically later on, as the war in Vietnam took an ever greater share of movement attention.

It is important not to let the simplicity of a two-step model blind us to these forms of overlap between the functions of the critical community and those of the movement. But nor should the blurring of boundaries between critical community and movement deny us the profit of distinguishing between the two. There are times when ideas developed in a critical community are discussed in limited circles for decades or even generations before exploding onto a wider social and political scene. We saw this in the case of the philosophes, and we will see it again in the case of alcoholism presented in chapter 3. Although the distinction can be subtle in practice, the shift from critical community to movement is a shift in audience from the members of the critical community itself to a wider audience of movement activists and

---

[19] For evidence on this point, see chapters 4 and 5.

other potential converts. Critical communities and movements are distinct actors whose contributions to cultural change come respectively from discourse and from action. It is important to keep them analytically separated, even when they are empirically intertwined.

Finally, I have defined movements as occurring through the union of critical discourse and collective action, with ultimate goals in the social and political arenas. This trait is intimately connected to the role of movements in the process of cultural change. For while other institutions, such as the mass media, political parties, and even advertising agencies may contribute to cultural change, only movements seek to develop support in both the social and political arenas for ideas that, at least initially, enjoy support among relatively restricted circles among the public. An understanding of the importance of the political and social arenas, in turn, requires that we take seriously the dual nature of movements. We can use this duality to develop an integrated perspective on the classic issues of movement mobilization, organization, tactical choice, and impacts.

In these first two chapters, we have seen in schematic form the two-step process by which critical communities create new perspectives on issues (or create new issues) and by which movements carry those perspectives to the wider society. These two steps do not guarantee that the ideas of the critical community will be adopted by the wider culture. But critical communities and movements, acting in partnership, do guarantee that there will be controversy about an issue that is likely to have previously been seen as unproblematic.

We shall pay a great deal of attention to the timing, behavior, and outcomes of critical community and movement activities during the course of this book. The second and third sections of the book will examine the tasks faced by movements in mobilizing activists and generating social and political influence. Before moving to these matters, however, we are best served first by considering in greater detail some examples of rapid changes in cultural values. Cultural change can take a variety of forms, depending on the relationship between established values and the new discourse developed in the critical community and publicly interpreted by the movement. This is the subject of the next chapter.

Chapter 3

THE ACCEPTANCE OF NEW CULTURAL VALUES

MOVEMENTS disseminate the new value perspectives of critical communities to the wider society, but not as they please. The set of values relevant to a given subject determines the standards by which new value perspectives will be judged. New value claimants are not considered in isolation, but are instead examined in light of those values already held.

We will in this chapter explore three modes of cultural change. The distinction between them hinges on the relationship between the proposed new values and the existing stock of values. "Value conversion" is the replacement of existing cultural values with new ideas on the same topic about what is important, equitable, or legitimate. "Value creation" is the development of new ideas, concepts, or categories of analysis that apply to situations that had not previously been the subject of explicit cultural values. Finally, "value connection" is the development of a conceptual link between phenomena previously thought either to be unconnected with each other or to be connected in a different way.[1]

In the case of value conversion, new valuations contradict and replace the old. Conversion is generally accompanied by a recategorization of familiar objects into new conceptual packages. This recategorization may have important consequences for how we think about an issue.

If African Americans are categorized as humans not fundamentally different from European Americans, then racial segregation is no longer a natural way to organize society and becomes instead one that is morally repugnant. Various related attitudes, behaviors, and institutions are also called into question. Disenfranchisment based on racial categories is no longer defensible. Socially imposed barriers to equality of achievement become more visible to us because the presumption no longer exists that differences in achievement reflect differences in ability.

If women are believed to have a legitimate right to work outside the home, then aspects of a career that conflict with the requirements of raising a family may be called into question. Differentials in salary and promotion

---

[1] The distinction made here between value conversion, creation, and connection parallels in some respects the distinction made by Snow and Benford (1988, 1992) on framing processes. Of the four framing processes they describe, frame bridging, frame amplification, and frame extension are all here subsumed under value connection. Their fourth process, frame transformation, could occur by either value creation or value conversion.

opportunities lose legitimacy when working women are no longer thought of as supplementing the income of a male head of household.

If nuclear weapons are reconceived as a means of fighting a war rather than deterring one, then such weapons come to be seen as reducing our security instead of enhancing it. Thinking about nuclear weapons conjures up images of the devastation that would be caused by a nuclear war, rather than of the stability associated with a strong military capacity.

These are all cases of cultural change by value conversion. Each case involves a recategorization of some core value, resulting in revision of a variety of related attitudes and behaviors. The arguments that segregation is wrong, that women deserve equal opportunity in the labor force, or that adding to the nuclear arsenal reduces security make sense only if the basic discourse on each topic is first reconceived.

Unlike value conversion, value creation does not demand a confrontation with existing ways of thinking. New values constitute additional considerations brought to bear on a topic. They represent an expansion of culture.

There have been numerous examples of value creation on environmental issues during the past century. The term "conservation" was itself coined during Teddy Roosevelt's presidency, when public land was first set aside for incorporation into what later became the National Forest system. More recently, the environmental movement has given us such terms as "biodegradable," "endangered species," and "global climate change," terms that bring new problems to our attention and that contain embedded within them perspectives on actions that need to be taken. The element of value creation in these examples resides in the fact that previous values did not advocate the use of nondegradable phosphates in detergents, the extinction of species, or thinning of the ozone layer. Instead, these phenomena were simply not taken into account in judging human behavior.

Value connection involves forging a conceptual link between phenomena previously thought to be unconnected. As Benford and Snow point out in their seminal article on frame alignment, it is a matter of achieving cultural resonance between new and established values. Similarly, Kempton, Boster, and Hartley (1995) find that environmental beliefs are often melded to existing religious and aesthetic values. Thus, "It is wrong to abuse the Earth because God created it," and "We must conserve the beauty of Nature." As Kempton et al. (1995: 218) conclude, "laypeople do not passively receive environmental news, but rather, they actively interpret what they hear via their preexisting cultural models."

The success of the civil rights movement rested largely on the connection made by its leaders to political and religious values. To African Americans who formed the potential base of support for the movement, Martin Luther King connected the struggle for civil rights to stories of struggle and redemption in the Bible. As Andrew Young (as cited in Hamilton 1972: 132–133) observes,

> when Martin would talk about leaving the slavery of Egypt and wandering into a promised land, somehow that made sense to folks. . . . And when they heard that language, they responded. You could go into Mississippi and tell people they needed to get themselves together and get organized. And that didn't make much sense. But if you started preaching to them about dry bones rising again, everybody had sung about dry bones. Everybody knew the language.

To America's white culture and to the political establishment, King placed more stress on the relationship between civil rights and the ideals of American democracy. Thus, the movement had more than one form of value connection to draw upon, and different connections were made for different audiences. McAdam (1994: 38) points out that King was able "to frame civil rights activity in a way that resonated not only with the culture of the oppressed but with the culture of the oppressor as well." At the beginning of the Montgomery bus boycott, King summarized these two forms of value connection succinctly and powerfully: "If we are wrong, the Supreme Court of this nation is wrong. If we are wrong, God Almighty is wrong" (cited in Evans and Boyte 1986: 58).

Value connections may evolve within a movement over time. In the environmental realm, beliefs about the link between environmental protection and economic growth have changed from the "limits to growth" claim of antagonism to the "sustainable development" idea of searching for complementarity. As a result, the connection of environmental virtue to reduced consumption has been severed in favor of viewing environmental soundness as linked to patterns of consumption that take into account environmental consequences. One consequence of this shift has been to rethink environmental policy making in a way that downplays reliance on governmental regulation and increases reliance on market incentives by developing price mechanisms for the real costs of environmental degradation (Shabecoff 1993). Such changes in the connections between values alter the substantive focus of environmentalism by placing its objectives in a new value context.

Altering values by creating new conceptual linkages is an exercise in what we might call applied philosophy. In nineteenth-century England, extension of the franchise to the unpropertied working class (and then later to women) was aided by the new claim, developed by John Stuart Mill and other liberal democratic theorists, that giving these groups a role in political life would increase their public-spiritedness. This argument created a new connection between rights and responsibility, and those who accepted it were less likely to fear that extension of the franchise would result in the confiscation of property by the unpropertied majority. At about the same time, American abolitionists led by William Lloyd Garrison were altering the public's thinking about slavery by decoupling it from the search for compromises that would hold the Union together (the context of the issue since the Constitution was drafted), and connecting it instead to a debate over moral imperatives. Abolitionists argued that slavery was sinful and morally degrading not only for the slaveholder but also for those who passively allowed slavery to continue. As the abolitionist perspective became an increasingly common understanding of the nature of slavery, regional polarization increased and it became more and more difficult to sustain a Republic that was half slave and half free.

Value conversion, value creation, and value connection are each forms of cultural change, but each has a different impact on the stock of cultural concepts we use to organize the world. Value conversion involves the revaluation of existing concepts. Conversion results in the repudiation of old behaviors and laws, and a demand for new ones. Value creation is the formation of new concepts, resulting in an expansion of our collective concerns and of the political agenda. Through value creation, problems previously left unconsidered or defined as being outside the political realm become subject to community norms and political contest. Value connection is the development of new linkages between concepts. All three forms of value change make possible new coalitions of social forces, but value connection is especially potent in this regard. Through value connection, utility companies support the idea of pollution rights vouchers, the English middle class came to support expansion of the franchise to the working class, and increasing numbers of Americans in the North concluded that some means had to be found not just to contain slavery in its existing territory, but to end it.

These processes of cultural change are best examined by means of concrete examples. The remainder of this chapter consists of three case studies representing value conversion, creation, and connection. In any instance of cultural change, some elements of value conversion, creation, and connection may all be found. But we will see that different processes of cultural change are predominant in different instances. We will also see in each case study the operation of the two-step process of cultural change. The first step is the incubation of new values within a relatively small, interacting, self-conscious critical community. The second step is the diffusion of these values to a wider public through the creation of social and political movements. The wider significance of cultural change will be indicated in each case by presenting evidence that new cultural values were followed by changing patterns of behavior among individuals, as well as by altered institutional design, rules, procedures, and laws.

VALUE CONVERSION: THE CASE OF DESEGREGATION

The story of the civil rights crusade that won for African Americans both desegregation and the right to vote has been told often and well. The successes of the civil rights movement have been convincingly attributed to the rise of a black middle class, the development of powerful black institutions such as the Negro college and church, and the migration of many African Americans to Northern cities where their votes counted dearly in a competitive party environment (Woodward 1955; McAdam 1982; Morris 1984). These developments are an important part of the story, but they represent background conditions that enabled people to undertake the real work of the movement: the cultural delegitimation of segregation.

The central success of the civil rights movement lies in the fact that values related to segregation were fundamentally altered over the span of a single generation. A pattern of race relations seen in 1930 as inevitable and in some ways natural came to be viewed by the 1960s as morally repugnant. The civil rights movement not only demonstrated that continued segregation was intolerable to blacks, it also highlighted the fact that it was shameful for the nation. The cause of integrating public facilities came to be seen as a struggle between good and evil, and the antisegregation campaigns of the civil rights movement have since come to be mythologized as one of America's shining moments.

Today, it is tempting to dismiss pre–World War II arguments for segregation and the racial superiority of whites as mere bigotry, a self-interested ideology backed by the ruthless use of violence and intimidation. But in the early part of the twentieth century most white people, and the evidence suggests many black people as well, believed in the appropriateness of segregation as a way of managing race relations. The earliest available survey evidence dates only from 1942, but at that time integrated transportation was supported by fewer than half of white Americans, and integrated schools by fewer than a third (Schuman, Steeh, and Bobo 1985: 194). Such questions were not asked of African Americans till much later, but a survey of Southern blacks in 1961 found that even at that late date 16 percent favored segregation and another 15 percent supported "something in between segregation and integration."[2]

The foundation of segregationist sentiment was belief in the racial superiority of whites, and the consequent justifiability of white domination of society and politics. It was not always this way. Gossett (1963: 3) observes that "Before the eighteenth century physical differences among peoples were so rarely referred to as a matter of great importance that something of a case can be made for the proposition that race consciousness is largely a modern phenomenon." By the mid nineteenth century, however, an ideology of racial distinctiveness was taking shape. There were three central claims to what I shall call the racialist ideology.[3] First is the belief that racial groupings, dis-

---

[2] "The Negro Political Participation Study, 1961," Donald Matthews and James Prothro, principal investigators.

[3] This terminology is used to distinguish the racialist ideology from racism, which is the contemporary holding of the same belief in racial difference, in a cultural context that no longer supports these views. Fredrickson (1971) uses the term "race thinking," which he believes was developed as a defensive response to the movement for abolition of slavery.

tinct in their capacities and potentials, exist within the human species. Racial differences were held to be a result of the environments in which the races evolved.[4] Africans were claimed to have developed to an inferior level due to the forgiving environment of the continent where plentiful food and a mild climate made teamwork, technological advancement, and an ethic of work and savings unnecessary (Newby 1968: 4; Fredrickson 1971: 254). Differences in the harshness of natural conditions around the globe were thought to have led to an evolved hierarchy of races in which whites were naturally fit to be socially, economically, and politically dominant.

The second premise of the racialist ideology was that there is a natural antipathy between all races, who tend innately to feel repelled by each other and who desire as little contact as possible. This was a newly discovered "law of nature" in the late nineteenth century, not present during the slavery period, which had entailed extensive contact between the races. Even at the end of Reconstruction "an excessive squeamishness or fussiness about contact with negroes was commonly identified as a lower-class white attitude, while the opposite attitude was as popularly associated with 'the quality'" (Woodward 1955: 31). The justification for such segregationist devices as separate railroad coaches for whites and blacks lay in the threat to public order that could arise from unrestrained contact between the races. As Whitelaw Reed, later editor of the *New York Tribune*, wrote in the 1850s, "Where Negroes reside in any great numbers among the whites, . . . both parties are the worse for it, and it is to the interest of both that a separation should be made as soon as possible" (cited in Fredrickson 1971: 135). The Southern historian Phillip Alexander Bruce (as cited in Newby 1968: 77) put the matter even more pointedly in 1911:

> as the regular volume of travel increased, the physical repulsiveness of indiscriminate race mixture in public conveyances grew more acute, and the danger of personal conflicts also augmented. . . . No one who remembers the former promiscuous commingling of whites and blacks in the Southern trains can fail to recall the scenes of violence witnessed there in consequence of the aggressive attitude of negroes inflamed by drink.

The ultimate purpose of the enforced segregation of the races was to prevent the greatest nightmare of the racialist ideology, the fear that "promis-

---

[4] An earlier nineteenth-century theory, polygeny, held that God created the races separately and gave them differing capabilities at Creation. When evidence for the theory of evolution established a common origin for all humans and a much longer time scale of human development than foreseen by Creationists, the natural selection account described here was substituted to make the same points about white racial superiority. See Fredrickson 1971: 71–96, 230–245, and Gossett 1963: 144–175. The evolutionary development of more and less intelligent strains of *homo sapiens* could in principle occur, according to Gould (1981: 323), except that the time scale is all wrong. *Homo sapiens* is at most a few hundred thousand years old, and it would take a much longer period of complete genetic compartmentalization for significant differentiation to develop.

cuous commingling" in railroad cars and elsewhere would create a mixed race. This was, again, a late nineteenth-century cultural innovation, for interracial unions between white slaveowners and black slaves had been common before abolition. It was to "prevent amalgamation [that] the Creator had, it was thought, implanted in each race an instinct of aversion toward all other races which tended to maintain the races in pristine purity" (Nolen 1967: 31). The belief was firmly held that mixing the blood of different races invariably led to the downfall of civilization; as Dr. Josiah Nott put the matter in 1856, "The superior race must inevitably become deteriorated by any admixture with the inferior" (cited in Fredrickson 1971: 80). Senator Ellender of Louisiana offered a history of the dire consequences of "race amalgamation" during a 1938 filibuster against a proposed antilynching law[5] (as cited in Newby 1968: 129, 131):

> What I fear is that political equality will lead to social equality, and social equality will eventually spell the decay and the downfall of our American civilization. . . . Such decay has followed wherever there has been a mixture of the colored races with the whites. . . . [I]f the amalgamation of whites and negroes in this country is permitted, then there will be a mongrel race, and there will come to pass the identical condition under which Egypt, India, and other civilizations decayed.

The obvious contradiction between the claim that there are instinctive racial aversions and the need to be concerned about "the amalgamation of whites and negroes" is an especially pernicious example of the inconsistencies found in the racialist ideology (as in any cultural belief system). Similarly, comments about the link between racial mixing and the fate of civilization in Egypt and India show the flimsiness of the empirical basis for wild speculations about racial differences. But that weakness of evidence is obvious to us only in retrospect. It is almost impossible to overestimate the power of cultural ideas to condition observers to see certain facts but not other facts, and above all to suggest interpretations of the facts that are seen. The power of culture to shape everyday observation is illustrated in the conclusions of Filipo Manetta, who toured antebellum slave plantations to observe the intellectual development of black children. Manetta found that "the negro children were sharp, intelligent, and full of vivacity, but on approaching the adult period a gradual change set in. The intellect seems to become clouded, animation giving place to a sort of lethargy, briskness yielding to indolence" (quoted in Shufeldt 1907: 35).

The mind leaps to causal explanation of these developmental differences,

---

[5] Lynchings became more frequent, more public, and more exclusively targeted at black males in the late nineteenth century. Their most common purpose was to spread the word that sexual congress between black men and white women would not be tolerated (McPherson 1975: 303).

and it would seem to be self-evident that children growing up with the realization that they are slaves (and prohibited by law and custom from receiving even a basic education) would follow a different trajectory of intellectual and personality development than children growing up in freedom. But the explanation that today seems obvious appears never to have occurred either to the author of these lines or to the man who quoted them in 1907. The very next sentence in Manetta's account reaches a different conclusion: "We must necessarily suppose that the development of the Negro and White proceeds on different lines."

From the perspective of a culture permeated by the racialist ideology, such differences as those observed by Manetta are evidence of Negro racial inferiority. Gould (1981) has made the same point about the theory of white intellectual superiority, which also rests on unexamined assumptions, logical fallacies, inadequate statistical control, and systematic errors and inconsistencies in measurement. Ashley Montagu (1942) generalizes the problem when he points out that findings of racial difference were based on an initial unproved assumption that there are significant genetic differences that underlie racial traits. The power of cultural assumptions to screen our perceptions and interpretations of facts turns on its head the conventional wisdom about the utility of the scientific method in correcting errors and biases. There is nothing in scientific procedure that guarantees detection and correction of errors due to cultural bias. As G. R. Boynton (1982: 37) has observed, "Science is the connection of ideas and descriptions." As a result, belief in racial difference came to dominate nineteenth-century American science and culture.[6]

There were of course significant differences among nineteenth-century Americans on such race-related issues as slavery. But belief in inherent racial hierarchies transcended such divisions. Slaveholders trumpeted racial hierarchy to justify slavery, while abolitionists attacked slavery based partly on a variant of the racialist ideology that Fredrickson (1971) calls "romantic racialism." Typical are the 1835 sentiments of the Reverend William Ellery Channing that, "We are holding in bondage one of the best races of the human family. The negro is among the mildest and gentlest of men" (Fredrickson 1971: 106; see also Stange 1977: 58, 94, 162–164). The message of Harriet Beecher Stowe's antislavery novel *Uncle Tom's Cabin* (first published in serial form in 1851–1852) was that Negroes are human beings who deserve to live in freedom, despite their inferiority to whites. In one of his debates with Stephen Douglas, Abraham Lincoln opined that "There is a physical difference between the two [races] which in my judgment will forbid their living together on the footing of perfect equality" (Fredrickson 1971: 150; see also Gossett 1963: 254–255). Even the Progressives at the

---

[6] On the influence of racial thought in various academic fields, see Newby 1965.

turn of the century, for all the strength of their belief in democratic equality, professed themselves at a loss to know how true democratic citizenship could be extended to an inferior race. In his book *Social Organization* (1909), Charles Horton Cooley lamented "the impotence of democratic traditions to overcome the caste spirit when fostered by obvious physical and psychical differences" (Fredrickson 1971: 318).

In short, belief in the racialist ideology was a widespread cultural value, at least among whites. All nineteenth-century sources of authority—religious, literary, political, and scientific—concurred on the basic propositions of racial hierarchy and the attendant need for segregation in a multiracial society. Religious leaders found the reasons for African inferiority in the curse of Ham; one authority on the Bible claimed that the serpent who tempted Eve with the apple in the Garden of Eden was actually a "Negro gardener" (Fredrickson 1971: 87). Any acculturated white American of the nineteenth century would hold as self-evident the "truths" of the racialist ideology: that there are innate and hierarchical racial differences, that there is a natural antipathy between the races, and that degeneracy of all racial groups comes from biological mixing.

Was this prejudice? Yes, of course it was. But from the perspective of the time, "The inferiority of the negro race, as compared with the white race, is so essentially true, and so obvious, that to assume it in argument, cannot be justly attributed to prejudice. If it is prejudice, it is rare prejudice, which affects nearly all the white race, and proves the existence of a deep-seated race aversion" (Morgan 1890, cited in Newby 1968: 23).

It is hardly surprising that the racialist ideology informed the thinking of the Supreme Court in its decision in *Plessy v. Ferguson* (1896):

> Legislation is powerless to eradicate racial instincts or to abolish distinctions based upon physical differences, and the attempt to do so can only result in accentuating the difficulties of the present situation. . . . [The State of Louisiana] is at liberty to act with reference to the established usages, customs and traditions of the people, and with a view to the promotion of their comfort, and the preservation of the public peace and good order. Gauged by this standard, we cannot say that a law which authorizes or even requires the separation of the two races in public conveyances is unreasonable. . . . If one race be inferior to the other socially, the Constitution of the United States cannot put them upon the same plane.

Plessy justified segregation as a practice rooted in "racial instincts," accepting without apparent regret the inevitable breeches of civil and political equality that followed from it. Whatever the Constitution might say, there could be no end to segregation as long as the racialist ideology was dominant in American culture.

How, then, did the end of segregation in public facilities actually occur? It has become common to say of the Supreme Court decision in *Brown v. Board of Education* (1954) that it departed from *Plessy* largely because of the accumulated experience that separate cannot be equal. But the Court in 1896 was already aware of the inequality inherent in racial separation, and that inequality was accepted as necessary. Under the prodding of a series of judicial victories won by the National Association for the Advancement of Colored People (NAACP) in its cases before the Supreme Court, separate had in fact become gradually more equal since the *Plessy* decision, at least in the realm of education. The condition of inequality, then, does not account for the shift in judicial logic between *Plessy* and *Brown*.

The explanation of change between 1896 and 1954 lies instead in the delegitimation of the racialist ideology on which *Plessy* had been based. *Plessy* refers to "racial instincts," "distinctions based upon physical differences," and segregation based on the "established usages, customs and traditions of the people." None of these ideas were acceptable in educated circles by the mid twentieth century. Led by anthropologist Franz Boas in the 1920s and 1930s, scholars jumped off the bandwagon of the racialist ideology in specialties as diverse as anthropology, sociology, education, and neural psychology, with a new generation of research in each field leading to the conclusion that no innate basis of racial differentiation could be found (Gossett 1963: 425–430; Sitkoff 1978: 190–203). These scholars, drawing on and referring to each others' work, formed a critical community. Within twenty years of Boas's pathbreaking research, they were successful in discrediting all scientific evidence for the very existence of genetic racial classification, much less for the existence of a hierarchy of races. By the mid 1940s these writings were being popularized by people like Ashley Montagu, whose 1942 book title summarized an argument increasingly accepted in educated circles: *Man's Most Dangerous Myth: The Fallacy of Race.*

The racialist ideology had held that separation of the races was necessary for the fullest development of members of each race, but by 1954 the antiracialist critical community, and particularly its specialists in education, were coming to precisely the opposite conclusion. The Supreme Court drew upon this research for its opinion in *Brown*: "To separate them [children in grade and high schools] from others of similar age and qualities solely because of their race generates a feeling of inferiority as to their status in the community that may affect their hearts and minds in a way unlikely ever to be undone."

In its logic as well as in its ruling, the Court's decision in *Brown* reflected an entirely different set of beliefs about the natural relationship between the races than that illustrated in *Plessy* fifty-eight years earlier. The Court in 1954 was following the lead of the academy in its opinion, but it was ahead of the cultural beliefs of most white Americans, particularly in the South. Moreover, the ruling in *Brown v. Board of Education* did little in the near term to integrate schools. Compliance with desegregation in the South was negligible until the early 1960s, and only after 1970 did as many as half of black schoolchildren attend schools with whites. As Rosenberg (1991: 30–36) has pointed out, the Supreme Court is not able to promote social change by virtue of its decisions alone. This is certainly true in the case of the Court's mandate for desegregation, which was criticized by President Eisenhower (Sitkoff 1981: 25) and ignored by education administrators. Only half of Americans expressed support for school integration in May 1954, shortly after the *Brown v. Board of Education* ruling, and just under a quarter of Southern whites did so.[7] These numbers had not moved a year later. America was on the cusp of a cultural revolution in race relations in 1954, but neither the twenty-year cumulation of scholarship denying the existence of racial hierarchies nor the Supreme Court decision in *Brown v. Board of Education* served as the turning point.

Although the Supreme Court was not responsible for it, there was in fact a sea change in support for school integration between the mid 1950s and the late 1970s. Howard Schuman and his colleagues (1985) have compiled the available survey data on attitudes toward segregation in this period, and a portion of their findings appear in figure 3-1. In 1956 the data show the existence of two cultures of racial belief, one Northern and one Southern, with stark differences within each region by level of education. Differences between education levels are most likely due to greater exposure of the more educated to the growing criticism of school segregation (Sniderman, Brody, and Tetlock 1991; Zaller 1992). The regional differences in figure 3-1, of course, reflect long-established subcultures in white American society.

From this starting point in 1956, there was a rapid growth of support for school integration that affected every region and demographic group in the country. After 1970 the growth of support for integration slowed in the North, if only because ceiling effects were reached as the percentage supporting school integration neared 100. The rate of change in the South, by contrast, continued unabated for another decade. By 1976 the South was virtually indistinguishable from the North in support for school integration, except among Southerners with less than a high school education.

Figure 3-1 is in effect a sketch of the collapse of the racialist ideology. Within a generation, integration of the schools (and of other public places) went from being a highly contested and regionally divisive value to a general cultural norm. As late as 1962 James Kilpatrick could write a book like *The Southern Case for School Segregation*, in which he concluded that the South would maintain segregated schools, churches, and private clubs "for

---

[7] The question asked was "The United States Supreme Court has ruled that racial segregation in the public schools is illegal. This means that all children, no matter what their race, must be allowed to go to the same schools. Do you approve or disapprove of this ruling?"

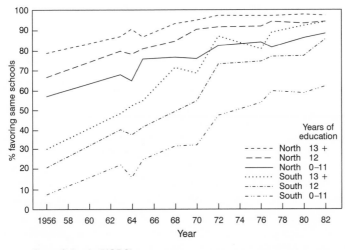

Same Schools (NORC):
"Do you think white students and black students should go to the same schools or separate schools?"

Source: Howard Schuman, Charlotte Steeh, and Lawrence Bobo, *Racial Attitudes in America* (p. 78). Reprinted with the permission of Harvard University Press. Copyright 1985 by the President and Fellows of Harvard College.

Figure 3-1   Acceptance of school integration among whites, 1956–1982

years to come." Kilpatrick's reasoning was that Southern white resistance to integration is culturally rooted, and that this culture would change only over the span of generations. He was correct about the cultural values, but wrong about their persistence. Within twenty years, Southerners at each level of education were about as favorable to integration of the schools as Northerners had been when Kilpatrick was writing. During the same period, adherents of the racialist ideology ceased being regarded as defenders of common-sense cultural values and came instead to be despised as racists. The Center for Political Studies at the University of Michigan dropped segregation/ desegregation questions from its National Election Studies in 1978 because public opinion had become so one-sided as to render the questions all but useless (Carmines and Stimson 1989: 103).

As we noted in chapter 1, change this rapid cannot be the product simply of generational turnover. Detailed analyses of these data by Schuman et al. (1985: 129–132) show that change occurred within age cohorts as well as between them.[8] Zaller (1992: 179) finds that the youngest age groups were most likely to undergo conversion to the new values of racial integration, but

[8] See also the reports of Mayer (1992) and Firebaugh and Davis (1988), who find the same pattern of declining support for segregation in all age groups and in all regions—with change particularly rapid in the South.

conversion on the issue occurred in all age cohorts. This is an instance not only of rapid cultural change, but of rapid change involving large-scale conversion on a topic that is subject to strongly held convictions.

African Americans underwent a conversion on acceptance of segregation that was in some ways more startling than the conversion by whites. In 1954 just 53 percent supported the *Brown* decision mandating school integration. Their reluctance to endorse school integration may have had more to do with fear of the harm that could come to their children in white schools than with acceptance of the racialist ideology. But there was also genuine adherence to the segregation ethic of race relations among Southern blacks, particularly among those who were older and had less education.[9] According to Schuman et al. (1985: 144–145) only about 80 percent of blacks were in favor of desegregation between 1964 and 1970, a percentage that actually waned a bit later in the decade as black nationalism gained in adherence. Even so, by 1973 only 9 percent of blacks said they were opposed to school integration.

What force caused the wholesale abandonment of the racialist ideology among people of all races, all regions, and all levels of education? The cultural delegitimation of segregation has been attributed to respect engendered by the Harlem renaissance, horror at the Nazi use of a similar racialist ideology, and newfound American pride in its role as leader of the free world (Newby 1968: 9; Sitkoff 1981: 16). These factors, however, all existed well before opposition to segregation began to melt away in American society. The timing of the shift in attitudes on segregation, and particularly the steep increase in support for desegregation among Southern whites and blacks between 1956 and 1970, points unmistakably to a single precipitating factor. This is precisely the period of peak mobilization in the civil rights movement.

The power of the civil rights movement to force a public reassessment of the racialist ideology stemmed from its undeniably Southern origins, its widespread support among African Americans, and its firmness of purpose in abolishing segregation. These traits enabled the movement to strike at the heart of the racialist ideology. The movement's articulate leaders and disciplined supporters, with their steadfast commitment to peaceful demonstrations in the face of violent reprisals, were a powerful blow to the claim of superior levels of intellectual and moral development in the white race. Belief in instinctive racial antipathy, thought to be felt by blacks as well as by whites, was also shattered by the obvious determination of a large movement, composed primarily of blacks but with many white supporters as well, to achieve integration. "I believe, and in fact I know, that the negro of the

---

[9] Gallup (1972) reports from a survey completed on July 14, 1954, that 90 percent of African Americans between twenty-one and twenty-nine years old, who had a college education, supported the *Brown* decision.

South loves the white people of the South," according to a common refrain from the racialist period (cited in Newby 1968: 132). The civil rights movement was a constant reproach to this view; it became what Schuman et al. (1985: 209) called "the demand that would not be silenced."

James Baldwin has captured the sense of delusion that set in among whites in 1955 and 1956 when the bus boycott took hold in Montgomery: "It was as though the white people of Montgomery Alabama had gotten their feelings hurt. They just did not understand how their former slaves, who they loved so much, could be guilty of such a tremendous repudiation. . . . White women and white men were walking by like wounded lovers: 'How could you do this to me?' It was strange, it was pathetic, it was revelatory."[10]

The role of the civil rights movement in fostering acceptance of school integration is also suggested by the relative lack of change in some other beliefs about race relations. The one element of the racialist ideology that was not directly addressed by the civil rights movement was beliefs about the consequences of biological mixing between the races. And antipathy to interracial marriages is the sole element of the racialist ideology that can still be found in American culture. As late as 1972 only 25 percent of whites and 58 percent of blacks approved of racially mixed marriages.[11] Schuman et al. (1985) find that regional differences in support for laws against intermarriage did not diminish between 1962 and 1982, unlike the diminution of Southern distinctiveness in values connected to other areas of racial segregation. This lack of change adds to the evidence of the influence of the civil rights movement on the changing culture of race relations.

The significance of these sweeping changes in attitudes toward segregation has been challenged by some investigators who note that support for a federal role in implementing school desegregation actually fell between 1964 and 1976, even as support for school segregation as an abstract principle was becoming a cultural norm.[12] The increasing divergence between principles and practice has led some to conclude that commitment to school integration remains superficial. Since overt support for segregation is no longer culturally acceptable, support for the abstract idea of integration is combined with opposition to busing and to other mechanisms that would actually bring integration about (Jackman 1978; Sears, Hensler, and Speer 1979; Kinder and Sears 1981; Sniderman, Brody, and Kuklinski 1984). Schuman et al. (1985: 196–197) also demonstrate that support for measures to implement principles of racial equality generally lags behind acceptance of the principle of integration.

---

[10] James Baldwin, interviewed in the Public Broadcasting System's film *Martin Luther King: An Amazing Grace* (1991).

[11] The *Gallup Poll Index*, report no. 88 October 1972 (Princeton, NJ).

[12] The decline in support for federal involvement in school desegregation occurred in both the white and black populations.

These findings show that behavioral change does not follow swiftly and neatly from attitudinal change. Yet culture does count, and social institutions are altered when cultural values change. Hochschild (1984: 30) reports that the percentage of black students attending schools with over 90 percent minority enrollment declined from two-thirds to one-third between 1968 and 1980 (see also Sitkoff 1981: 232). The largest changes occurred in the South, which was the most segregated region in 1968 and the most integrated region in 1980. Although nearly 90 percent of whites objected in the abstract to school busing for racial integration, two-thirds of white parents whose children have been bused said that busing has worked out in a "very satisfactory" way (Hochschild 1984: 183). Attitudes and behavior may not change in perfect harmony, but change has been sizable in both realms.

The delegitimation of the racialist ideology led to a fundamental alteration of American race relations between 1950 and 1980. The country had two distinctive regional cultures of racial belief in 1950; by 1980 it had only one. Integration became the norm; support for segregation came to be viewed as an expression of bigotry. Before segregation ever lost its political muscle, it first lost its cultural legitimacy.

VALUE CREATION: THE CASE OF SEXUAL HARASSMENT

The tumultuous history of race relations in the South during the period of the civil rights movement suggests that the conversion of social values is a highly conflictual form of change. People must be persuaded to question their existing values, abandon them, and adopt new ones. This is almost certainly not the path by which most value change occurs. A smoother path to value change is by the creation of new social values in contexts where there were none before.

In March 1972 suit was filed in the Newark Federal Court by a secretary whose boss, a vice-president of the Scholl Manufacturing Company, had threatened to fire her if she would not have sex with him.[13] To the contemporary eye, the secretary's allegations represent a straightforward and particularly egregious claim of sexual harassment. However, the phrase "sexual harassment" never appeared in the complaint filed at the time—simply because the concept was not yet invented. The employer was instead charged with employment discrimination. The reasoning was that the Scholl vice-president would not have asked a male subordinate to provide sexual services as a condition of employment, and therefore to have asked this female secretary to do so was to treat male and female employees differently. In its report on the case, the *New York Times* noted that this suit was believed to be the first of its kind.

[13] *New York Times*, March 30, 1972, p. 22, col. 3.

Almost exactly twenty years later the American television-viewing public was riveted by the spectacle of a nominee to the United States Supreme Court defending himself against detailed allegations of having initiated unwelcome conversations about sex and having made repeated suggestions of a sexual relationship to a subordinate who had worked for him in the U.S. Civil Rights Office. The charges against Judge Clarence Thomas were summarized by his accusers, by the media, and by millions of Americans with the phrase "sexual harassment."

Entry of the term "sexual harassment" into the American vocabulary sometime during the mid 1970s was an act of value creation that gave people a tool for debating the range of appropriate workplace interactions between men and women.[14] Incidents such as the one at the Scholl Manufacturing Company in 1972 are sure already to have been offensive to the moral sensibilities of most Americans. But it requires a crystallizing term like sexual harassment to stigmatize actions that might previously have been viewed with indifference or resignation. The term also turns a private issue into a public issue, partly by embedding sexual harassment in a workplace context that connects it to the existence of distinct roles for men and women in the workplace. Under the influence of the phrase, making co-workers uncomfortable with sexual remarks or jokes is considered comparable with demanding sex as a condition for continued employment. In short, diffusion of a new term like sexual harassment causes the standards of appropriate behavior to be given systematic reconsideration.

Development of the concept of sexual harassment rested on three claims that have emerged from the critical feminist community in the past two decades. Feminists working with the concept have claimed that sexual harassment is far more widespread than usually admitted, that the problem is systemic rather than being attributable solely to the behavior of individuals, and that the predominantly verbal unpleasantness referred to as a hostile environment or "conditions of work harassment" constitutes an abuse comparable with the sexual blackmail of "quid pro quo harassment." These three claims comprise the core elements of the concept of sexual harassment as developed within the critical community. All three have proved to be influential in the drafting of federal and state regulations, and in the growth of case law on the topic.

The first of these claims is that sexual harassment is far more widespread than generally known. The argument made within the feminist community is that employers often tolerate sexual harassment, fellow employees look the other way, and female victims feel powerless to complain of their treatment. As MacKinnon (1979: 1) put it, "working women have been subject to the social failure to recognize sexual harassment as an abuse at all. Tacitly, it has

---

[14] MacKinnon (1979: 27) dates the term from 1976.

been both acceptable and taboo; acceptable for men to do, taboo for women to confront, even to themselves." Early initiatives related to sexual harassment, then, focused on the need to show that quid pro quo harassment was not an occasional or isolated incident, but was instead very common. This was the purpose of such events as the Speak-out on Sexual Harassment organized in Ithaca, New York, in the mid 1970s (Farley 1978). Survey studies were also publicized to show that anywhere from 45 to 80 percent of working women believed themselves to have been victims of sexual harassment at some time (MacKinnon 1979: 26–27; see also the citations in Riger 1991).[15]

The second aspect of sexual harassment elaborated within the critical community is that the problem is not personal but social. The argument is that sexual harassment does not occur as a result of uncontrolled desire or interpersonal insensitivity on the part of an individual, but is instead rooted in the nature of authority relations within workplaces. Women in the workplace are often hired in part for their attractiveness and their pleasant demeanor. It is a small step from viewing an employee's appearance to be a job-related characteristic, to engaging in sexual teasing or innuendo. When this behavior occurs between male superiors and female subordinates, sexual harassment can be connected directly to hiring practices and job descriptions developed within a firm.

Viewing the problem of sexual harassment as rooted in the work environment enabled the critical community to claim that the employer or corporation is legally responsible for maintaining an environment in which job descriptions, allocations of authority, and the distribution of women and men in different roles do not encourage sexual harassment. The systemic view of the problem serves to hold employers liable for sexual misconduct in the workplace, just as employers are held liable in cases of racial discrimination.

The third element of innovation to come from the critical community of feminist thinkers is expansion of the concept beyond quid pro quo harassment to include conditions of work harassment, or harassment due to a hostile environment. Conditions of work harassment occurs when a working environment is created in which women are routinely subjected to unwelcome sexual remarks, propositions, touching, or embraces. The range of actions that may be interpreted as creating a hostile working environment has been the subject of much discussion within the critical community. Farley (1978: 15) and others include blatant staring as a form of sexual harassment. Tuana (1992: 57) defines sexual harassment as any action embarrass-

[15] An October 1991 Gallup survey of the entire adult population found that 14 percent claimed at some time to have been the victim of sexual harassment on the job, including 21 percent of women (*Gallup Poll Monthly*, no. 313, October 1991, Princeton, NJ).

ing to women, and discusses the case of a physics professor who drew a "shapely woman" on the chalkboard to illustrate the effects of a vacuum on the body.

As developed in its critical community, then, sexual harassment is viewed as widespread, inextricably linked to workplace authority patterns, and a problem not only of making employment opportunities dependent on sexual favors but also of the existence of work environments hostile to the comfortable participation of women. These ideas were developed in a flurry of papers, articles, and book chapters beginning in the mid 1970s. Different arguments favoring distinct legal remedies for sexual harassment were advanced in this period (for reviews, see Paul 1991 and Wall 1991). The authoritative treatment, though, proved to be the approach laid out by Catherine MacKinnon in her widely cited book *Sexual Harassment of Working Women*. MacKinnon argued that sexual harassment is a form of sex discrimination in violation of Title VII of the 1964 Civil Rights Act. This was soon taken to be the definitive legal approach to fighting sexual harassment. Authoritative support for action against sexual harassment came from the Equal Employment Opportunity Commission (EEOC), which in 1980 adopted Catherine MacKinnon's view that sexual harassment in the workplace is a form of employment discrimination. The 1980 EEOC guidelines became the standard definition of sexual harassment (as cited in Riger 1991):

> Unwelcome sexual advances, requests for sexual favors, and other verbal harassment or physical conduct of a sexual nature constitute sexual harassment when (1) submission to such conduct is made either explicitly or implicitly a term or condition of an individual's employment, (2) submission to or rejection of such conduct by an individual is used as the basis for employment decisions affecting such individuals, or (3) such conduct has the purpose or effect of unreasonably interfering with an individual's work performance or creating an intimidating, hostile or offensive working environment.

The EEOC definition covers both quid pro quo harassment, in which "conduct of a sexual nature" is linked to employment decisions, and conditions of work harassment, the creation of "an intimidating, hostile, or offensive working environment." Within the relatively brief span of about five years, then, the significance, causes, and scope of sexual harassment were given shape within the critical community of feminists. What remained was to spread this understanding of the concept widely and convincingly into the society.

There is, of course, no single means by which the ideas of a critical community may be diffused. In the case of sexual harassment, the particular path chosen was to work through the EEOC to define sexual harassment as illegal, and then to use this ruling to file complaints both within the EEOC and in the criminal justice system. This process served gradually to solidify legal recognition of the problem of sexual harassment during the first fifteen years after invention of the term in the mid 1970s.

The means of deciding what is an offensive working environment is particularly interesting from the perspective of cultural values because courts have employed the "reasonable person rule" to evaluate workplace behavior. This standard is not based on the perceptions of either the accuser or the accused, but on whether a reasonable person would be offended by the conduct that forms the basis of the grievance. Adoption of the reasonable person rule to evaluate the presence of a hostile working environment makes the definition of sexual harassment directly contingent on social norms about acceptable workplace behaviors. Changing cultural values would thus come automatically to be reflected in changing legal standards of permissible and impermissible workplace behavior.[16] Among the actions that have led to complaints of sexual harassment under the "reasonable person" rule are being the subject of rumors about a sexual relationship with a superior, standing too close to someone while conversing with them, working in a firm that uses sexually suggestive images in advertisements for its products, and being subjected to "suggestive looks."[17] This list could be greatly extended; the point is that the reasonable person rule on what constitutes a sexually hostile working environment makes the task of determining cultural standards part of the authoritative handling of the issue.

Under the influence of the critical community and the EEOC guidelines, the body of case law on the subject gradually accumulated.[18] The first judicial finding of harassment in a case claiming a hostile work environment came in the Washington, D.C., District Court in 1981 (*Bundy v. Jackson*, described in Cole 1986: 269). The 1986 U.S. Supreme Court ruling in *Meritor Savings Bank, FSB v. Vinson* gave the imprimatur of the highest court to the clause of the EEOC regulations concerning offensive conditions of work, using language that reflected in part the *amicus curiae* briefs filed by Catherine MacKinnon and others from the critical community.

With the general issue of hostile work environments settled, the next focus

---

[16] Some feminists have argued that the "reasonable person" should be replaced by the "reasonable woman," who may find offensive behaviors that are acceptable to either a "reasonable man" or a "reasonable person." This position has not so far found legal acceptance.

[17] These examples are all from formal complaints filed between January 1990 and December 1992.

[18] Anna-Maria Marshall (1996) has shown that some of the private lawyers who took on early cases of sexual harassment were able to share experiences, strategies, and legal research through their connections to the National Conference on Women and Law. Others were not part of this network, but they were very likely to have just graduated from law school, where they were exposed to critical community arguments on litigating sexual harassment. This example illustrates the potential for members of a critical community to undertake action themselves, bypassing (temporarily) the social and political movement.

of legal controversy became what kind of harm a plaintiff must suffer in order to prove that he or she has been working in such an environment. Lower courts continued to differ in their interpretations of what level of harm would constitute evidence of an offensive environment. Those within the critical community argued that no harm had to be shown, only the potential for harm to a "reasonable woman." As a *New York Times Sunday Magazine* feature story on Catherine MacKinnon put the issue, "A woman might remain a victim of a hostile environment for years, until she rejected it and was consequently fired, or until she was forced to leave. . . . For a court to require such a rejection, MacKinnon argued, amounts to forcing 'the victim to bring intensified injury upon herself in order to demonstrate that she is injured at all.' "[19]

Authoritative resolution of the question of what harms are necessary to demonstrate a hostile environment awaited the Supreme Court decision in November 1993, in the case of *Harris v. Forklift Systems.* In its ruling on this case, the Court determined that harassment consists of any conduct that "would reasonably be perceived, and is perceived, as hostile or abusive, [with] no need for it also to be psychologically injurious." Once again, interpretations of sexual harassment developed within the critical community became influential in the formulations of the Supreme Court.

In instances of value creation, and in contrast to situations where the task is to alter existing values, it would appear that an energetic and resourceful critical community can have a great deal of influence over development of a new cultural concept in the legal and regulatory codes. In this respect, the case of sexual harassment is typical of the general phenomenon of value creation. Sexual harassment is an atypical example, however, in one important respect. It happened that the date of publication by the *New York Times Sunday Magazine* of its feature story on Catherine MacKinnon was the last day of an era. Beginning the following Monday, on October 7, 1991, the issue of sexual harassment was changed forever in American culture.

It was on that date that the charges made by Anita Hill against Clarence Thomas became public knowledge. Professor Hill claimed that while she was working for Judge Thomas at the U.S. Civil Rights Commission, he had on several occasions initiated discussions with her of sexual practices that he had seen in pornographic movies, that he had engaged in himself, and that he would like to engage in. Her charges became public just after the nomination of Judge Thomas for a seat on the Supreme Court had been supported by the Senate Judiciary Committee and reported to the full Senate. The charges led to a reconvening of the Judiciary Committee for new hearings, at which Hill, Thomas, and a variety of supporting witnesses for each were called to testify. The three days of hearings were carried live on every televi-

---

[19] *New York Times Sunday Magazine*, October 6, 1991.

sion network, and an edited version was rebroadcast each evening. In a Gallup poll taken immediately after the hearings, 86 percent of the American public said they had watched at least part of the proceedings on television. The median length of viewership was two to four hours, with 18 percent saying they had watched ten hours or more.[20]

It is perhaps of minor historical interest to note that in her first public comments on the matter, Anita Hill did not use the phrase "sexual harassment." In response to a direct question as to whether what she had experienced was sexual harassment, the law professor declined to use the term, arguing that this was an issue of character rather than whether a law had been broken. The American public was not so cautious in its assessment, and the formulation of the issue as it swept the country was whether Clarence Thomas had sexually harassed Anita Hill.

It has become a truism to say that the Hill-Thomas hearings dominated conversations at workplaces across America, conversations that dealt not just with what might have happened between Thomas and Hill, but also about what happens at one's own job. There is no means of gauging the extent or impact of these conversations, but it is clear that the publicity surrounding the Hill-Thomas hearings had an extraordinary galvanizing effect on every medium of social communication. In the immediate term, the story saturated the news media, both in the form of news reports and in the production of numberless editorials, op-ed pieces, and letters to editors. In the following months, the entertainment portion of the media developed television movies and thematic episodes of regular television series on sexual harassment. There was also a variety of quickly produced books about Anita Hill, about the Hill-Thomas episode, and about sexual harassment more generally. The National Organization for Women (NOW) and other women's groups organized open forums on the issue. Public opinion research firms, including all the national television networks, *Time* and *Newsweek*, Gallup and Harris, most leading newspapers, and a variety of private pollsters and survey laboratories connected to universities conducted a burst of polling on sexual harassment.[21] Within a few months of the Hill-Thomas hearings, Americans would have a hard time *not* being informed about the state of public opinion on such questions as what constitutes sexual harassment and what proportion of working women believe they have experienced harassment.

In this new public phase of value creation, the same critical community that had influenced formulation of the issue of sexual harassment by the EEOC and by the courts now became influential in the way the issue was

[20] Another 18 percent said they had watched over five hours, according to Gallup 1992.

[21] Rutgers, the University of North Carolina, Eastern Montana College, Florida International University, the University of Tennessee, and the University of Kentucky are among those who asked questions about sexual harassment between October and December 1991, according to the *American Public Opinion Index* (Tallahassee, FL: Opinion Research Service, 1992).

phrased in opinion polling. On the day the Thomas story broke, the *New York Times* published a primer on the issue. This included both a definition of sexual harassment taken directly from the EEOC regulations and a brief legal history of the concept in which the executive director and the legal director of the NOW Legal Defense and Education Fund were cited as authoritative sources. The *CBS/New York Times* poll reported on October 11 that 81 percent of women and 75 percent of men agreed that sexual harassment "could just involve unwanted sexual conversations" and did not need to include physical contact. The critical community concept of conditions of work harassment had become part of the public discourse. This diffusion of critical community ideas occurred with some simplification but with remarkably little watering down of the concept as it was originally developed.[22]

The extraordinary amount of attention given to Anita Hill's charges took the concept from the feminist critical community and the courtroom and put it in every workplace and living room in America. But such "successes" are not made overnight. Attention to sexual harassment was already growing in the print media in the year prior to the Hill-Thomas hearings. Nor was this an instance of media attention serving to make an issue (in)famous for fifteen minutes. The number of stories about sexual harassment actually rose in 1992 compared to 1991, and in 1993 the reduced number of stories was still more than eight times the 1990 rate of media attention.

The Hill-Thomas case itself did not remain newsworthy for long after the final confirmation vote for Justice Thomas in the Senate. The continued high rate of attention to sexual harassment came instead from the revelation to media managers that this issue was now the focus of wide interest and concern. Thus, when future instances of sexual harassment became known, they received much more publicity than had comparable events in the past.[23]

The significance of the Hill-Thomas hearings for cultural change is captured by the fact that evaluations of Judge Thomas came to be conditioned by the accusation of sexual harassment. Prior to the hearings, public opinion on whether Judge Thomas should be confirmed were dominated by partisan considerations, as one would expect in the absence of much specific information about the nominee. Partisan differences declined rapidly after the hearings. Instead, gender (women more opposed to the nomination) and race (blacks rallying around the nomination, whites becoming more negative) became substantially stronger predictors of opinion (Nixon and Glean 1994; see also Gimpel and Wolpert 1996).

Hearings also provided an opportunity to probe the boundaries of sexual

----

[22] The critical community's own assessment of its influence is less sanguine. This is a function of the single-mindedness with which any critical community regards the issues with which it is concerned.

[23] The causes for fluctuations in media attention are further developed in chapter 6.

harassment, as for example when Senator Alan Simpson asked if it really is improper for a supervisor to ask an employee for a date or to describe the plot of an X-rated movie.[24] It was not inevitable that the story even be understood as one of sexual harassment: in other cultural settings the hearings were portrayed differently. British newspapers greeted news of Thomas's confirmation with headlines like "Judge Beats Sex Rap," and "Sex Scandal Judge Wins Vital Battle."[25] Even allowing for the stylistic tics of the British tabloid press, it is clear that the British frame of reference for these events was shaped by notions of immorality attached to an illicit affair, rather than by the concept of abuse of authority attached to sexual harassment. Even in the United States, much of the media attention and popular interest in the case centered on the question of whether Judge Thomas had demonstrated sexual perversion (Scheppele 1995). But considerable attention was devoted as well to the use and abuse of workplace authority, and to the dilemmas faced by an ambitious subordinate (particularly in a "company town" like Washington, D.C.) when her boss becomes sexually suggestive or demanding. The lack of attention to abuse of authority issues in British press treatments suggests the influence of the critical community in shaping perceptions of the issue in the United States.

The Hill-Thomas hearings also had an impact on behavior, both among the American public and in political institutions. It is impossible to know what effect the hearings had on everyday behavior in the typical workplace. But one thing is clear: the sight of Anita Hill testifying against her former supervisor emboldened many women to take equivalent action. Nine to Five, a Chicago-based advocacy group for working women, was soon fielding two hundred calls per day on its hotline for complaints of sexual harassment. Existing channels of appeal, primarily the EEOC grievance procedure at the federal level and the fair employment practices agencies (FEPA) at the state level, were swamped with new complaints. Figure 3-2 shows that the number of complaints filed with EEOC-FEPA nearly doubled in the two years after Anita Hill took the stand.

The overall correlation between year and the number of sexual harassment complaints to EEOC-FEPA is $r = .86$, indicating an upward trend in complaints over time. That trend is closely associated with the extent of media coverage of the issue, as the correlation between number of complaints and stories in the broadly based *Reader's Guide to Periodical Literature* is $r = .78$. But there is an even stronger correlation between number of complaints and media coverage lagged by one year ($r = .89$). In other words, the best predictor of the number of EEOC-FEPA complaints in any given year is the

---

[24] American public opinion gave an overwhelming answer to the latter question: yes.

[25] According to Fay Weldon, "Sex and Paradox across the Atlantic," op-ed page of the *New York Times*, November 18 1991, p. A31.

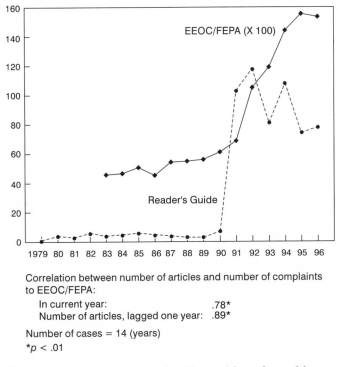

Correlation between number of articles and number of complaints
to EEOC/FEPA:

In current year: .78*
Number of articles, lagged one year: .89*

Number of cases = 14 (years)
*$p < .01$

Figure 3-2   Press coverage and formal complaints of sexual harassment, 1979–1996

amount of media attention to sexual harassment in the *prior* year. The chain
of influence from critical community to mass media to social behaviors
seems clear.

Political institutions responded as well. The Congressional Research Service produced its first-ever report on sexual harassment in late 1991, in the
form of a bibliography of existing research on the topic. The Senate, embar-
rassed by its handling of the Hill-Thomas episode, scheduled hearings on the
sexual harassment of women in government and passed a law that for the
first time allowed employees of the Senate itself to take harassment complaints to federal courts. Civil rights legislation considered weeks after the
Thomas confirmation was passed with an added provision to allow victims
of sexual harassment to collect damages. When Senator Brock Adams of
Washington was accused in 1988 of having drugged and molested an aide,
the case was set aside for lack of corroborating evidence. Those same
charges, renewed five months after the Hill-Thomas hearings (with an increased number of accusers), led Senator Adams to announce his retirement
from politics. Four years later, allegations of sexual harassment over a

twenty-year period against Oregon Senator Robert Packwood led to the compilation of a ten-volume report by the Senate Judiciary Committee and pressure on the senator from his colleagues that resulted ultimately in his resignation. In the nine years from 1983 to 1991 there were five congressional hearings related to sexual harassment. In the four years from 1992 to 1995 there were forty-three such hearings.

American public opinion did not stop changing after the Hill-Thomas hearings either. Gallup Poll surveys showed that at the time of the hearings a large plurality of the public found Clarence Thomas's denials credible (48 percent), compared with only 29 percent who believed Anita Hill. One year later, Gallup found substantial movement toward believing Professor Hill (43 percent), compared with only 39 percent who now believed Justice Thomas's denials. This change appears to have been broadly based in the population, though it was particularly concentrated among those over thirty years old, the college educated, and among nonwhites.

According to *The Gallup Poll—Public Opinion 1992*,[26] the reasons for this shift in opinion included Professor Hill having "remained in the public eye as a rallying point," and Justice Thomas's alignment with the antiabortion side of a Supreme Court ruling on a Pennsylvania law. But the truth is that few Americans were likely to have seen or heard anything from Professor Hill after the hearings, or to be even vaguely familiar with Justice Thomas's decisions on the Court. What they *had* done in the intervening year is to be engaged by a social movement on the subject of sexual harassment. It was impossible in October 1992 not to be more aware of the prevalence of sexual harassment and of the difficulties in combating it faced by women in subordinate positions in the workplace. Professor Hill was considered credible by more people not because of more information about her or about Justice Thomas. Rather, people's general estimates of the likelihood of such events having occurred were now increased.

These reactions suggest that sexual harassment, a concept that did not exist in 1975, became within twenty years part of the social and political culture of American society. Compared with the conversion of American culture from support for segregation to support for integration, the development of a culture of opprobrium toward sexual harassment occurred relatively quickly, with little conflict, and with a particularly large role for the critical community in defining the issue in terms that would later influence EEOC regulations, judicial decisions, media stories, and public understandings. These contrasts between sexual harassment and school integration exist because sexual harassment was a new cultural value, not in direct conflict with existing cultural values the way racial integration conflicted with prior views about race relations.[27]

---

[26] Gallup 1993, October 1–3, p. 178.

[27] The case can be made that the concept of sexual harassment overturns earlier attitudes that

The case of sexual harassment, then, illustrates once again the role of a critical community in developing a new value concept and of a social movement in diffusing that concept to the wider society. The development phase occurs in discussion groups, conferences, books, journals, and private correspondence. The diffusion phase occurs in public meetings, rallies, and through highly publicized court cases. Members of the critical community help define the scope of the issue by gathering evidence concerning its incidence, developing strategies of litigation and filing *amicus* briefs, drafting model regulations and corporate policies, testifying before congressional committees, and being available for citation by journalists. But these activities were possible only because of the existence of an ongoing movement on behalf of women's rights, a movement in which members of the sexual harassment critical community were highly likely to be involved. When the movement predates the critical community it creates a value context within which the specific critical community operates. The rapid diffusion of the idea of sexual harassment was facilitated by its isomorphism with the established discourse of feminism.

Despite the efforts of both critical community and movement, awareness of the issue remained limited until some galvanizing event caused it to break out into wider society. Events like the Hill-Thomas hearings are sometimes seen as exogenous bolts of lightning for which movement organizers must wait. Such a view misses the fact that the Hill-Thomas episode would have played out completely differently, or would not have occurred at all, without fifteen years of prior work by critical community and movement activists. The Hill-Thomas hearings were a powerful crystallizing moment, but that moment could have come about only after extensive preliminary work.

In 1979 Thomas Emerson could plausibly write in his forward to Catherine MacKinnon's book (1979: vii) that "Sexual harassment of working women has been one of the most pervasive but carefully ignored features of our national life." That statement was no longer true thirteen years later. Sexual harassment had become a national issue, based on a new social value cultivated within a critical community and then spread to the wider society in the ongoing context of the women's movement.

Value Connection: Movements against Alcohol Abuse

The third form of value change, connection, is a hybrid of value conversion and creation. Value connection involves destroying old values and creating new ones by altering the context in which an idea is evaluated. The success of the civil rights movement in linking desegregation to equal rights and

---

"boys will be boys." Such beliefs, however, are nowhere near as central to American culture as was the racialist ideology described earlier in this chapter. They are also beliefs about private behavior. The concept of sexual harassment placed these private behaviors for the first time into the realm of public concern and action.

opportunities is an instance of value connection. So is the connection later made by women's advocates between racism and sexism, a connection that enabled feminists to draw upon the more highly developed moral language and legal apparatus that existed to fight racism.[28]

Changing beliefs about the causes of alcohol abuse illustrate the significance of the way in which values are connected to particular contexts. Successive generations of antialcohol movements during the past three hundred years have connected the problem to different root causes and have thereby activated different segments of the population on behalf of different proposed remedies. Changes in value context led as well to altered social behaviors and governmental policies.

According to Harry Levine, it was only at the end of the eighteenth century that some Americans reported for the first time that they were addicted to alcohol. "During the 17th century and for most of the 18th, the assumption was that people drank and got drunk because they wanted to, and not because they 'had' to. . . . Drunkenness was a choice, albeit a sinful one, which some individuals made" (Levine 1978: 144, 149). The "sinful choice" of drunkenness had made it an issue to be addressed primarily from the church pulpit until the end of the eighteenth century. But as the idea took hold in the early nineteenth century that drunkenness was a matter of compulsive behavior rather than of moral weakness, new voices began to be heard. Studies by Dr. Benjamin Rush led him to designate drunkenness, or inebriety, as a "disease of the will." This addiction concept of inebriety led to development of the nineteenth-century temperance movement, which incorporated Dr. Rush's view that inebriety was a compulsion into the largest social movement of the nineteenth century. The only sin remaining in inebriety—though it was a grave one to all temperance activists—lay in exposing oneself to the addiction by tasting alcohol in the first place. The inebriate was viewed in temperance speeches as a victim to be pitied. Moderate drinkers were the prime object of temperance fury, for they were flirting with disaster. The moderate drinker had to be stopped while it was still possible to do so. Temperance forces thus took to heart Dr. Rush's injunction that " 'Taste not, handle not, touch not' should be inscribed upon every vessel that contains spirits in the house of a man, who wishes to be cured of habits of intemperance" (Rush 1814, cited in Levine 1978).

---

[28] Early use of the words sexist and sexism generally defined the terms by analogy to racist and racism. The *OED*'s first recorded use of the term sexist is from a speech by one P. M. Leet, given in November 1965: "When you argue . . . that since fewer women write good poetry this justifies their total exclusion, you are taking a position analogous to that of the racist—I might call you in this case a 'sexist'—who says that since so few Negroes have held positions of importance . . . their exclusion from history books is a matter of good judgment rather than discrimination." See the *Oxford English Dictionary Supplement*, vol. 4, SE–Z (Oxford: Oxford University Press, 1986), p. 84.

If addiction is the problem, then prohibition is the cure. Knowledge of the damage done by alcohol to the human body grew rapidly between 1890 and 1914, leading to increased support for Prohibition. Only five states were dry in 1900, but after the Prohibition amendment was sent to the states in December 1917 it took only fourteen months for forty-five of the forty-eight states to ratify it (Timberlake 1963). The ballplayer-turned-preacher Billy Sunday greeted Prohibition with the exclamation that "The reign of tears is over. The slums will soon be a memory. We will turn our prisons into factories and our jails into storehouses and corncribs" (cited in Rubin 1994: 12). Prohibition was the crowning achievement of the perspective linking inebriety to addiction, and addiction to any contact with alcohol.

Repeal of the Prohibition amendment in 1933 was the death knell not only for the temperance movement but also for any concept of addiction that viewed every use of alcohol as an invitation to habitual inebriety. The belief that alcohol was inherently addictive had evolved at a time when it was thought that only distilled beverages—hard liquor—contained alcohol. Fermented beverages such as wine, beer, and hard cider were thought to contain the elements of alcohol, but not the substance itself. Once the alcoholic content of fermented drinks was established, the large numbers of regular social drinkers who did not lapse into inebriety became an unanswerable reproach to the temperance movement. Although movements against alcohol consumption would continue, they required a new value context in which to press their case.

That value context was expressed by the term "alcoholism," a concept that had already existed in the pages of medical journals since the mid nineteenth century.[29] The idea of "alcoholism" provided a fresh twist on the addiction theme by locating the source of addiction in the individual user of alcohol, rather than in the alcohol itself. That is, some people are considered to be more vulnerable to alcohol addiction than others. This view, and its consequences for public policy, was elaborated in the Yale Summer School of Alcohol Studies over a period of years just before and during World War II (Yale University 1945). The Yale School summarized the four key beliefs that composed the alcoholism concept: "first, that the problem drinker is a sick man, exceptionally reactive to alcohol; second, that he can be helped; third, that he is worth helping; fourth, that the problem is therefore the responsibility of the healing profession, as well as the established health authorities, and the public generally."[30]

Meanwhile, the work of Alcoholics Anonymous (AA), founded two years

---

[29] The first reference to alcoholism noted in the *OED* comes from a medical book published in Germany in 1852; others have traced the term to Dr. Magnus Huss in 1849 (Keller 1982). By the end of the nineteenth century the term appears to have been common in medical journals.

[30] Dwight Anderson, in Yale University 1945; cited in Room 1982: 371.

after the repeal of Prohibition, popularized the disease concept of alcoholism as well as developing a program of treatment that relies heavily on interaction between alcoholics. Between the work of Alcoholics Anonymous and of a medical establishment eager to take on the treatment of alcoholics, the disease concept spread rapidly in American culture. Already by the end of 1954, 63 percent of Americans believed that "drunkenness is a disease and should be treated as a disease in a hospital when trying to cure it."[31]

Just as had occurred with the transition from drunkenness as moral weakness to inebriety as helpless addiction, the transition from inebriety to alcoholism also brought with it a shift in how the problem was seen and in who would be involved in leading the fight against it. As Gusfield (1982: 405) put it, the alcoholism concept created a "turn away from the definition of alcohol use as a morally suspect form of behavior and its redefinition as a matter of personal taste made problematic only by a group of people with a form of sickness." Public sympathy for the alcoholic may have been increased still further by accounts of the origins of the disease. The factors that make an individual susceptible to alcoholism are said to be environmental (e.g., stress), personality (sense of self-worth), and biological inheritance (White 1982). This was a long way from the view of the inebriate as personally responsible for his condition because of failure to keep the temperance pledge of abstention.

Public policy goals also shifted in response to the new alcoholism concept. The willful drunkard of the eighteenth century was condemned; the addicted inebriate of the nineteenth century was pitied and held up as an example of why Prohibition was necessary; the alcoholic of the twentieth century was treated. As a disease, alcoholism cannot be banned any more than one might legislate against the common cold. Appropriate government policies are therefore to make treatment available rather than to ban alcohol use or to punish the alcohol abuser.

Since 1945 publicly funded alcoholism treatment agencies have been created in every state. This development crested in 1970 with the establishment of the National Institute on Alcohol Abuse and Alcoholism (NIAAA) within the Department of Health, Education and Welfare. In its first decade of operation (1971–1980), the NIAAA dispensed over $1.3 billion for research grants and treatment programs (Lewis 1982). The growth of governmental funding for research, in turn, further increased the medical respectability of the problem and led to heightened professional interest in the area. One consequence of the quest for federal dollars was the expansion of treatment programs from those dependent on alcohol to those who are codependent—family and friends of the alcoholic (Wiener 1981).

---

[31] The proportion agreeing that alcoholism is a disease had risen to 87 percent by 1987, according to the Gallup poll.

As long as alcohol issues remain connected to a medical analysis, thinking about alcohol use is constrained to evolve with broader trends in the medical field. Observers of the issue point out that the current generation of social values connected to alcohol use has adopted an emphasis on disease prevention that has recently grown within the medical profession (Gusfield 1981: 333; Wiener 1981: chap. 13). This new thinking, characterized as the public health movement, places increased responsibility on the individual to make healthy life-style choices, including alcohol use at a level that minimizes the chances of becoming an alcoholic or of suffering the other health and social debilitations associated with chronic alcohol use.

The public health movement represents a partial return to the philosophy of the temperance movement, in that it once again expands the field of vision from acute cases—alcoholism—to include the social costs of even moderate, "controlled" drinking. One symptom of the shift in emphasis in the professional community was the decision of the NIAAA to purge its literature of all reference to "responsible drinking."[32]

Even as the NIAAA and the medical community have backed away from the idea of responsible drinking, the surge of political mobilization around the twin themes of reduced governmental involvement in society and increased individual responsibility have also had their impact on cultural values concerning alcohol use. When Candy Lightner learned in 1980 that the drunk driver who had just killed her thirteen-year-old daughter was on probation for one conviction of driving under the influence and out on bail for a similar hit-and-run charge, she decided that the law was too lenient with those who drink and drive. Rather than challenge directly the medical establishment's view of the alcoholic as victim of a disease, Lightner's organization, Mothers Against Drunk Drivers (MADD), focused on the individual's responsibility not to put others at risk while impaired by alcohol. MADD's perspective is that regardless of whether alcohol abuse is an individual choice or a disease, driving while impaired is not a compulsion. Reinarman reports that Lightner prevailed in the MADD executive committee against those who would connect the organization to more general policies against alcohol use, such as legal restrictions on advertising alcoholic beverages. "Lightner's argument [was] that it is not alcohol itself that causes death and injury, but rather irresponsible users and abusers of alcohol" (Reinarman 1988: 102).[33] This perspective shift—from the consequences of alcohol

---

[32] See Lewis 1982. The connection between the public health perspective and renewed concern about moderate drinkers is shown by the existence of dissenters in the field, who argue that alcohol abuse is a habit rather than a disease, and believe that one can choose to develop good habits (drinking in moderation) or bad habits (drinking in an uncontrolled fashion). See Vogler and Bartz (1982).

[33] The one restrictive measure on which MADD acted vigorously was to raise the legal drinking age to twenty-one, a campaign that represents one of its most striking policy successes.

abuse for the drinker to the consequences for others—made possible yet another reformation of the social coalition involved in alcohol abuse issues. Finding MADD's focus on drinking and driving to be more palatable than efforts to restrict alcohol consumption, major beer brewers and broadcast executives dependent on beer advertising supported MADD with donations and public service announcements.

The existence of a growing social movement against alcohol abuse in the 1980s was marked by all the usual signals: significant increases in media attention and in congressional hearings (Baumgartner and Jones 1993: 162–163), as well as shifts in public opinion. MADD itself had 85 percent name recognition in 1985, twice the percentage able to name their representative in Congress (Reinarman 1988). MADD's efforts in calling attention to the social costs of alcohol abuse also had measurable impacts on public opinion and behavior. Gallup surveys show that the proportion of respondents who said they sometimes use alcohol fell from 70 percent in 1981 to 56 percent in 1989 (only to recover to 64 percent in 1992, when the social movement against drinking abated).[34] Despite this reduced incidence of alcohol use during the 1980s, an increasing percentage of Americans admitted that they "sometimes drink more than they should," up from 23 percent in 1978 to 32 percent in 1985 and 35 percent in 1989.[35] The percentage of people who said that "drinking has been a cause of trouble" in their family was also at unusually high levels during most of the 1980s, reaching a peak of 24 percent in 1987 and again in 1992.[36]

The linkage of alcohol use to the context of individual responsibility has also brought with it a shift in public policy on driving while under the influence. MADD has successfully lobbied for state policies reducing legal blood-alcohol content from .10 to .08 or .05, adding as well a "per se" standard that defines driving under the influence as having this blood-alcohol level regardless of whether there is other evidence of impairment. For those charged, plea bargaining has been eliminated in many states, first offenders face mandatory jail in some states and mandatory license suspension in others, and fines have been substantially increased. Accidents resulting in injury have been reclassified as felonies, fatal accidents have sometimes resulted in murder charges being filed, server liability laws have been passed, and sobriety checkpoints have been instituted and have survived constitutional challenge.

The cultural effect of these policy changes was to place drunk driving

[34] The smallest proportion of Americans previously recorded as drinkers in the periodic Gallup surveys was 55 percent, in 1958. The highest level of drinking was 71 percent, recorded several times in the late 1970s. See also Jacobs 1989: 4–5.

[35] Gallup, various years.

[36] The forty year average in Gallup polls between 1950 and 1984 was 16.5 percent. Gallup 1989, p. 206.

high on the list of crimes of moral turpitude, in a category fully distinct from both the alcoholic who stays off the roads and from the driver involved in an accident for reasons other than alcohol impairment. These legal and cultural changes reduced drunk driving fatalities by one-third in the ten years between 1983–1993, with drunk driving fatalities among teenagers down 60 percent over the same period. Compared with the situation fifteen years earlier, America was in the mid-1990s a society that drank less, was particularly less likely to drink and drive, and consequently suffered far fewer alcohol-related casualties on the road. At the very same time that the problem of drinking and driving was becoming substantially less severe, Americans were becoming more concerned about the issue and more intolerant of problems created by drinking and driving.[37] New cultural values may heighten concern about an issue even when the problem is becoming less severe.

The example of antialcohol movements shows that a single phenomenon, alcohol use, may be connected to different contexts by successive generations of concerned activists. The physical effects of alcohol on the human body have been understood in largely the same terms (though in ever greater detail) for the past two centuries. But there is great variation in beliefs over time and between cultures about the reasons people drink to a level of self-impairment and about the social consequences of drinking.[38] The problem may be defined as one afflicting primarily those who have fallen away from God, the lower classes, recent immigrants, those with a genetic weakness, or youth. The negative consequences of chronic alcohol abuse have at times been viewed primarily in terms of effects on the individual, and at other times in terms of effects on society.

In each phase of redefinition, the ideas of critical communities provided an interpretation, a language, and a body of evidence about the causes, effects, and needed policy responses to alcohol abuse. And in each of these successive phases, social movements played a key role in elaborating and publicizing a perspective that had previously existed only within the critical community. What the Women's Christian Temperance Union and the Anti-Saloon League did for Dr. Rush's theory of addiction, and what Alcoholics Anonymous did for the alcoholism concept, Mothers Against Drunk Drivers has done for the idea of individual responsibility for the consequences of alcohol use. The role of the movement has in each case been to place alcohol abuse in a new value context and to articulate a political agenda reflective of these new values.

[37] This is not the first time that a crusade against alcohol use occurred at a time when the problem was actually becoming less severe. The best evidence is that the nineteenth-century temperance movement actually gained in strength at a time when per capita alcohol consumption was in sharp and long-term decline (Barrows and Room 1991: 19).

[38] For additional perspectives on alcohol use from other cultures, see Barrows and Room 1991.

The specific value connections that are made also determine who will get involved in the issue. When chronic drunkenness was a moral issue, church ministers took the lead role from their pulpits. The temperance movement retained the religious fervor of the antidrunkenness crusades, but their analysis of the social ills caused by chronic inebriation engaged the late nineteenth-century network of progressive social reformers. The alcoholism concept, in turn, disenfranchised the temperance movement and activated the medical establishment on behalf of a new approach to studying treatment methods.[39] The more recent transition from alcoholism to the social consequences of alcohol use has again shifted the ground by expanding the issue from medical treatment to community control, thereby engaging a wider public.

Unlike the case of school segregation, the effects of alcohol consumption have always been judged to be negative. Unlike the case of sexual harassment, awareness of the problem of alcohol consumption is not new. The evolution of the alcohol use issue is not a case of either value conversion or value creation. In each phase of the issue, the element of change has been the context in which the problem of alcohol use is viewed. Each new cluster of value connections has brought with it a new set of activists and organizations, as well as a new approach to policy making on the subject.

These case studies of value conversion, creation, and connection each illustrate the ways in which new ideas developed in a critical community are diffused by a movement. In practice, successful movements typically blend all three forms of value change. The civil rights movement fostered the conversion of values on segregation, the connection of desegregation to constitutional principles, and the creation of a new sense of self-worth among African Americans. The environmental movement has sought to delegitimize subordination of the natural environment to the purposes of mankind (its least successful struggle), to create new values on the importance of a healthy and diverse natural environment for human quality of life, and to make new connections between daily behaviors and environmentally sound practices.

Although movements mix the three types of value change, it is nonetheless worth distinguishing between them because the process of change dif-

---

[39] Jay Rubin (1979) has shown that leaders of the temperance movement, after first embracing the new alcoholism approach, soon realized that medicalization of the issue created a push toward treatment rather than prohibition. Temperance writers began to express anger at alcoholism researchers, whom they accused of having been bought off by the liquor industry. As the alcoholism concept became dominant in the culture, however, the remnants of the temperance movement joined in this perspective. The 1956 presidential platform of the Prohibition Party broke ground in this respect by calling for "increasing psychiatric aid to treat alcoholics and help others in need of counseling," even while maintaining their demand for the enactment of laws to prohibit the manufacture, distribution, and sale of alcoholic beverages.

fers markedly in each case. Value conversion is the most difficult to accomplish, for it requires alteration of existing values. The delegitimation of segregation was a drawn out and conflictual process when compared with the creation and spread of a norm against sexual harassment or the connection of alcohol abuse to beliefs about individual responsibility. By focusing attention on new values, or by placing an established value into a new context, people can be led to draw novel conclusions about what is proper or necessary. The most promising path of cultural change may be for creation of a new concept (e.g., alcoholism as a disease) to lead to the forging of new connections (e.g., between chronic alcohol abuse and the medical establishment), and only then to convert people to new ways of thinking about the issue (e.g., the responsibility of society to assist in the treatment of alcoholics).

THE POLITICAL CONSEQUENCES OF VALUE CHANGE

Each case of value change examined here demonstrates that innovations in the way we think about a particular topic have the potential to alter our values and behavior. But any account of the impact of cultural change must include an understanding of how such changes in values affect politics. Societies are not altered solely, or even primarily, by value change at the individual level. Rather, change occurs in varying degrees in different groups in the population, as new values are incorporated into the ideological packages used to cement political coalitions. To understand this process, we must examine the diffusion of new cultural values not just as a social process but also as a political process.

Cultural change ultimately requires the diffusion of beliefs within circles of like-minded people, or among people with ideological affinities for each other. From the political perspective, critical communities are composed not just of innovative thinkers but also of networks that have a particular ideology and (perhaps) a partisan orientation. The ideas of these communities are most likely to find acceptance among those whose political sympathies are generally in alignment with the critical community and movement. People look to the reactions of party and other group leaders to help them evaluate new issue claims. When the stances of political parties shift and polarize on an issue, then voters take these party positions as cues to orient their own thinking. New values are accepted outside of their ideological home only by people whose own level of political information is too low to enable them to decipher cues about the partisan source of the message. To the extent that new values spread at all beyond those with an ideological affinity for them, this will occur among those least informed and among the young, whose prior beliefs are less firmly entrenched.

A good example of this process is the growth of sentiment against the Vietnam War, which expanded from very limited circles in the middle 1960s to encompass (by many measures) a majority of the American population by 1970. John Zaller (1992: chap. 9) has demonstrated that antiwar sentiment was quite limited as long as political leaders and media reports were united in support of the war. When antiwar protest succeeded in getting other viewpoints expressed, however, public sentiment began to change. First to change were liberals with the greatest levels of political awareness—presumably because they were the first to receive and accept the antiwar message. Next in the timing and extent of change came liberals who were not as attentive to politics. Finally, Zaller found some degree of opinion change among conservatives with low levels of political interest and information, though conservatives with high levels of awareness remained steadfast in their support of the war. Zaller concludes from his research that acceptance of the new value claims occurred most readily among those who were predisposed to share the political or partisan identity of those advocating an antiwar position.

The extent to which value change is associated with partisan beliefs depends in part upon the degree of differentiation of party positions on the issue. Carmines and Stimson (1989) have shown that the Democratic and Republican parties offered a clear choice on civil rights issues beginning in 1964. Public beliefs on racial segregation were already crystallized before that time, as one would expect of such a fundamental issue in the polity. But the connection of racial views to party loyalties grew substantially in the wake of the 1964 presidential election, which offered "a choice, not an echo" on race as on other issues. Members of the public shifted their party loyalties to conform to the new party polarization on race, with African Americans becoming more Democratic and Southern whites becoming more Republican. The effect of this polarization was to heighten the salience of race issues in people's evaluations of the political parties during the course of the 1960s (Geer 1991).

Carmines and Stimson's account of the reciprocal influence between party programs and partisan divisions among the public is an insightful variation on the party realignment theme, focused on a specific issue area. But it is worth noting that the dynamics described by Carmines and Stimson come into play only after what they call an "external disruption to the established order" (1989: 6). That is, leaders of the Democratic Party, and President Kennedy in particular, had to be tempted by expanding African American mobilization into increasing the clarity and intensity of their appeals for the support of black voters. The Republican strategy of moving in a conservative direction on race issues became possible only after the Democrats made the opening move in favor of desegregation and civil rights. And the public pronouncements of Presidents Kennedy and Johnson on the subject would not have occurred had the existence of the civil rights movement not indicated that there was electoral profit to be reaped.

It might seem as though there is a contradiction between the idea that cultural change in the 1950s and 1960s was rapidly marginalizing support for school segregation, and the observation that the Republican Party could become more conservative on race issues. But it is important to be clear that the party polarization on race described by Carmines and Stimson is only a relative polarization of one party compared with the other. Even during the 1964 Goldwater candidacy, much less during the 1968 and 1972 Nixon campaigns, the Republican Party was not as conservative on race issues as the Democratic Party had been in the 1950s. Republicans were also more liberal on race issues in the 1960s than they had been in the 1950s. In the context of rapidly changing cultural values, party polarization occurs when one political party moves to follow the new cultural current more decisively than the other.

If all diffusion of new political values took place within existing political, partisan, or ideological groupings, then value change would be constrained by the cleavage structure of the polity. In practice, the value perspectives developed in critical communities and disseminated through movements will not always be tied to existing ideological and partisan cleavages. In the case of value creation, popular acceptance of new values may well tempt both parties into advocating the critical perspective.

Value connection offers an even greater opportunity for new values to be accepted across lines of political cleavage, because forging new connections between values implies reshaping political coalitions. Value connection results from application of what William Riker (1986) has called the heresthetic arts, the strategic redefinition of an issue by placing it in a new context. In the hands of politicians, heresthetics is primarily a means to refashion issue coalitions. But heresthetic reconfiguration also changes the way in which the issue is seen, the aspects of the issue that are most salient as a policy problem, and the types of policy responses that will be considered. Heresthetics is not simply a matter of altering coalitions, but also results in a reinvention of the issue itself. New values brought to the political agenda by heresthetical means are likely to find supporters across the lines of prior partisan division. These considerations suggest that the process by which new values are brought to public attention—conversion, creation, or connection—will affect the political patterning of diffusion of that value.

CONCLUSION

In each of the examples of value change explored in this chapter, critical communities have functioned as innovators of new ways of thinking about problems and movements have introduced the values of the critical community into the wider society. Of course, neither critical communities nor movements operate in a contextual vacuum. Changes in the physical world, in the structure of society or in the state of knowledge may all create a context in which a particular problem area becomes visible to people, or more urgently visible, or visible in a new light. New knowledge about the minimal degree of genetic differentiation between races and about the long-term physical effects of alcohol abuse played important roles in spurring cultural reevaluations of the racialist ideology and the temperance ethic. Increases in the number of working women contributed to the pressure to examine the relationship between authority and sex in the workplace. Increasing educational and occupational accomplishments of African Americans and women gave each group a growing number of capable leaders for the causes of civil rights and feminism. In the area of alcohol abuse, a far-reaching network of researchers, foundations, hospitals, insurance companies, care givers, and governmental agencies exert constant pressure on the definition of alcohol abuse, specification of its causes and consequences, and the range of approaches used to deal with it.

Social, technological, and physical environments matter in producing cultural change, but such change cannot be viewed as an automatic reaction to changes in the environment. Increasing concern about a problem may occur when the problem is becoming objectively less severe. Even when the existence and severity of a problem are matters of incontrovertible fact, naming the causes of the problem and the best solution to it are not. The facts do not speak for themselves.

Critical communities and their associated movements develop the link between brute data and cultural interpretation. Claims of racial hierarchies and of instinctive aversion between races were important props to the policy of segregation, and when those props were removed the entire structure of Jim Crow segregation was fatally weakened. The concept of sexual harassment would certainly have developed without the advocacy of Catherine MacKinnon, but the way in which the legal system addressed the issue would possibly have been quite different. Medical researchers played a key role in developing and legitimizing the alcoholism concept, while victims of drunk drivers have become an important influence on policies dealing with the charge of driving under the influence.

The significance of perspectives developed within critical communities on the causes and consequences of a problem is appreciated by engaging in a thought experiment. If sexual harassment had been considered the autonomous act of a boorish person, then the remedy would be to punish that person. If the propensity to commit acts of sexual harassment had been defined as a disease, we would fund research on the problem and build centers where offenders could receive treatment. Had the issue first been pushed by corporate personnel managers, sexual harassment may well have come to be seen primarily in terms of its effects on employee morale and productivity. The employer would then become a victim along with the actual target of the harassment. Remedies adopted to combat sexual harassment would almost certainly have been directed at offending employees rather than at employers. In practice, sexual harassment is considered to be the act of a person whose behavior reflects accepted norms of interaction in the workplace. The remedy, then, has been to place responsibility on the employer to create and maintain an environment in which sexual harassment does not occur. And it is the employer (along with the offender) who is punished when sexual harassment does occur as a repeated pattern.

That there is no preordained direction of cultural change is suggested by contrasting the recent histories of sexual harassment and drunk driving. At the same time as the idea of collective responsibility for sexual harassment was being developed and implemented, MADD took the treatment of drunk drivers in the opposite direction of individual responsibility. In most social settings, the idea of the alcoholic as a disease victim in need of treatment is still dominant. Behind the wheel of a car, the disease concept falls away and the alcoholic is held responsible. These diverging developments provide further evidence for the importance of the critical community–movement partnership in defining an issue.

Value conversion, creation, and connection are three specific relationships that new values may have to the established discourse on the subject. By employing some combination of the three types of value change, critical communities and movements seek to have an impact on the problems we think about and how we think about them. The contribution of movements to this process is to shape the perspective of a critical community in such a way as to make possible mass mobilization for the cause. Movements articulate for a large public the moral shame of segregation. Movement activists engage people in discussions of sexual harassment, and press the EEOC to commit resources to sanctioning it. Movements make us aware of the human costs of everyday social drinking and link that growing awareness to a campaign against drunk drivers. The centrality of movements to rapid cultural change gives us reason to examine them more closely in the chapters to come.

PART TWO

Microfoundations

Chapter 4

THE CREATION OF SOLIDARITY

My experiences at Tent City . . . opened my eyes.
I hadn't really thought of myself as part of an
oppressed group before.
—Arnie, participant in a homeless protest
(cited in Wagner and Cohen 1991: 555)

THE THEORY of cultural change elaborated in the first part of this book suggests a two-step process in which new values are first developed in critical communities and then disseminated by movements to the wider society. Critical communities are composed primarily of scientists, academics, and a variety of social analysts and commentators. The ideas of the critical community are reshaped by leaders and activists in social and political movements, in accord with the demands of mobilization and the experience of movement struggle. Once the issue becomes public, the movement takes center stage and the critical community fades to the background.

The first and most fundamental issue that movements face is the problem of mobilizing activists. The potential that movement organizations have for diffusing change in cultural values can be realized only if they are able to overcome the notorious free-rider problem. Public choice analysts and movement organizers know that a widespread desire to remedy some social or political problem is not in itself enough to guarantee the mobilization of a movement. Ever since Olson's (1965) clarification of the barriers to mobilizing for collective goods, scholars have understood the necessity for movements to push people out of an individualistic, expected utility calculus and to foster an alternative set of calculations involving the group welfare.

Movement participation is unlikely to be rewarding in the same ways as participation in other types of organization. Movements cannot pay wages, as corporations do. They often cannot rely on intrinsic interest in their activities, as hobby clubs do. The opportunities they offer for political influence are more uncertain than those of other forms of political association.

At the same time, the costs of movement participation can be high, for movement protests are not infrequently punished by the community or by authorities. Consider the case of Prudence Crandall, a Connecticut schoolteacher in the early nineteenth century. After reading William Lloyd Garrison's abolitionist newspaper, *The Liberator*, Miss Crandall decided in 1832 to admit an African American to her girls' school, a "young lady of pleasing appearance and manner." This action became the center of a statewide uproar over the proper place of African Americans in the society, resulting in a state law, passed in May 1833, making integrated schools illegal. When Miss Crandall refused to segregate her school, she was sent to jail. Freed after an inconclusive trial, the community took over: her students were harassed, her well was poisoned, her home was set on fire. Miss Crandall married in late 1834, closed her school, and moved to Illinois (Stange 1977: 27–28).

Prudence Crandall sacrificed her career, home, position in the community, and personal safety for the sake of participation in a cause whose course her own actions were unlikely to affect. Her story is heroic and it is unusual, but it is hardly unique. One hundred twenty years after Prudence Crandall was forced from her home in Connecticut, freedom riders traveled by bus through the South, certain they would be beaten and fearing they might be murdered. Civil rights volunteers engaged in community organizing and voter registration projects faced daily harassment and lived in fear of their lives. Nothing in their prior middle-class existences had prepared them for this. As Sara Evans (1979: 72) summarizes, "There were obscene phone calls, narrow escapes, highway chases at 80 to 90 miles an hour. One woman found it most difficult to accept the fact that the police were not on her side, that in effect she had no protection."[1]

Hundreds of thousands of activists have taken risks in dozens of major movement mobilizations during the nineteenth and twentieth centuries. As a purely statistical matter, advocates of expected utility analysis may take comfort in the hundreds of *millions* of Americans who have never made a substantial personal sacrifice for a collective goal. For example, Walsh and Warland's (1983: table 1) study of inhabitants in the area surrounding the Three Mile Island nuclear power plant showed that 84 percent of those opposed to restart of the nuclear reactor contributed no time or money to the community groups leading the opposition. But that predictive success is reduced to a Pyrrhic victory when one considers that the minority of people who do engage in collective action are the ones who have shaped nearly every element of the social and political landscape with which we are today familiar. Sometimes it is more important to understand the unusual than it is to predict the typical.

As a number of students of movement mobilization have pointed out, the factor that motivates mobilization, overlooked in rational choice models based on an individual calculus, is that people assess their environments and decide on a course of action based on formal and informal networks, which

---

[1] On personal sacrifice in the civil rights movement, see also Sitkoff 1981: 117–124; Farmer 1985; and McAdam 1986.

are expressive of feelings of group solidarity. When people see their own fates as being inextricably tied to the fate of some larger group, and when the extent of solidarity in that group leads one to expect that others will participate in the movement as well, then the expected utility of participation in a movement is transformed. The choices that are rational for an individual in an atomized environment are not necessarily the decisions reached by someone in an environment rich in organizational networks and group solidarities.

The existing literature on movement mobilization tends to divide between work based on rational choice modeling and work based on networks and solidarities. But the difference between these perspectives has been narrowing in recent years. Consider for example the range of solutions to the free-rider problem that has been proposed by scholars working within the rational choice models. Olson (1965) proposes that movements organized in small groups will have greater success in mobilizing support because the impact of their efforts is likely to be greater in a small group setting than in a large group. Reliance on established group networks lowers the costs of communication and increases the expectation that others will also join the movement (Marwell and Oliver 1993). Solidarity makes movement mobilization possible by fostering a collective rationality that operates alongside individual rationality (Klandermans 1988). Mutual assurances and commitments made by people who know and trust each other reduce the expected costs of mobilization (Chong 1991).

These are among the considerations that would increase the probability of a rational individual deciding to become active in a movement. And every one of these considerations is closely tied to the presence of group identification and group solidarity. As we will see in this chapter, group identification refers to the extent to which group interests are taken to be identical to individual interests. Feelings of solidarity increase the belief that others in the group are likely to become active in the movement; solidarity is thus the mechanism that generates the mutual assurance so important to rational mobilization.

GROUP IDENTIFICATION

The central theme of this chapter is that movements mobilize public support by linking their cause to existing group identifications and by strengthening solidarity within the group. Identification involves the belief that members of the group share a common fate by virtue of their group affiliation, and that the fate of the individual cannot be separated from the fate of the group. The feeling of group identification is illustrated in the reaction of a black college student to news film on the Greensboro lunch counter sit-ins: "My identification with the demonstrating students was so thorough that I would flinch every time one of the whites taunted them. On nights when I saw pictures of students being beaten and dragged through the streets by their hair, I would leave the lounge in a rage" (Sitkoff 1981: 86–87).

When identification with the group leads one to feel the physical and emotional stress of other group members, it is impossible to avoid the conclusion that what is good for the group is worth doing. Group identification is necessary for mobilization into a movement because the more people believe they share a common fate, the more they value the kinds of outcomes that can only be produced by collective action (Brewer 1979). Movement organizations do not usually create group identification de novo, but instead build on existing group ties and networks, either actual or latent.

Solidarity is the belief that the group is capable of unified action in pursuit of the group's goals. It is not possible for one to feel solidarity with a group with which one does not identify, but on the other hand it is possible to identify with a group without feeling solidarity. It is a task of movement organizations to heighten the sense of solidarity within the group(s) linked to the movement cause.

One of the messages conveyed by the leadership of a solidary group is that unity is essential to success. Ben Franklin understood the mobilizing power of belief in the necessity of unity when he exhorted his colleagues to present a united front for independence of the American colonies: "Gentlemen, we either hang together or we shall surely hang separately." A Chicago community organizer used a different metaphor to express the same sentiment, noting that "We're in this boat together. We either row together, unite, and safely go across, or we drown separately. It's as simple as that" (cited in Hirsch 1986: 379).

Given the importance of group solidarity for mobilization, it is clear that movements must be centrally concerned with cultivating solidarity among potential members. At the time of Italian unification, Massimo d'Azeglio said "We have made Italy, now we must make the Italians." With movements, the required sequence runs in the other direction: in order to make a working-class movement, a feminist movement, or an environmental movement, one must first make the working class, feminists, and environmentalists. As Sabel (1982: 187) notes, "workers standing side by side in a factory do not necessarily view their work in the same way." It is the task of a labor organizer to teach workers to view their work, their lives, and the sources of their grievances in the same way.

Fortunately for movement leaders, solidarity is a labile social construction, created by interaction among group members. Both identity and solidarity are by-products of the effort each of us undertakes to make sense of our environment by locating ourselves in relation to other people. This we do by deciding what groups we are part of and what our group affiliations mean to us. Although group boundaries generally exhibit a great deal of continuity over time, they are nonetheless susceptible to transformation as the social values that underlie particular group distinctions are altered.

Even such seemingly immutable groups as those that compose the socio-economic classes are creations of the nineteenth and twentieth centuries, the period in which what Asa Briggs (1960) has called "the language of class" was still evolving. The idea of a class hierarchy based on occupation took hold during the industrial revolution, replacing an older hierarchy of social ranks or estates that had existed in preindustrial Europe. The estates most commonly identified were the nobility (including landowners and warriors), the clergy, and those who worked with their hands. The latter group encompassed both craftsmen and peasants, both those who owned their land or shops and those who did not. Distinctions that later became important, based on the degree of skill required in a job or on whether one was master or apprentice of a shop, had far less significance as an indicator of social status in the eighteenth century. Even in England, terms like working class or middle class came into use only after 1812. Reference to the prior system of "ranks," "orders," "degrees," or "estates" did not disappear until after 1850 (Briggs 1960).

This transition represented more than a substitution of one terminology for another. The old language contained in it ideas of duty, deference, mutual responsibility between ranks, and a hierarchical *social* order. The new language of class emphasized the commonality of *economic* interests within classes and the separation of interests—even the conflict of interests—between classes. Social stratification was replaced by economic stratification. What had been a complex set of social obligations was narrowed to an economic relationship based on ownership of factor endowments. Although taken for granted today, this was a striking aspect of capitalism both to its early champions and critics. Marx and Engels (1848: 475–476) noted that creation of the bourgeoisie has

> pitilessly torn asunder the motley feudal ties that bound man to his "natural superiors," and has left remaining no other bond between man and man than naked self-interest, than callous "cash payment." . . . It has resolved personal worth into exchange value. . . . It has converted the physician, the lawyer, the priest, the poet, the man of science, into its paid wage-laborers. The bourgeoisie has torn away from the family its sentimental veil, and has reduced the family relation to a mere money relation.

In short, the development of class consciousness involved a change of values that affected every culturally defined relationship between people.

Fortunately for organizers of non-class-based movements, capitalism has not reduced all group identities to "a mere money relation." People feel a personal connection to groups on a variety of grounds that transcend economic interest. Thus, an abolitionist expresses her commitment to fellow

activists because they are people "who, living in the world, have yet . . .
lived apart from it, bearing . . . in their lives, a continual testimony against
its evil habits" (cited in Hersh 1978: 157). Thus, a member of the gay rights
group ACT UP says that only by working through the group is it possible
"to express the anger and rage that is righteous and justified" (cited in Gamson 1989). Even class-based organizations thrive, in part, on noneconomic
sources of group identification. Thus, the farmers most likely to join the
American Agriculture Movement are those who see farming not just as an
occupation but as a way of life rooted in rural values and the work rhythms
of nature (Cigler and Hansen 1983: 93).

As with other types of cultural values, group identities are responsive to
changes in economic and social structure. But, as with other types of cultural
values, the contents of group identities also depend on human agency—they
cannot be extrapolated directly from economic and social structures. When
these structures are in flux, there is a period of experimentation in which
new group identities are proposed, generally by drawing on analogies from
the past. The Knights of Labor, for example, sought to create a labor movement that rested on preindustrial artisanal notions of the "nobility of toil."
The Knights extended membership in the Order to shopkeepers and small
manufacturers who "showed respect for the dignity of labor" (Fink 1983: 9–
10). The enemy was not only big industry and big finance, but also idlers,
gamblers, speculators, liquor dealers, and lawyers—none of whom were
viewed as producing a socially worthwhile product.

The Knights of Labor did not survive, and its conceptions of a group
identity encompassing all who engage in productive labor died with it. Labor
organizations of the twentieth century came to accept the commodification
of work, and dropped arguments about the nobility of toil in favor of claims
for a fair share of the firm's profits. The boundaries of group identity in
modern unions are accordingly narrowed to fit the distinctions between manual and nonmanual labor that constitute contemporary understandings of
economic class. General Master Workman Terence Powderly, leader of the
Knights of Labor, would have been puzzled to learn that a small independent
supplier of parts to Honda of America does not today join the United Auto
Workers. He would be shocked to learn that the hauler of liquor is welcome
to join the Teamsters. The boundaries of class identity that today seem so
firmly rooted in our culture, and that to some are viewed as the natural order
of things, have come to be that way only as the product of more than a
century of organizing and struggle in the context of industrialization. As
Tilly (1985), Fantasia (1988), and others have pointed out, the creation of a
group prepared to pool its resources for common purposes comes about as
the result of a continuous history of communication, interaction, and struggle. Class consciousness, like other forms of group identity, is created and
shaped by collective struggle for various political goals.

The Elements of Solidarity

Group identities set the pattern of movement mobilization by determining the boundaries of collective interests. To be aware of one's group identity is to be conscious of belonging to the group. But group identity is not a sufficient condition for mobilization to occur. Group solidarity provides the motivation for collective action by linking the welfare of the group to a program of political or social change, and by creating the expectation that the group will act cohesively to bring about that change. As Klandermans (1984) notes, people must decide whether to participate in a movement without having full information on how many others will participate. They must, then, develop expectations about the participation of others based on their belief that the group has a legitimate grievance, has identified a reasonable strategy of remedial action, and will act cohesively. These beliefs are the constituent elements of the feeling of solidarity.

Group solidarity is, in effect, a politicized group identity.[2] In addition to awareness of belonging to the group (identity), solidarity consists of three additional attitudes about the group. First, feelings of solidarity require dissatisfaction with the group's existing power or status. Second, responsibility for low group status must be placed outside of the group—either on some other group or on the political, social, or economic systems themselves. And finally, members of the group must believe that collective action can improve the group's position. Group identification is a necessary foundation that makes group solidarity possible, but it is only the additional confluence of discontent, external blame, and approval of collective action that creates feelings of group solidarity. Identification determines the boundaries of the relevant groups; solidarity determines the likelihood that group identities will be translated into collective action.

Group solidarity is thus the psychological foundation of movement mobilization. People who feel a politicized discontent with the status of their group are likely to adopt the logic of collective rationality that is necessary to overcome the free-rider problem. As a result, movement organizations "have much to gain by undertaking the difficult process of strengthening solidarity relations within the constituency. . . . Political education, ideological discussion, study groups, consciousness-raising sessions, newsletters, and political tracts frequently are intended to raise personal interest in the collective goods being promoted" (Fireman and Gamson 1979: 23, 26).

We shall see that movement organizations do indeed go to great lengths to create and sustain feelings of solidarity among members of a group. Before moving to that point, however, we must first create an operational measure

---

[2] Group consciousness is a term used in a similar sense elsewhere in the literature. See, e.g., Miller et al. 1981; Klein 1984; and Conover 1988.

of group solidarity and demonstrate its connection to movement mobilization.

MEASURING IDENTIFICATION AND SOLIDARITY

Because the presence of group identification and group solidarity cannot simply be assumed within movements, we must have a means of measuring each. The problem is that identification and solidarity are states of mind, and clues to states of mind are not readily prised from historical records. As Charles Tilly (1964: 83) put it, "In the world of history, true love leaves fewer memorials than the sale of a sow." Even so, the determination of group identities is generally an easy enough task; the strength of group solidarities is more difficult to measure.

Group identification is often ascertainable through the claims, activities, icons, artifacts, and language of movements (Gamson 1992). As Tarrow (1992: 197) has noted, group identities are best observed "through the study of how people struggle, against whom they struggle, and in the name of which symbols and points of concern they struggle." It may be hard to chant a slogan like "Down with moderates, royalists, and administrators that are enemies of the people, and up with the *sans culottes!*" (Rudé 1964: 119), but at least such a motto leaves little room for doubt about the boundaries of group identification.

Unlike group identification, group solidarities are not as easily determined from an external inspection of protest activities or slogans. To infer the strength of group solidarity from the existence of movement protest would be to engage in tautology, since it is precisely the point of this chapter to establish that solidarity leads to collective action. For recent movements, however, the states of mind that constitute solidarity can be directly measured. In their study of political belief and action in the South in 1961, Donald Matthews and James Prothro provide us with a wealth of measures relating to group identification and solidarity. Group identification, in this context, is the feeling of closeness to other members of the same race. Group solidarity consists of an expression of interest in how other members of the same race are getting along, discontent with the conditions of racial segregation, *and* approval of collective action to promote integration.[3]

---

[3] The measure of group identification (a sense of closeness with the group) is "Would you say you feel pretty close to Negroes in general, or that you don't feel much closer to them than you do to other people?" The measure of group solidarity relies on four questions: (a) "How much interest would you say you have in how Negroes as a whole are getting along in this country?" (b) "Are you in favor of integration, strict segregation, or something in between?" (c) "Now thinking of the NAACP, do you generally agree with what it does, or do you generally disagree?" (d) "What is your feeling about the sit-in movement (in which some of the young Negroes go into stores, sit down at lunch counters, and refuse to leave until they are served)?" It is worth noting that the group term "black" came into widespread use only a few years

This is a demanding test of group solidarity. At the lowest threshold of solidarity, the feeling of having "a good deal of interest in how Negroes as a whole are getting along" was held by 76 percent of this 1961 sample of African Americans in the South. But the existence of group solidarity requires as well that one connect the welfare of the race to the systemic conditions of racial segregation and electoral disenfranchisement.[4] Of those who had "a good deal" of interest in the welfare of others of their race, 72 percent also supported full integration. Thus, 54.9 percent of the total sample passed these two hurdles.

Finally, group solidarity requires that one believe in the possibility of changing the group's status through collective action. At the time of the survey, the civil rights movement was engaged in challenges to segregation through the court system as well as direct action protests, such as marches, boycotts, and sit-ins at segregated public facilities. The survey provides two measures of approval of the tactics employed by the movement. Maximum solidarity exists when a respondent approves of both the legal appeals mounted by the NAACP *and* of the more militant direct action tactics adopted by the student sit-in movement. Of the 55 percent of respondents who were interested in the welfare of fellow African Americans and were supportive of integration, 83 percent gave unqualified support to the NAACP and 41 percent "strongly approved" of the sit-in demonstrations. It is apparent that approval of illegal forms of collective action represents the most demanding test of group solidarity. This rate of approval of the sit-ins, however, compares favorably with approval of illegal protests found in other settings.[5]

Overall, 21 percent of the sample achieved a maximum score on this four-part measure of solidarity. The lowest level of solidarity, found among 33 percent of the sample, occurs when interest in the welfare of other African Americans is not found together with a clear position against segregation. The remaining 46 percent of the sample scored at one of two intermediate levels of solidarity. Respondents in the midrange of solidarity had an interest in the welfare of African Americans and were supportive of integration, but

---

after this study was completed, so that declining to express interest in how "Negroes" are getting along cannot be attributed to a preference for other terms expressing the group identity of African Americans.

[4] At a later point in the civil rights movement, race solidarity could also be expressed by endorsing the segregation proposed by Elijah Muhammad. His beliefs were publicly stated by the time of the survey in 1961, but they were at that time seen by few African Americans as a means of improving their group status.

[5] A survey of protest approval and participation in the United States conducted in 1974 by Barnes, Kaase, et al. (1979) found that only 2 percent of the sample approved of occupying buildings. This is substantially lower than the 41 percent approval of lunch counter sit-ins found in 1961 among African Americans in the South. Approval of illegal protest appears to be contingent not just on a generalized attitude about the law, but also on one's beliefs about the particular cause.

did not approve of the NAACP's legal challenges and/or the illegal student sit-ins. This is the measure of group solidarity with which we will test the relationship between group identification and group solidarity, and between solidarity and participation in the civil rights movement. Table 4-1 shows that group identification among African Americans in the South was widespread (89 percent), though not quite universal. Apparently, it was still possible for Southern blacks in the late days of segregation not to feel that one has "a lot in common with other Negroes." This is a salutary reminder of the fact that group identity, much less group solidarity, cannot be taken for granted even under conditions of pervasive discrimination overtly directed against the group. Some African Americans reacted to racial prejudice precisely by denying their own connection to the group.

The first hypothesis is that group identification is a necessary but not sufficient foundation for group solidarity. Twelve percent of those without a feeling of group identity nonetheless scored high or very high on the solidarity scale, compared with 37 percent of respondents who felt they had a lot in common with others of their race (see table 4-1). Of the total sample, only 1.2 percent scored in the upper reaches of the group solidarity scale without expressing group identification. The hypothesis that group identification is a necessary foundation for group solidarity is thus confirmed in nearly all cases.

The second hypothesis is that group solidarity is a necessary motivation for movement mobilization. The connection between solidarity and participation in the civil rights movement is shown in figure 4-1. Those scoring very high on the measure of group solidarity are seventeen times more likely than those very low in solidarity to have joined a civil rights organization.

TABLE 4-1
Group Identification and Solidarity

	Group Identification	
Solidarity	No	Yes
Very low	42.6	31.1
Low	45.6	31.9
High	5.9	13.8
Very high	5.9	23.2
All	11.1	88.9

Source: Negro Political Participation Study, 1961–1962.
Note: Pearson's $r = .15$ ($p < .01$). With education controlled, Pearson's $r = .16$ ($p < .01$). Number of cases is 611. Entries are the percentage active in the civil rights movement.

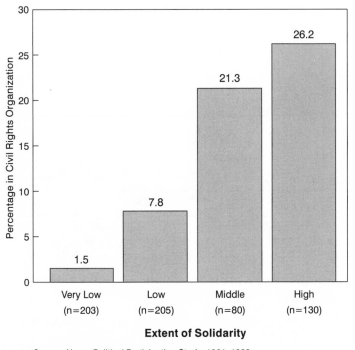

Source: Negro Political Participation Study, 1961–1962.

Note: Correlation between solidarity and participation: r = .28; with education controlled: r_{ed} = .21

Figure 4-1   Racial solidarity and civil rights participation

By contrast, group identification is almost completely unrelated to the likelihood of joining a civil rights organization: 11.8 percent of those who feel they have more in common with other African Americans are members of a civil rights organization, compared with 8.8 percent of those who do not feel they have more in common with others of their race (Pearson's r = .03). It is clear that group solidarity, rather than group identification alone, is required for movement participation.

The solidarity theory of movement participation makes a second claim as well. The component elements of solidarity are a syndrome that must be present in its entirety in order to motivate participation in a movement. Interest in the welfare of the group, desire for change in the group's status, and acceptance of the forms of collective action are all necessary for mobilization; no one or two of them are sufficient to overcome the free-rider problem.

The effects of solidarity on civil rights activity are decomposed into their separate elements in table 4-2. The table shows that there are relatively low

TABLE 4-2

Components of Solidarity and Movement Participation

	Pearson Correlation	OLS Beta
Interest in how Negroes are getting along	.12	.06
Is R in favor of integration?	.19	.08
Does R generally agree with the NAACP?	.16	.07
Does R approve of the sit-in movement?	.23	.17
Solidarity Index	.28	na

Source: Negro Political Participation Study, 1961–1962.

Note: The correlations reported are with membership in a civil rights organization; that is also the dependent variable in the regression. All correlations are significant at the .01 level. In the OLS regression, only the coefficient for approval of the sit-in movement is significant at the .01 level.

The Solidarity Index is constructed from the preceding four variables on the principle of a Guttman scale. Each variable represents a "harder" threshold toward full solidarity.

correlations between membership in a civil rights organization and interest in the welfare of other African Americans ($r = .12$), or being in favor of racial integration ($r = .19$). Agreement with the activities of the NAACP is only moderately correlated with movement participation ($r = .16$). The strongest correlate of membership in a civil rights organization is approval of the sit-in movement ($r = .23$).[6] But even that relationship is weaker than the relationship between membership in the movement and the index created by combining all four components of solidarity. It is the interaction between the components of solidarity, rather than any of them taken separately, that most powerfully predicts civil rights involvement.

MODES OF CHANGE IN GROUP SOLIDARITY

The analysis to this point has shown that group identity is a necessary but not sufficient condition of group solidarity. Moreover, when the elements of group solidarity are all present, they are potent in motivating participation in the civil rights movement. This leads to two questions: what are the factors that produce group identity, and how are group identities converted into feelings of group solidarity?

Because group identities are a type of cultural value, the ways in which

---

[6] This pattern of bivariate relationships is maintained in the beta weights from an OLS regression, shown in the second column of table 4-2. Approval of the sit-in movement absorbs all the covariation between civil rights activity and the more widespread elements of group solidarity.

they are created and reshaped can be analyzed with the same conceptual categories developed in chapter 3 to describe changes in cultural values. Identity conversion, creation, and connection are special instances of the more general phenomenon of value conversion, creation, and connection.

As is true of other cultural values, conversion is the most difficult and conflictual strategy for generating changes in group identity. It is likely to be difficult to convince the members of one social group that they should transfer their loyalty to a different group, unless the old group identity has first been discredited or made irrelevant by changes in the environment. Such environmental changes account for the transition in group identities from social ranks to economic classes. The industrial revolution altered the specific forms of work that people do, as well as the organization of work. The social status and economic security of manual workers were transformed. The industrial revolution brought with it the decline of small craft shops, with their relatively egalitarian division of labor between master and apprentices (Darnton 1984: 79–83). Workers were more likely to be employed in large factories; owners no longer worked alongside them as skilled practitioners of the craft. In these changed conditions, group identities that emphasized hierarchical distinctions between owners and workers came to replace solidarity between master and apprentice within a trade.

The spread of a feminist identity in this century has gained adherence partly in consequence of technological advances and changes in the social structure. Klein (1984) has demonstrated that a later age at marriage, higher educational attainment, fewer children, reduced time burdens of housework and food preparation, increased opportunities in the workplace, and higher rates of divorce have all made labor force participation more attractive for American women. With greater participation in the labor force, identities centered on the family have lost their exclusive appeal. The result has been the spread of a new public identity for women, found especially among feminists but not limited to them, which today coexists with the traditional identity centered on the family.

Comparing the experience of women in different countries is instructive in the ways new group identities are shaped by their relationship to established identities. In the United States, a feminist identity has been constructed around a variety of issues that converge on the principle of creating equal opportunity to fill any economic, political, or social role. The central principles of American feminism were developed by analogy with the principles of racial equality, in no small part because many American feminists in the 1960s had prior experience in the civil rights movement (Evans 1979; Ferree 1987).[7]

[7] Despite this formative experience, the American women's movement has not been very successful in developing solidarity or participation among women of color.

In Sweden, these principles of social equality are not associated with the struggles of a racial group, but rather with the struggles of the labor movement. Whereas the women's movement in the United States sought to extend the group rights analysis pioneered in the civil rights movement, the task for Swedish feminists has been to establish the legitimacy of group interests that are not class interests. Swedish feminists have at times been frustrated by the ease with which women's demands are channeled through a policy process dominated by the (usually male) representatives of economic classes. Public policies are highly favorable to women's participation in the labor force, but this is seen by some feminists as an impediment to the creation of group solidarity (Gelb 1989). As one Swedish champion of women's equality put it, "How do you fight satisfaction? How do you fight politicians who say, 'We are with you all the way?'" (cited in Scott 1982: 157).

Identities that are institutionally and culturally entrenched have the upper hand in any confrontation with emergent group identities. An alternative means of changing group identity that runs into less resistance is to change only the content rather than the boundaries of group identity. This is identity change by connection, which involves developing a link between a new critical community discourse and existing group identifications.

It is not uncommon for movement organizations to attach their cause to regional, ethnic, or nationalist loyalties, since these group identifications produce exceptionally powerful feelings of solidarity. Many struggles around the world that are, at root, conflicts over the distribution of social prestige or of economic resources, are nonetheless cast by movement leaders as struggles for ethnic justice or for national liberation. Leaders of the Contra movement in Nicaragua, working as contract employees of the U.S. Central Intelligence Agency (CIA), proposed that Contra rebels connect their cause to existing nationalist identifications by "mak[ing] it clear that the Sandinista regime is foreignizing, repressive, and imperialistic, and that even though there are some Nicaraguans within the government, they are puppets of the power of the Soviets and Cubans." The Contras were further instructed to capitalize on religious identities by emphasizing the atheism of Sandinista socialism and portraying themselves as religiously inspired. Their training manual suggested that the Contras foster an "identification process of the people with the Christian guerrillas."[8]

The Contras were building on a venerable tradition of connecting movement causes to religious sentiment. In nineteenth-century America, religious belief was one of the few sources of group identity that transcended identities based on ethnic and national origins. Leaders of the abolition and temperance movements were careful to link their causes with moral strictures

---

[8] Citations are from the *New York Times*, "Excerpts from Primer for Insurgents," October 17, 1984, p. A12.

found in the Old and New Testaments. Thus, for example, Prohibitionists wrestled with the fact that Jesus Christ drank wine, and that his first miracle was turning water into wine at a wedding.[9] When William Lloyd Garrison and the "comeouter" faction of the abolition movement began "excommunicating" congregations that refused to give an unequivocal endorsement to immediate emancipation, their actions created a split within the movement.[10] Large numbers of abolitionists continued to work through the churches, believing that no movement could be successful if it did not enlist denominational group identities.

The moral force of religious solidarities is so significant that connection to religious identities has been an important component of mobilization strategy even in movements operating in relatively secular societies. The 1980s European peace movements, despite having primarily secular leadership, organized many events to cultivate support from religious people. Easter marches, prayer vigils, candlelight parades, and the building of rudimentary chapels outside of missile bases were all designed to facilitate the transfer of group identity from church to movement. Those countries where such tactics were used most extensively had the highest rates of movement participation among churchgoing people (Rochon 1988: 146–149).

Identity creation is the final alternative open to movements. Creation of new group identities is surely more difficult than is value creation more generally, but there are times when connection to existing group identities is not possible. Identity creation requires ideological innovation. The identities of "environmentalist" and "feminist," to name two prominent examples, have resulted from the elaboration of environmentalist and feminist value systems. These new identities are then further developed in the course of collective action. As people engaged in a cause meet resistance from authorities or other social institutions, their sense of having a shared fate—of being a group—is enhanced.

Identity creation is an uncertain process, one that is full of false starts and failed efforts. The student movement in the mid-1960s experimented with an identity based on Marxist ideas about the capitalist exploitation of labor. Despite the awkward fact that most student radicals had middle-class backgrounds, a theory of the exploitation of the student class was developed in which the university's role was "to shape, train, and funnel manpower, for the needs of the American capitalist enterprise."[11] As Berkeley student leader

---

[9] One Prohibitionist response to this, never fully persuasive even to those committed to the cause, was that all references to "wine" in the Bible refer to unfermented grape juice.

[10] "Comeouterism" took its name from Revelations (18:4), "Come out from her, my people, that ye receive not of her plagues." Dissociation from congregations that extended fellowship to slaveholders was seen more as a way of avoiding personal moral contamination than as an effective means of altering church policies. See McKivigan (1984), especially chap. 9.

[11] Kunen (1968: 102), citing the head of the SDS theoretical group at Columbia University.

Mario Savio put it, "the university is part and parcel of this particular stage in the history of American society; it stands to serve the needs of American industry; it is a factory that turns out a product needed by industry or government."[12]

As the war in Vietnam became central to student protest, the identity centered on "students as products of the university factory" was deemphasized in favor of another identity in which university students joined the emerging global alliance of oppressed peoples. Racism at home and imperialism abroad were two fronts in the same struggle. Common cause was to be made with Vietnamese peasants, those fighting around the globe for national liberation, and racial minorities in America: "The struggles of Third World movements abroad and black America at home have marked the beginning of the end of US corporate capitalism. . . . The conclusion we must draw is that the primary task for the radical student movement at this time is to develop a political strategy of anti-imperialism."[13] Solidarity with freedom fighters in North Vietnam, in the Middle East (Al Fatah), in Cuba, and elsewhere reflects the attempt to create a new identity of the revolutionary student. This effort was a failure because few students felt close to or sympathetic with a global network of revolutionaries.[14]

The student movement's greatest mobilization successes occurred, logically enough, when the movement focused on the interests of students *as students*: concerned with social justice in university admissions policies, with participation in university governance, and with the vulnerability to being drafted and sent to Vietnam. When Students for a Democratic Society (SDS) and other student organizations abandoned their appeals to student identification and shifted to the revolutionary identification, they went into rapid decline. "The SDS revolutionaries were on the barricades, but they had forgotten to look behind: their troops were no longer following" (Sale 1973: 528).

The women's movement, although ultimately more successful in creating a new feminist identity, went through a similar phase of early experimentation. Many of the original activists in the women's movement came from prior involvement with the civil rights and student movements, and so their search for a group identity initially took the forms developed in those move-

---

[12] Cited in Vickers 1975: 98. See also the SDS policy statement written by Carl Davidson in 1966, titled "A Student Syndicalist Movement," which is extensively quoted in Sale 1973: 290–292.

[13] Carl Davidson and Greg Calvert, "Ten Days to Shake the Empire," a proposal for ten days of direct action on and off campus that was not adopted by SDS in April 1968 but which nonetheless accurately reflected the direction that the organization was moving. Cited in Sale 1973: 400. See also Sale's chap. 21 on the growth of an antiimperialist analysis within SDS.

[14] Indeed, the existence of a global network of revolutionaries was itself a fiction necessary to the creation of the identity of student revolutionary.

ments. One such identity was, again, the third world, revolutionary identity. The report of a "Women's Liberation Workshop" held at an SDS National Conference in June 1967 concluded: "As we analyze the position of women in capitalist society and especially in the United States we find that women are in a colonial relationship to men and we recognize ourselves as part of the Third World."[15] The very phrase "women's liberation" was meant to underline the connection between the women's movement and other movements of oppressed groups in the United States and elsewhere. Just as leaders in the women's movement in the nineteenth century drew on their experience in the abolition movement to denounce "the slavery of sex,"[16] so were twentieth-century American feminists at first likely to see their collective experience through the prism of other contemporary movements.

The difference between the student movement and the women's movement at the end of the 1960s, though, is that the women's movement moved beyond its derivative origins to develop a new synthesis that serves as a model of identity creation. There are fierce debates within the critical community between "difference feminists" and "equity feminists," but the feminist identity that has come to be widely diffused contains elements of both. Group identity in the women's movement has ultimately centered on an amalgam of beliefs about the superiority of women in human relations and the right of women to participate in all aspects of social, economic, and political life on an equal basis with men.

By creation and connection, and occasionally by conversion, group identities are shaped to enable movement organizations to mobilize activists to their cause. There is competition between alternative identity formulations within most movements, and a number of formulations may be tried out in the early phases of a movement. The winner (or winners) in that competition are not decided on the basis of philosophical analysis, but on the basis of which identity formulations are successful as a basis for mobilization. When a particular group identity comes to be accepted within a movement, it defines the boundaries of the constituency of the movement and determines the broad purposes of collective action.

DEVELOPING SOLIDARITY

To motivate costly action on behalf of group goals, however, group identification is not enough. The movement must also develop solidarity within

---

[15] Cited in Evans (1979: 190). Evans appends the wry comment that "The evident inadequacies of this analysis made it a short-lived one."

[16] As Lucy Stone put the matter, "Marriage is to woman a state of slavery. It takes from her the right to her own property, and makes her submissive in all things to her husband." Cited on p. 197 of Blanche Hersh's (1978) book titled *The Slavery of Sex*, which explores the connections between the abolition and women's movements.

the group. Solidarity has been studied in an enormous array of contexts ranging from small-group dynamics to studies of national character. These studies converge in suggesting two basic processes that foster strong feelings of solidarity. First, interaction strengthens solidarity by giving people common experiences. Second, ideology itself strengthens solidarity by offering a shared interpretation of the group experience. All group solidarities, whether in clubs, corporations, political associations, or nations, are founded on interaction and shared ideology.

The issue of how movement organizations use interaction and ideology to strengthen group solidarity is, therefore, central to understanding how movements mobilize support. It is a question best examined by looking at instances where solidarities are particularly well developed. This is generally the case in religious cult movements, which often induce people to immerse themselves in group-directed activity and to undergo great sacrifices on behalf of the cult's aims. The solidarities generated within cults are sometimes stronger even than the desire for self-preservation. The suicide of 914 residents of the Jonestown People's Temple in Guyana in 1978 and the hold-out of Branch Davidians during a siege by federal agents in 1993 are but two striking examples of people accepting or risking death as the price of their solidarity with the group. Residents of Jonestown who survived the suicide ritual, usually because they were elsewhere that night, later expressed regret at missing the chance to die with their friends. Many had difficulty reintegrating into the looser solidarities characteristic of mainstream society (Chidester 1988). Much the same phenomenon afflicted Heaven's Gate members who did not die with their brothers in Rancho Santa Fe, California, in March 1997. Several of them later attempted suicide on their own or in groups.

The intense group solidarity produced by cults rests on both ideology and interaction.[17] Ideology creates feelings of distinctiveness among members by proclaiming that those in the movement will be saved while those outside are damned. Cult ideologies claim to offer members special insight that will enable them to transcend the dilapidated circumstances of most human lives. The paradigm case is the millenarian movement, which predicts the imminent end of the world due to human folly, but offers salvation to those who adhere to the movement's precepts. Solidarity with a millenarian movement offers a means of survival.

The ideology of group distinctiveness found in cults is reinforced by ar-

---

[17] Rosbeth Kanter's (1972) analysis of commitment to millenarian cults includes sacrifice, renunciation of outside ties, communion with fellow members, symbolic rebirth within the movement, transcendent connection to a higher power, and belief that the cult has access to a truth revealed only to members. Each of these elements is connected to interaction and ideology within the cult. For a related exploration of interaction and ideology in relation to movements more generally, see Ferree and Miller 1985; Fantasia 1988; and Taylor and Whittier 1995.

rangements that isolate members from the outside world. In the case of communal movements, where members live and work together, this isolation may be nearly complete. Hutterite communities speak Tyrolean German, effectively limiting unauthorized contact with the surrounding English-speaking society (Lee 1970).

The solidarity-producing powers of ideology and interaction reach their zenith when everyday experiences reinforce faith in the shared ideology, and the shared ideology in turn lends special meaning to daily interactions. As Kanter (1972: 241) puts it, "ideologies that promote transcendence . . . tend to invest with meaning even the most minute daily acts and include every part of a person's life under their wings." The Hutterites illustrate exactly this encompassing character of the ideology.[18]

> What is in our society a routine function, such as the gathering of a family around the dinner table, becomes to the Hutterites an expression of worship as the entire community assembles in the colony dining hall to partake of a meal in almost complete silence. The taking of nourishment to them is more than just that; it is a religious service, a tribute to the glory of the Provider of all.

The importance of interaction and ideology as factors productive of solidarity shows us why cult movements have a substantial advantage over other types of movements in creating strong group solidarities and in motivating individual sacrifice. Interactions are especially dense in cults that create a communal life-style. Cults are also advantaged by their ideologies, since their beliefs involve claims to special insights that link everyday behavior to higher truths. Movements that are both communal and religious may produce ties of solidarity stronger than the ties of family.

In size and influence on the wider society, cults and communal movements tend to be fringe phenomena. The same isolation that fosters intense solidarity among members also inhibits the spread of cult influence. But the experience of religious cults in producing solidarities is nonetheless useful as a guide to what to look for in other types of movements. Secular movements must also create a sense of group solidarity in order to motivate participation based on collective rationality. And their tools for developing solidarity are the same tools used in religious cult movements: ideology and interaction.

The importance of interaction for movement participation is reflected in the tendency of movement organizations to recruit members through existing social networks (Snow, Zurcher, and Ekland-Olson 1980; Opp 1989: 88–89). Those who join a movement organization are disproportionately likely to know others who are active within the movement (Klandermans 1984; Walsh 1988: 125). As Marwell and Oliver (1993) point out, the use of existing networks of formal and informal interaction reduces the costs of

---

[18] Victor Peters, cited in Lee 1970: 170.

communication within the group and increases expectations of cohesive action.

Some movement organizations benefit from the existence of natural communities that can serve as a basis of mobilization (Lo 1992). People who live and work in close proximity to each other have the kinds of interactions that require only a uniting ideology to create group solidarity. Environmental organizations that require the active involvement of members are overwhelmingly likely to be community-based, a limitation that has had a powerful impact in defining which environmental problems lead to mobilization and which do not. Student movements are much larger among college students (who live in close proximity to each other) than among high school students. They are also found primarily at residential universities rather than at commuter schools. Eldridge Cleaver (1968) reports that the Black Muslims gained numerous converts among prison inmates, and that the public split between Elijah Muhammad and Malcolm X was echoed in the development of rival factions of prisoners. Few of these inmates were involved with the Nation of Islam before beginning their prison terms, but close confinement served to engage many of them in the struggles between rival movement leaders.

Movement leaders who are not able to draw on residential communities may nonetheless design their organizations so that contact between activists is maximized. The Weathermen insisted that interactions with nonmembers be limited to the greatest extent possible. Even in the absence of such rules, an activist's interactions with those outside the movement are often reduced over time. As participants become increasingly immersed in movement activities, they tend to reorient their friendships and interests so that people and ideas connected with the movement assume increasing prominence while everything else is diminished. Entry into the movement may mark a turning point in the life of an activist. Lydia Maria Child, a popular writer of children's books, became a prominent author of abolitionist appeals after meeting Garrison (as cited in Filler 1960: 59):

> I little thought then that the whole pattern of my life-web would be changed by that introduction. I was then all absorbed in poetry and painting, soaring aloft on Psyche-wings into the ethereal regions of mysticism. He got hold of the strings of my conscience and pulled me into reform. It is of no use to imagine what might have been if I had never met him. Old dreams vanished, old associates departed, and all things became new.

Using the somewhat different language of sociological analysis, Useem (1972: 463) makes a similar point on the effects of participation in the student antiwar movement of the 1960s:

> It was a period of diminished contact with the non-movement world and alienation from some groups. The college community, graduate department, church,

profession, workplace, and other associations all receded in significance. People in these non-movement settings seemed less interesting and less relevant, and there was at least a mild estrangement. Severe strains were also experienced with close associates and parents, and in several instances relationships with girl friends and fiancées eventually collapsed.

In the end, there is nothing as productive of solidarity as the experience of merging group purposes with the activities of everyday life. This is an insight acknowledged by every organization that has convened a retreat in place of a regular meeting held on the business premises during regular hours. Movement organizations, with their need for strong group solidarity, build the "retreat" concept into many of their activities. Long meetings in which all participants are active in the discussion and in which the personal and the political are freely mixed may be very demanding of time, but they leave participants with an enhanced sense of having a great deal in common.

Many forms of protest, such as sit-ins and other types of site occupation, also have profound effects on the group spirit of their participants. As McAdam (1989) points out, activities that involve large risks and great costs may give activists a conversion experience that binds them to the movement for life. Barbara Epstein (1991) describes the experience of being swept up in a mass arrest as having produced a euphoric feeling of solidarity with other participants in the protest. An Illinois-based director of the National Abortion Rights Action League (NARAL) comments that movement activities organized during election campaigns are especially effective because "it's usually cold, and people feel a lot of solidarity going out together in the cold" (Staggenborg 1991: 100). The longer the group stays together and the greater the privations it faces, the greater the solidarity-building impact.

The Greenham Common Women's Peace Camp, set up outside an anticipated cruise missile base in Britain in 1981, offers an example of solidarity building through intense interactions under difficult circumstances. The Greenham women remained encamped (albeit with much turnover in participants) for a decade. The collective experience of dodging the local constabulary as they tried to evict the campers fostered an increasingly close bond between camp residents. As occurs in communal religious movements, the elements of everyday life at Greenham Common came to be imbued with special significance as part of the camp's resistance. Returning after one eviction during which virtually all their supplies had been confiscated, one camper summed up the general mood in saying that "I'm so pleased to be back here on this patch, the fire in the same place, no caravans, no tents. It's like it was when the camp first started. Nothing except a fire, blankets, plastic, a bit of food and spirit, determination, joy—yes, joy—we feel great. We know they're not going to get rid of us" (cited in Harford and Hopkins 1984: 68). The relationship between participation and the development of group solidarity was even more directly expressed by a student protester against the Vietnam War, who reported that "When I turned in my card I felt I was being welcomed into the best group I had ever been welcomed into. There was real warmth and tenderness in this group, and complete equality" (Useem 1973: 252).

Where movements do not find residential communities in which to take root, it may be part of the organizational strategy to strengthen solidarity by other means. The adoption of characteristic forms of dress, behavior, or language sets movement members apart from others. Movement activists, for example, commonly develop a shared language for describing themselves and their opponents. Russian revolutionaries, Black Muslims, and members of the Greenham Common Women's Peace Camp all adopted new names as a symbol of personal rebirth in the movement. Fellow activists are brothers, sisters, or, more generically, comrades. Naming the opponent is also an important part of identifying group boundaries. Thus we have male chauvinist pigs, Anglos, honkies, blue-eyed devils, and a very long list of names for police officers and other governmental authorities.

Giving a new name to the group itself is a further means by which movements strengthen the power of a group identity. Thus, Negroes became blacks, who later became African Americans. Ladies became women, and some women became feminists. The crippled became the handicapped became the disabled became the challenged. Homosexuals became gays, some Mexican-Americans became Chicanos, and many conservationists became environmentalists. Movements may protect the distinctiveness of their group labels by rotating them with a swiftness bewildering to outsiders, or by adopting for themselves labels that are anathema to polite society outside of the group (nigger, queer).

Adoption of these labels implies adoption of a group-centered way of looking at the world (Tajfel 1974). Gutierrez and Hirsch (1973) found that high school students who called themselves Chicanos in the early 1970s had a more politicized sense of ethnicity than those students who preferred the label Mexican-American. Self-described Chicanos were more likely to believe that the only way for the group to get ahead was by collective protest. The importance of naming the group to increase solidarity is summarized by black power advocate Stokely Carmichael in his claim that "we must first redefine ourselves. Our basic need is to reclaim our history and identity. . . . We shall have to struggle for the right to create our own terms through which to define ourselves and our relationship to society, and to have those terms recognized" (Carmichael and Hamilton 1967: 34–35; see also Melucci 1995).

The act of defining the group is, in practice, the act of declaring what is special, separate, or superior about the group. This act contributes to group identity and solidarity. Naming is a means of creating collective interpretations of group experience. Ideology and interaction ultimately contribute to solidarity by fostering acceptance of the movement's way of describing (or renaming) the world. But even in movement organizations that do not provide an environment of total immersion comparable with that of cult movements, the activities of organizing, sharing viewpoints, and protesting are all occasions for strengthening solidarity.

SOLIDARITY IN THE CIVIL RIGHTS MOVEMENT

These examples of the circumstances that produce solidarity within movements suggest four hypotheses about the conditions under which group solidarity develops. First, solidarity is a learned value that is absorbed through social networks that conform to group lines. Second, solidarity is strongest among those for whom movement ideas of group identity are discussed in everyday interactions. Third, solidarity is learned most readily in isolation from people who are not members of the group. And fourth, solidarity is associated with perceptions that the outside world is uncomprehending of the group and unjust in its treatment of group members. The final part of this chapter will put these hypotheses to the test using data from the 1961 Matthews-Prothro study of participation by African Americans in the South.

Our first investigation is into the means by which feelings of group solidarity are learned. If solidarity is arrived at experientially—for example, through exposure to group discrimination—then there is relatively little that a movement organization can do to increase the strength of solidarity. If, on the other hand, solidarity is learned in social settings where the ideas of the movement are discussed, then social arena activities of the movement will be rewarded by increases in the solidarity of the group.

Figure 4-2 gives us a means of discriminating between the experiential and the social network hypotheses about the sources of solidarity by displaying the relationship of solidarity with education and age. As is generally true in the study of political values and behaviors, the strongest single correlate of feelings of solidarity among African Americans is education. More than 40 percent of those with an education beyond high school achieve the highest levels of solidarity, compared with only 11 percent of those with four or fewer years of elementary education.

Higher levels of education are associated with solidarity presumably because education increases one's exposure to the ideas and activities of the civil rights movement. This effect may be magnified in figure 4-2 because at the time of the survey college students were deeply involved in civil rights protest, particularly by sitting in at segregated places. In any case, the impact of education on movement solidarity is so powerful that all other relationships examined here will be considered both in bivariate form and with education controlled.

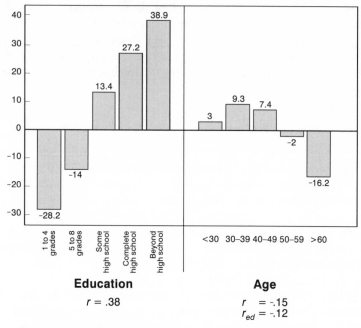

Source: Negro Political Participation Study, 1961–1962.

Note: Bars are the percentage "high" in solidarity minus the percentage "very low" in solidarity.

Figure 4-2   Demographic bases of solidarity

The relationship between solidarity and age goes to the heart of the question of whether solidarity is learned through experience or in social networks. If group solidarity results from the experience of discrimination, then solidarity should increase with age. If solidarity is the result of exposure to movement ideas through social networks, then the relationship between age and solidarity is indeterminate and will be a by-product of the composition of the social networks connected to the movement. The data in figure 4-2 show that solidarity is strongest among people between thirty and forty-nine years of age, and falls off both among those who are younger and those who are older. The hypothesis that solidarity increases with the length of exposure to group discrimination is not sustained.

The failure of length of experience of discrimination to increase solidarity suggests that we examine the proposition that solidarity is developed through exposure to the social networks of the movement. Figure 4-3 compares respondents who were immersed in settings where the movement was active with those who were not. One important distinction in this respect is between people living in rural and urban areas. African Americans in rural

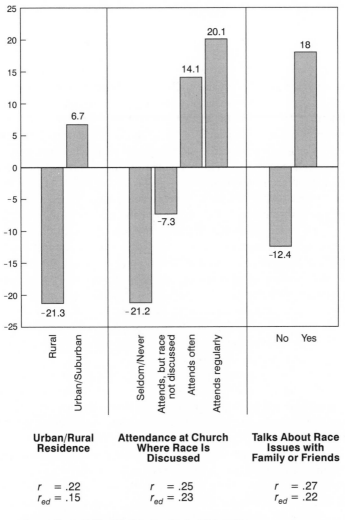

Source: Negro Political Participation Study, 1961–1962.

Note: Bars are the percentage "high" in solidarity minus the percentage "very low" in solidarity. All correlations are significant at the .01 level.

Figure 4-3   Effects of interaction on solidarity

areas were dispersed and were commonly subject to oversight by white land-owners for whom they worked. African Americans in Southern cities, by contrast, developed a much denser network of ties with each other. McAdam (1982: 112–116) points out that the rate of urbanization among African Americans from 1900 to 1954 was closely associated with the growth of civil rights organizations. Figure 4-3 extends this evidence on the importance of urbanization by showing that those living in rural areas were less likely than their urban counterparts to feel racial solidarity, even when their lower levels of education are controlled.

A second channel of exposure to movement ideas was in church. Black churches were a mainstay of the civil rights movement, both in the recruitment of leaders and in the organization of specific campaigns.[19] Matthews and Prothro (1966: 181) found that one-third of respondents named a minister or preacher when asked to identify a leader in the African American community. This was nearly three times the percentage that named members of any other occupational group. Figure 4-3 shows the importance of the black church as a force in developing movement solidarity. Those who did not attend church, or who attended a church where issues of race relations were not discussed, scored very low in solidarity compared with those who "often" or "regularly" attended a church where race relations were discussed. This correlation is barely diminished by controls for education, a fact that shows the ability of the church to reach out to all parts of the black community.

The final measure of involvement in movement-oriented social networks is the extent to which race relations are discussed in one's circle of family and friends. This measure takes us to the importance of "everydayness" in the development of strong feelings of group solidarity. Figure 4-3 shows that those who talk about racial problems with family or friends score substantially higher in solidarity than those who do not.

It is likely that solidarity is both cause and effect of these conversations. Feelings of solidarity impel one to discuss movement issues in one's social circle, and those discussions create the kind of environment in which solidarity is further strengthened. A static correlation cannot tease apart these interactive relationships, but the mere existence of the relationship is sufficient to confirm our hypothesis on the association between solidarity and the integration of movement topics in everyday interactions.

The third hypothesis is that solidarity is stronger in segregated environments, where interactions tend to be exclusively with other members of the group on which the movement is based. While cult movements may seek the isolation of their members in order to increase solidarity, it was of course precisely the point of the civil rights movement to overcome racial segregation. If our understanding of the origins of group solidarity is correct, though, the very conditions of segregation that aggrieved those within the

---

[19] See Morris (1984). Verba et al. (1993) find that church attendance was still closely related to political participation among African Americans twenty years after the end of the civil rights movement. African Americans were almost twice as likely as whites to hear in church a message on the importance of voting.

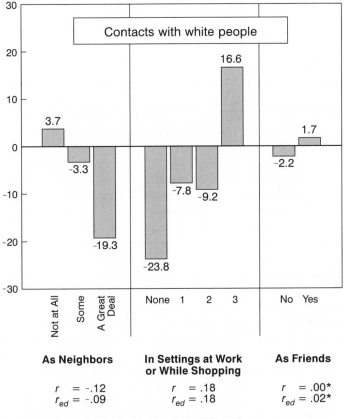

Figure 4-4   Effects of segregation on solidarity

civil rights movement may also have contributed to the feelings of solidarity
that made the movement so successful.

The evidence in figure 4-4 presents a mixed picture that requires some
refinement of the hypothesis about the effects of a segregated environment
on solidarity. Residential segregation does indeed have the hypothesized effect, as people who live in completely segregated neighborhoods feel the
highest levels of group solidarity. On the other hand, those who report more
contact with whites in public places, such as at work or in shops, are higher
in solidarity than people who work and shop in a segregated environment.
And the presence or absence of racially integrated friendships, which one

might expect to be the most powerful of these conditions, makes no difference whatsoever to solidarity.[20] Consistent with the experience of cult movements, it would appear that residential segregation is a powerful tool for
building solidarity. The evidence presented here, however, also suggests that
segregated work and friendship environments do not increase solidarity.

Finally, we investigate the relationship between solidarity, perceived polarization between groups, and criticism of the segregation system. Studies
of group solidarity are divided on the subject of its association with polarized perceptions of differences between groups. One school of thought
agrees with Eric Hoffer's (1951: 86) assessment that "Common hatred unites
the most heterogeneous elements." The experimental studies summarized by
Brewer (1979) generally reach the opposite conclusion: that group solidarity
is associated with favoritism to the in-group but not with any pronounced
hostility to out-groups. It should be noted, though, that such studies are conducted on randomly assigned and experimentally induced group identities
that are not based on a lifelong real-world experience of prejudice and discrimination.

Given the deeply troubled history of race relations in the South prior to
this survey, the data in figure 4-5 tell a remarkable story. African Americans
who felt a high level of racial solidarity in 1961 did not have more polarized
images of whites and blacks, although they did have distinctive images of
the two groups. Those with higher levels of solidarity gave higher estimates
of the percentage of their own race in favor of segregation, demonstrating
the belief in group unity that Chong (1991) has shown is important for mobilization. However, the high solidarity group was also more optimistic
about the percentage of whites who accept integration. Because of their
greater optimism about the antisegregation attitudes of both blacks and
whites, those with high solidarity have only a slightly (and statistically insig-
nificant) more polarized view of the difference in beliefs between the races
than do those at the lowest levels of solidarity. The lack of polarization in
the beliefs of high solidarity African Americans is also confirmed by their
unwillingness to agree that all white people are alike in the extent of their
racial prejudice.[21]

The relatively optimistic views among high-solidarity African Americans

---

[20] The measures of residential segregation and segregation at work and while shopping are
based on multiple indicators. Each of the separate indicators behaves in the same way as the
overall index. It is therefore unlikely that these results are an artifact of measurement error. The
friendship measure is, by contrast, based on a single variable. The question appears to be
straightforward: "Have you ever known a white person well enough that you would talk to him
as a friend?" Being a single indicator, though, it may be more vulnerable to measurement error.

[21] In their analysis of the same data, but focusing on black college student protesters, Matthews and Prothro (1966: 476) find that the protesters are exceptionally optimistic and tolerant,
"as far from an embittered, alienated group of professional radicals as one can imagine."

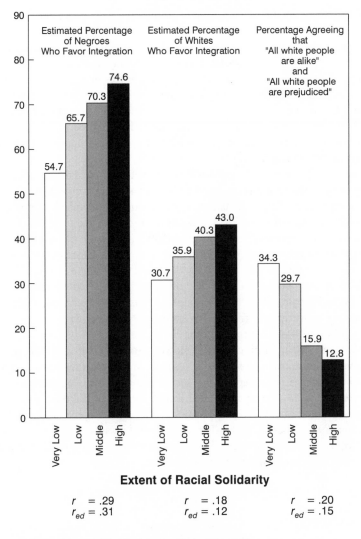

Source: Negro Political Participation Study, 1961–1962.

Note: All correlations are significant at the .01 level.

Figure 4-5   Effects of solidarity on racial polarization

about the desire of all Americans for racial integration may be one reason why they were disproportionately likely to become involved in the civil rights movement. High-solidarity respondents were not only more committed to the goals and the tactics of the movement, but they were relatively sanguine about the readiness of the rest of society to accept racial integration.

The association of racial solidarity with optimism about the beliefs of whites in 1961 does not mean that high-solidarity African Americans viewed the segregation system with equanimity. They were in fact most likely to see the current political and social system as racially biased and in need of change. Figure 4-6 shows that those with high levels of solidarity were more likely to believe that the legal system does not offer "Negroes . . . fair treatment." Because of their pessimism about the current state of race relations, high-solidarity African Americans were more likely to believe that government should intervene in private markets for housing and electric power, which they saw as operating in a discriminatory fashion.

The data in figures 4-5 and 4-6 suggest that high solidarity is associated with perceptions of injustice and a belief that structural change must occur. Those high in solidarity are also more optimistic that members of both races are ready to support an end to segregation. Of course, the civil rights movement was at a midpoint in its career when this survey was carried out in 1961. The movement had just obtained a string of successes in ending segregation in public places. Between 1957 and 1963 there was civil rights activity in over 900 cities, and 261 of those protests led to desegregation (Evans and Boyte 1986: 66). Throughout this period as well, there were increasing signs that the federal government was preparing to become more active in protecting civil rights in the South.

With accelerating aspirations and slowed progress later in the decade, the relative optimism of high-solidarity African Americans found in this survey may have been a temporary phenomenon. Studies of movement activists in other contexts have generally found a high degree of political distrust and cynicism about the views and commitments of the general public (e.g., McKean 1980; Rochon 1988). The findings of this survey, however, suggest that solidarity, mobilization, and optimism are found together when a movement enjoys success in the political arena.

CONCLUSION

In 1958 William Kornhauser hypothesized that mass movements arise in atomized societies as rootless individuals seek attachment to some radical cause. We now know that movements flourish in precisely the opposite circumstances. Group identity links the individual interest to group interests, and group solidarity creates assurances that the movement will mobilize large numbers of people. For movements to play their part in the diffusion of new cultural values, they must be able to rely on existing networks of group identity and to develop an ideology and a pattern of interaction that heightens the sense of group solidarity.

By developing roots in group identities and by strengthening group solidarities, movements motivate people to make sacrifices for collective causes.

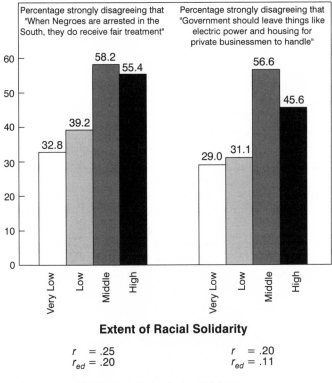

Figure 4-6 Effects of solidarity on system blame

No social or political movements achieve the levels of group solidarity characteristic of cult and millenarian movements, but we find in all movements a similar dynamic in which solidarity motivates individual sacrifice for the collective good of the group. Just as members of cults feel born to a new life upon entry into the cult, so too do movements inculcate activists with the feeling of undergoing a watershed experience.

The significance of solidarity for movement mobilization is that it creates the conditions for the first wave of activists to break with the calculus of individual rationality that mandates free ridership in movements for collective goods. African Americans with strong feelings of racial solidarity believed that ending segregation was both necessary and possible. These are the values that enable high-solidarity group members to convert their beliefs into strategic action on behalf of a collective good.

Solidarity was most highly developed among African Americans who had relatively few interactions with whites in churches and neighborhoods, who were involved in discussions of race relations in those settings, and who combined a strongly negative view of segregation with a relatively positive perception of black and white levels of support for integration. These traits all suggest that the keys to civil rights participation were exposure to movement ideas and extensive interaction with other African Americans. In the civil rights movement, and in other movements as well, interaction and ideology are productive of high levels of group solidarity. Group solidarity, in turn, fosters movement mobilization.

Because of the close linkage between movement activity and group identities, the distribution of identities in a society tells us a great deal about the history of movement mobilizations. Over the past decade I have asked students in my course on social and political movements to make a list of "their most important social identities, the groups they feel most connected to." The results are closely reflective of the history of movement activity in America. One-quarter of all group identities are connected to gender, race, or ethnicity. Women are far more likely to mention gender as part of their social identity (54 percent) than are men (17 percent).[22] All African Americans in the course referred to their race as part of their social identity, as did about two-thirds of Hispanics and Asian Americans. By contrast, less than 4 percent of white students referred to their race as being a component of their social identity. Social class was mentioned as a source of identity by only one student in twenty, reflecting the relatively slight influence of class-based movements in America.

Unsystematic surveys of college students do not constitute firm evidence, but the correspondence of student identities to recent movement mobilizations is too close to discount. Social movements mobilize support based on their connection to group identifications. Movement mobilizations, in turn, strengthen some group identities at the cost of others.

Movement organization, patterns of recruitment, and choice of activities appear well designed to emphasize group identities and to strengthen group solidarities. Movements recruit through existing social networks and, in so doing, they link their causes to the group identities found in those networks. Some movement organizations are able to develop intense patterns of interaction by recruiting within a residential community, such as college students or prison inmates. Movements that cannot do this may nonetheless design protests that involve occupying a particular space for a period of time. Demonstrations, sit-ins, blockades, and other site occupations all create oppor-

---

[22] The terminology as well as the content of group identities is subject to movement influence. Most female students referred to themselves as "women" and none referred to themselves as "girls." A small number of male students called themselves "boys" and none used the term "man," preferring instead "male." This suggests social roots for "women's" gender identity, and biological roots for the gender identity of "males."

tunities for movement activists to increase their awareness of sharing a common fate with the other members of the group.

Group solidarity is not the only requisite for movement mobilization. Potential activists must also be persuaded that the movement has a chance to succeed, and that success depends on unity within a fully mobilized group. Eric Hirsch (1990) reports that a student organization attempting to force Columbia University to divest its endowment of stock in companies doing business in South Africa during the apartheid regime had difficulty persuading students to attend meetings or rallies. When the organization initiated a three-week blockade of a campus building, however, an increased number of students turned out even though the commitment of time and the likelihood of university reprisal were clearly greater. A survey of participants revealed that many who joined the blockade but not earlier rallies felt that the blockade could succeed while the rallies were unlikely to do so. Moreover, the blockade continued to grow in response to threats of arrest and expulsion from the university, reflecting the mobilizing power of solidarity as sanctions against students became a salient part of the protest.

The examples of group identity and solidarity developed in this chapter have been primarily those of race, class, gender, and religious belief. These group identities are today so ubiquitous that it is tempting to think of them as natural to human thought, a matter of enduring realities. As Che Guevara is supposed to have said, "It's not my fault that reality is Marxist" (Sale 1973: 391).

But reality is only Marxist to the extent of our willingness to use Marxist categories of analysis when we look at the world. Group identities are social constructs. Some identities are important for a brief time: the phrase "Don't trust anyone over thirty" reflected the widespread but ultimately temporary belief (on both sides of the thirty-year age barrier) that young adults shared an outlook on life distinctive and antithetical to that of older people. This proved not to be an enduring group identity, but while it existed it was as real as any.

Some group identities, such as class, race, and gender, have proved to be more enduring. These traits have profound consequences for the patterns of one's life. Even in these cases, though, the social meaning of class, race, and gender categories has changed over time. Nineteenth-century farm and labor organizations articulated a particular sense of the dignity that resides in being a producer of goods, a sentiment that formed the basis of the Populist demand for economic democracy.[23] The identities of laborer and farmer re-

---

[23] As Herman Taubeneck, national chair of the People's Party, put it, "The Alliance, the FMBA [Farmers Mutual Benefit Association], the Grange, the Knights of Labor are nothing more or less than industrial schools whose one object is to teach the industrial masses the principles of economic government that we call for." Cited in Hicks 1961: 218.

main, but the linkage of manual work to aspirations for full participation in economic decision making has disappeared. Similarly, race has been a category of group identity since before the Republic was born, but the meaning of being colored, Negro, black, African American has changed from time to time (Cross 1971). As a prominent white Southern politician put it, observing the sit-in movement of the early 1960s, "These kids seem to be completely new Negroes, the likes of which we've never seen before" (cited in Fishman and Solomon 1970: 147).

Not all movements have an equally great capacity to create strong solidarities. The sense of shared fate among group members is most naturally developed in the case of ascriptive traits that are readily visible and to which the rest of society reacts. Race, ethnicity, gender, and linguistic origin are all easily observable, and all have been (and remain) bases of group discrimination. One of the mobilization strategies of the gay rights movement has been precisely to make homosexuality more visible in the society by encouraging gays to "come out." This strategy has created an identifiable community of gays for whom avoidance of discrimination by retreat to invisibility is no longer an option. An earlier strand in the homophile movement (as it was then known) sought legal protection for private behavior while counseling its members to seek in their public behavior the greatest possible degree of assimilation into the "straight" world (Adam 1987). Mobilization of the gay rights movement accelerated only after gays were first persuaded to be publicly different.

The potential range of movement mobilizations is limited by the kinds of group identities that can be converted into solidarities. This requirement introduces bias into the patterns of mobilization. Environmental organizations, for example, are heavily centered around neighborhood problems, such as the location of a polluting industry, a nuclear power plant, or a toxic waste dump. Environmental problems that do not have site-specific effects, such as global warming and the loss of biodiversity, are far less likely to be the subject of widespread mobilization. Issues that can be experienced as both personal and group predicaments are most keenly felt and lend themselves most readily to movement mobilization (cf. Iyengar and Kinder 1987).

We might refer to movements that are not rooted in some clearly identifiable (ascriptive) group identity as "movements of conscience." The importance of group solidarity to movement mobilization means that conscience movements not readily linked to group interest face an uphill struggle. Movements of conscience have most often connected themselves to religious beliefs, which owe their strong hold to the fact that they are learned early in life and are reinforced by numerous social institutions. Abolition, temperance, and the right-to-life movement all mobilized supporters by connecting religious beliefs to their causes.

Finally, an appreciation of the role of solidarity in movement mobilization widens our criteria for evaluating the success of a movement. Movement ideologies, organizations, and activities must be effective in creating group solidarities if they are to generate and sustain mobilization. Tactics like the occupation of a building or a march on Washington may fail to change any policies, but could nonetheless be highly efficacious in strengthening solidarities and enabling the movement to survive. Movement organizations use interaction and ideology to engage participants in activity that is collective, often risky, creates distinctions between group members and nonmembers, and is justified as an important contribution to a better world. Movements are able to initiate the diffusion of new cultural values only if they are founded on a powerful sense of group solidarity, one capable of overcoming all the disincentives of the individualist calculus against collective action.

APPENDIX

This chapter focuses on the importance of group identification and solidarity for movement mobilization, and on the things that movement organizations can do to increase solidarity. The problem of mobilization is often addressed from either a sociological or rational choice perspective, typically with distressingly little interaction between the two. Chapter 4 has taken a broadly sociological approach to the problem, but it could equally well have used the language of rational choice instead. It is worth remembering that our choice of tools is secondary to the goal of giving a theoretical account of empirically observable patterns of behavior. In this appendix, I offer a brief indication of how the language of rational choice can be used to express the same ideas as those developed in chapter 4.

The essence of the free-rider problem is that activity intended to foster change in cultural values is not a paying proposition from the perspective of a strictly individual calculation of how to use one's time and energy. The problem can be summarized succinctly by adapting to movement mobilization the classic equation expressing the costs and benefits of voting, as follows:

$$U_m = (I * p) - C \tag{1}$$

where

U_m is the utility of movement mobilization,
I is the level of individual interest in success of the cause,
p is the probability of making a difference by one's own participation, and
C is the costs, including opportunity costs, of being involved in the movement.

Under the terms of this formula, movement participation is never a good investment of one's time. It is true that the individual benefits from movement success may be substantial: one has only to think of the life of an African American living in the segregated South prior to the civil rights movement to recognize the significance of movement-led transformation. Even so, the $(I * p)$ term is necessarily close to zero, since the probability of making a difference in the success of a movement by one's own contributions is infinitesimal. This leaves the cost factor, the investment of time and energy involved in movement participation, the risk of being beaten, murdered, or sent to jail for participating in movement protests, and the opportunity costs of activities forgone in order to be active in the movement. Since expected returns from individual participation in a movement are negligible while costs are potentially considerable, even a person with an enormous interest in the success of the movement will not be motivated by that interest to take part in it. Movement participation can be understood as a strategic (rational) choice only if the balance between costs and benefits of activism is altered in some way.

In an important contribution to understanding movement mobilization from a game theoretic perspective, Chong (1991) has pointed out that the expected gains from participation in a movement depend on the perceived likelihood that the movement will be successful. Potential activists look for signals that the movement is succeeding, and the stronger those signals are, the more likely one is to become active. The signals most important for potential activists are the extent of participation by others (creating, in Chong's words, a "contagion effect") and the extent of government response to prior movement efforts (creating a "bandwagon effect"). Combining the bandwagon effect with the contagion effect, Chong's model can be formulated as follows:[24]

$$U_m = a + b(G) + c(M) - C \qquad (2)$$

where

> U_m and C are defined as in equation (1),
> G is the extent of governmental response to the movement to date,
> M is the current level of movement mobilization,
> a is the size of the "autonomous leadership,"
> b is the bandwagon rate in response to prior movement success, and
> c is the contagion rate in response to prior movement mobilization.

The bandwagon and contagion effects suggest that a movement, once started, can snowball in its rate of activity and ultimately effect a rapid transformation of cultural values and public policies.

---

[24] See Chong 1991: 150, equation (7.3). Chong examines the problem from the perspective of the aggregate level of mobilization, while the equation here expresses the probability of an individual joining the movement. However, equation (2) is functionally equivalent to Chong's (7.3).

This understanding of mobilization leaves us with the question of how movements get started. Chong is the first to acknowledge this problem, and he proposes two possible solutions to it. The first is that a sympathetic government may help create a movement by granting concessions (G) in advance of mobilization. This would encourage some activists to join due to the bandwagon effect, and that initial core of activists would in turn beget the contagion effect. We will see in chapter 7 that there are circumstances in which established political and social institutions may encourage the development of a movement, but generally we would expect governmental support for movement demands to be forthcoming only *after* the movement has demonstrated its mobilizing capacity. Movement organizers face the same catch-22 situation as people seeking loans to start up a new business: external assistance is needed to get started, but such assistance is not likely to be offered until it is demonstrated that the enterprise is already off the ground.

The second solution proposed by Chong to the problem of movement origins is contained in the inclusion of *a* in equation (2). This refers to an "autonomous leadership," understood as people who are willing to join a cause that has so far demonstrated slim prospects for becoming a mobilized movement. Chong calls these people "self-starters" and "gamblers." In a similar context, Elster (1989) calls them "Kantian altruists": people who act according to their notions of justice even if they do not believe that their actions increase the chances of achieving justice. As Chong (1991: 160) observes, "the only way that the level of mobilization can increase without the benefit of periodic concessions [by the authorities] is if there is an element of recruitment that is independent of this factor. The link between the rates of success and recruitment has to be broken."

Whether they are Kantians or risk-acceptant venture capitalists, the development of a mobilized movement depends on the existence of a first wave of activists willing to engage in costly activity under conditions that offer scant promise of success. These considerations sharpen our understanding of the free-rider problem by focusing our attention on the puzzle of how the first wave of activists comes to be engaged on behalf of a cause, before any glimmers of hope provided by governmental responsiveness (G) or a record of increasing mobilization (M). If we restrict our focus to the terms included in equations (1) and (2), then we must conclude that the first wave of activists is composed of Kantians, suckers, or just poor calculators.

To motivate initial mobilization rationally, movements must alter the very structure of the decision to become active. The argument of chapter 4 is that movements alter the calculations of potential activists as indicated in equation (3):

$$U_{mg} = (I * p) + (I_g * p_g * S_i) - C \qquad (3)$$

where

I, *p*, and *C* are defined as in equation (1),

U_{mg} is the utility of mobilization to the group,

I_g is the group interest in success of the cause,

p_g is the probability of the group being able to make a difference *if it mobilizes fully*, and

S_i is the extent of group solidarity felt by the individual.

Equation (3) differs from equation (1) in its blending of group-based calculation with the individual calculations typically incorporated into the rational model of participation. In equation (3) *individuals decide whether or not to participate based on the interest of the group in success of the cause, the probability that the fully mobilized group can prevail, and their own levels of solidarity.* This is similar to the model of "collective rationality" proposed by Finkel, Muller, and Opp (1989) (see also Ferree 1992).

The collective rationality embodied in equation (3), is activated only if the individual feels identity and solidarity (S_i) with the group.[25] Identification with the group means that one equates group goals with personal goals. Solidarity leads the individual to anticipate that the group will mobilize successfully. Therefore, solidarity must be present for the expected success of the *mobilized* group to become relevant. Feelings of group solidarity make it possible to act on behalf of the group interest without being a Kantian, because it is a decision based on anticipation that the group will achieve its objectives.

The incorporation of these factors in equation (3) is heterodox in the standard model of rational participation based on individual interests and atomistic calculations. Yet variations on these themes have had to be reinvented periodically in order to account for participation in elections. In his discussion of turnout, Downs (1957: 267) invokes group identity by saying that "rational men in a democracy are motivated to some extent by a sense of social responsibility relatively independent of their own short-run gains and losses." As Downs observes, the collective welfare may motivate participation even when the individual welfare does not.

Downs has been criticized for making ad hoc adjustments to assumptions in order to avoid the awkward conclusion that people cannot rationally participate in political activity (see, e.g., Ball 1976). But that criticism is misplaced if hypotheses about the mobilizing effect of collective interests and group solidarities are tested rather than simply asserted. The evidence in chapter 4 shows that movements do in fact mobilize those who have strong feelings of group solidarity, while those without such feelings are likely to be free riders. This perspective also makes sense of the common observation that movement mobilization occurs through established group networks.

---

[25] Recall from chapter 4 that group identification is a necessary precondition for solidarity. A positive S_i thus implies the existence of group identification.

We owe to the individual-centered rational model the understanding that movement mobilization for collective goods is very difficult. A compelling grievance or interest in the results of collective action is not sufficient to motivate participation. In order to overcome the free-rider problem, movements must heighten group solidarity. They must teach would-be activists to think of the potential impact of a fully mobilized group pressing for its goals, rather than the marginal impact of the individual's own participation.

Chapter 5

POLITICAL ENGAGEMENT

The worker's strike is a school of war.
—V. I. Lenin

IDENTIFICATION with a group encourages a person to associate group interests with individual interests. Solidarity with that group brings with it an expectation that other group members will be mobilized for the cause. People high in group solidarity spend a relatively large proportion of their time interacting with others in the group and talking about the issues that concern the group. They are more likely to believe that the group can act cohesively on behalf of its goals, and their expectations of success are therefore tied to the potential impact of the mobilized group, rather than to the impact one individual can have on collective outcomes. For all of these reasons, group solidarity alters the individual calculus under which it would not pay to become involved in collective action.

These are the conditions that lead to movement activism. But the history of activism does not end with the decision to become involved in a movement. The experience of mobilization also has an effect on the activist, by increasing one's awareness and understanding of the world in which one lives. Activism provides a sense of liberation from feelings of helplessness in the face of oppressive circumstances. Such experiences are an important motivation for activists to continue their involvement even when the movement falls on hard times. Equally important, the development of broadened understanding and increased organizational skills among activists enhances the ability of the movement to project critical values into the culture. Participation in movements, like the workers' strike referred to by Lenin, amounts to a "school of war" for activists. Graduates of the school are far better prepared to help the movement spread critical community ideas in the social and political arenas. This chapter is devoted to demonstrating the development of activist skills and engagement, a development that helps movements diffuse new cultural values.

TESTIMONIALS TO POLITICAL ENGAGEMENT

Movement participation increases an individual's ability to understand the political and social environment, and to take action in it. Participation enables people—in fact, it often forces people—to surpass what they had thought to be their limits. Joining a movement is not unlike entering graduate school: it is learning by doing, it is transcendence by undergoing trials.

The specific manifestations of the movement "school of war" are varied, but they can be reduced to a few themes. Most broadly, participation in movements increases people's feelings of engagement with politics. Political engagement can be defined as the feeling of being personally connected to the political world. This is reflected in high levels of attentiveness to politics, possession of a relatively large fund of political knowledge, belief in one's ability to influence politics, and participation in political activities beyond those connected to the movement itself.

The bundle of skills, orientations, and beliefs that make up political engagement is experienced by movement activists as a kind of awakening to the possibilities of a life devoted to public issues. In 1851 the fervor of abolitionist activism was growing steadily, even though the goal of ending slavery was apparently as far away as it had been at the beginning of the movement twenty years earlier. The prominent Boston abolitionist Wendell Phillips may have been speaking for many when he declaimed, "My friends, if we never free a slave, we have at least freed ourselves in the effort to emancipate our brother man [sic] . . . we have been redeemed into a full manhood—taught to consecrate life to something worth living for" (cited in Dillon 1974: 59).

Just over one hundred years later, Martin Luther King Jr. would speak in nearly identical terms of the benefits of activism to end segregation. Like the abolitionists, King emphasized the individual's responsibility to establish a relationship with God based on taking responsibility for his or her own actions. Cornel West (1990: 115) has pointed out that the verse from Luke 4:18 was a leitmotiv of King's message to those who would join the movement: "The spirit of the Lord is upon me because he hath anointed me to preach the gospel to the poor." Dennis Chong (1991: 87) summarizes King's mobilizing powers as residing in his ability to convince people that "the struggle itself was sufficiently worthwhile and ennobling to compensate for the great price that each participant would have to pay. The hostilities, threats, and injuries that each would have to endure were a testimony to their dignity, self-esteem, and courage."

The barriers to full social participation among members of oppressed groups are psychological as well as external, and so it is understandable that people will accept the sacrifices of movement participation when the reward is an increase in one's sense of dignity, self-worth, and control over the environment. But movement participation offers more than the possibility of elevation to a higher plane of spiritual and moral fulfillment. Participation in movements constitutes an education in the processes of social and political interaction, and in the channels of social and political influence.

The skills of organizing and persuading can be learned in almost any organizational environment. Brady, Verba, and Schlozman (1995) found that over half of their sample of the American public had the opportunity to write a letter, give a speech, organize a meeting, or take part in making a decision in the course of their jobs. One-third of the sample did these things in non-political organizations, and 20 percent did so in their church or synagogue. Only about 4 percent of their sample had ever taken part in a protest movement, which means that the opportunity to practice organizational and suasive skills within movements is much rarer than the opportunity to develop these skills on the job, in church, or in voluntary organizations.

Even so, a number of traits of movement participation make it particularly effective in skill development. Movement organizations are typically small, they stress member participation rather than leader direction in decision making, and they often define local targets of action that engage all available hands. One can be a devout but passive member of a church congregation, and one can be a loyal but passive member of a labor union. It is not possible to be a passive activist in a movement organization.

Consider the activities organized within the American nuclear freeze movement. At its peak, the freeze movement rested on a network of between 1,400 and 2,000 local freeze organizations throughout the country (Garfinkle 1984: 81; Katz 1986: 173). Meetings, forums, debates, video presentations, art displays, fasts, and vigils were organized by the thousands in local churches and clubs, in social and service organizations, and at county fairs, city councils, and town meetings (Bentley 1984; Solo 1988: 82–85). Activists in local freeze organizations lobbied hundreds of town meetings and city councils to go on record in support of the freeze. The campaign to put freeze proposals on the ballot in a number of states required activists to contact prominent politicians for endorsements and to knock on tens of thousands of doors to distribute literature, solicit contributions, and collect signatures on petitions. In California alone, a half million signatures were gathered in three months to put the freeze on the state ballot, requiring an estimated 200,000 volunteer hours. Local freeze groups also became active in the 1982 congressional elections in all fifty states, helping to elect a new Congress that by one estimate had twenty to thirty more pro-freeze votes than the outgoing Congress (Waller 1987: 165). The range of activities undertaken in the freeze movement provided experience and insights into elections and the legislative process that can be found in no textbook.

What Oliver and Marwell (1992) call "action technologies" include canvassing, organizing a meeting, speaking, writing letters, and other activities in which an individual must step out from the crowd, be noticed, and take a risk. The small scale of many movement activities, especially in the social arena, contributes powerfully to the sense that what an individual does can make a real difference. "I myself desegregated a lunch counter, not somebody else, not some big man, some powerful man, but little me," said a proud black student. "I walked the picket line and I sat in and the walls of segregation toppled. Now all people can eat there" (cited in Sitkoff 1981: 91).

The internal politics of movement organizations are also a training ground that enhances political skills. Much has been made of the virtues and vices of the consensus style of decision making adopted by many movement organizations. This is normally seen as offering the advantage of preventing an entrenched leadership from becoming too powerful, offset by the difficulties of arriving at decisions (see, e.g., Barkan 1979; Downey 1986). The perspective of skill development offers an additional consideration, namely that a participatory decision process demands a high level of member involvement and therefore encourages the same skills activists will need in order to carry out the movement's work in the social and political arenas. An observer of Farmer's Alliance activists (as cited in Hicks 1961: 132, 159) noted that

> People commenced to think who had never thought before, and people talked who had seldom spoken. On mild days they gathered on the street corners, on cold days they congregated in shops and offices. Everyone was talking and everyone was thinking. . . . Little by little they commenced to theorize upon their condition. . . . It was a religious revival, a crusade, a pentecost of politics in which a tongue of flame sat upon every man, and each spake as the spirit gave him utterance.

The format common to most hierarchical organizations, in which initiation, discussion, decision making, and implementation are dominated by the organization's officers, leaves the skills of ordinary members relatively untouched. Consensus decision making in movement organizations forces each member to cultivate the ability to formulate and convey his or her thoughts on organizational issues.

The skill development aspects of movement involvement begin as soon as a person attends a meeting or takes part in movement activity. The lack of paid staff positions in most movement organizations means that activists new to a movement are pushed to positions of responsibility in short order. Consider the testimony of a volunteer in the community organizing program of the Student Nonviolent Coordinating Committee (SNCC), on learning during her training period what her first assignment would be: "I was overwhelmed at the idea of setting up a library all by myself. . . . Then can you imagine how I felt when at Oxford [Mississippi], while I was learning how to drop on the ground to protect my face, my ears, and my breasts, I was asked to *coordinate* the libraries in the entire project's community centers? I wanted to cry 'HELP'" (cited in Evans 1979: 70–71).

In movements of the least privileged groups in society, it is less likely that activists will enter the movement with skills in organization and communication that have been honed in other settings. Increasing the skills and self-confidence of activists may in such instances be the organizational activity that consumes more time and energy than any other. Such movements are likely to seek help in activist training by drawing on the resources and experience of foundations, labor unions, and other social change institutions. Aldon Morris (1984: chap. 7) has coined the term "movement halfway house" for institutions such as the Highlander Folk School, the American Friends Service Committee, and the Fellowship of Reconciliation. These organizations, and others like them, are not part of a particular movement but instead work to assist the development of resourceful activists in a variety of movements. They may put together workshops on subjects ranging from techniques of community organizing to developing a repertoire of protest music.

The Highlander Folk School is in many ways typical of these organizations. It was founded in Tennessee in the 1930s as a tool for developing community organization among mountain people (Adams 1975). Highlander soon became involved in unionization efforts in the South, and then after World War II the staff began to bring people together to talk about means of fighting segregation. Rosa Parks attended Highlander four months before sitting down in the section of the Montgomery public bus reserved for whites (Morris 1984: 146). It was at a celebration of the twenty-fifth anniversary of Highlander's founding that Martin Luther King Jr. first heard the song *We Shall Overcome* sung by Pete Seeger, who found it in the trove of protest songs collected at Highlander by Zilphia Horton (*Social Policy* 1991: 51). Within a few years Highlander initiated a program in literacy and citizenship training for blacks across the South, a program so successful that it was picked up and expanded by the Southern Christian Leadership Conference (SCLC) (Morris 1984: chap. 5; Evans and Boyte 1986: 65).

Whether or not a movement organization creates explicitly educational opportunities for activists, the very fact of participation puts people in new situations and enables them to develop previously unsuspected abilities. The learning curve, and an activist's excitement about it, may be especially great for people with the least exposure to formal education, or for whom culture and circumstance have not provided the chance to express their convictions to an attentive audience. David Wagner and Marcia Cohen (1991) report on the effects of a 1987 "tent city" protest by the homeless of Portland, Maine, which was a response to the closing of two emergency homeless shelters. The one hundred participants not only organized a viable community in the encampment, but also joined with homeless advocate Mitch Snyder to negotiate a settlement with the city that included opening year-round shelters, liberalizing the general assistance welfare program, and gaining homeless representation on a variety of city boards. The skills bred in the context of this protest led to the formation of several groups of homeless and formerly homeless who acted as watchdogs over the city's performance in meeting these commitments. Wagner and Cohen (1991: 547, 557) report that

> At one point, nearly 30 homeless or formerly homeless people were carrying beepers as they served as "peer advocates" to other homeless people. . . . Three years after Tent City and the first creation of grievance committees in Portland, homeless and formerly homeless people continue to occupy seats on several city boards as well as in a number of service agencies. Groups representing the homeless appear at shelters, soup kitchens, and city hall to protest a wide variety of administrative actions.

Through their involvement in the movement, activists develop new political beliefs to go along with their organizing skills. Rather than a series of misfortunes, rather than a reflection of one's own shortcomings, grievances come to be connected to the structure of power that holds back the entire group. An activist's view of the world becomes politicized, sometimes before one is even aware of it. The wife of a striking English coal miner joined a women's support group in 1983 and found herself in a world so different that she did not immediately realize how profoundly it had changed her (as cited in Coulter, Miller, and Walker 1984):

> At first I was frightened to speak at meetings, but now I've spoken to a rally at Barnsley with 10,000 people. Before the strike I didn't get involved in politics. After we'd started to speak at meetings, people used to come up to us and ask us to get involved in their political parties. . . . I said I wasn't involved in politics, and people said to me, but you're a socialist. It frightened me at first because I didn't know I was talking politics until someone told me. . . . Now it cuts deep and I feel I have to voice my opinion about Thatcher's dictatorship.

Engagement among Civil Rights Activists

Does movement activism develop political skills and engagement? One means of examining the curriculum of this school of protest is to compare the political skills of activists and nonactivists in the population that a movement seeks to mobilize. Figure 5-1 returns to the data collected by Matthews and Prothro from African Americans and whites in the South in 1961. There are significant differences between civil rights movement activists and the rest of the black population in the propensity to read newspapers and newsmagazines, to remember a variety of political facts, and to declare oneself interested in politics.[1] Those who were active in the movement score well beyond those who were inactive on all three measures. In fact, those who

---

[1] Political information is measured by the number of correct answers to questions on the length of a term in the U.S. Senate, the number of members on the Supreme Court, the names of the two states most recently admitted to the Union, and the name of Franklin Roosevelt's party.

took part in the civil rights movement scored significantly higher than Southern whites in political information, interest, and news consumption—this despite their lower average level of education and the general nonresponsiveness of government to their interests.[2]

Those who were not members of any civil rights organization and did not take part in any of its protests are divided into two groups in figure 5-1, based on whether they approve of sit-ins at lunch counters or not.[3] Even among those not active in the civil rights movement, people who approve of the sit-ins score higher on reading about politics, having political information, and being interested in politics. It is true that passive approvers of the movement have more education than passive disapprovers of the movement (ten and a half years on average to only seven years of education among those not approving of the sit-ins). But the differences in political engagement between those who approve and those who disapprove of the movement are statistically significant even when education is controlled.[4] This is evidence of a ripple effect of movement activity on the political engagement of a population. That is, the existence of the civil rights movement and the character of its demands for political inclusion had an effect on the political interest and attentiveness of those who approved of the movement, even if they were not active in it. We shall see further evidence of ripple effects on the political engagement of nonactivists later in this chapter.

An additional effect of the civil rights movement on its supporters, and particularly on those who became active in it, is to increase feelings of subjective competence to take action in local instances of racism. Respondents were asked if they would take action were they to be mistreated in a store owned by whites, and whether they would try to put their child in a nearby all-white school if they felt that the white school was "much better than the Negro school." Those who said they would take action in either situation were asked what they would do. In the case of mistreatment in a store, the proposed actions ranged from speaking with the store owner, to complaining to local authorities, to organizing a boycott. In the case of integrating the local school, the predominant action proposed was to organize with others to demand admission, though a small handful said they would initiate "a direct personal attack on the situation."

Because these are the respondent's own statements about what they would

---

[2] Information, interest, and news consumption among southern whites is set to zero in figure 5-1, providing a baseline against which the same variables can be measured among different groups of African Americans.

[3] This is a relatively demanding test of approval of the civil rights movement, since sit-ins were its most controversial tactic at the time of the interviews in 1961.

[4] Those who were active in the movement had an average of just over twelve years of education. Differences between activists and nonactivists also remain significant with education controlled.

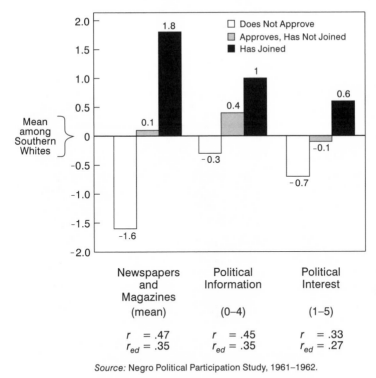

Source: Negro Political Participation Study, 1961–1962.

Note: All correlations are significant at the .01 level.

Figure 5-1 Civil rights involvement and political engagement

do in a hypothetical (though all too realistic) situation, we do not know what the respondent would actually do if the circumstances arose. But the point of these questions is *subjective* competence: the conviction that one would act (which means at a minimum that there is a belief one *should* act), and the ability to outline a plausible plan of action.[5] Movement activity, particularly in the social arena, demands the ability to confront local discrimination in its everyday forms. Change in the social arena can occur only if there is a high level of subjective competence among movement activists and sympathizers.

Figure 5-2 shows that activists in the civil rights movement had the highest levels of local subjective competence among African Americans in the South. Three times as many activists said they would take action to integrate

[5] Measures of subjective competence originated with Almond and Verba (1963), who used it to demonstrate that there are cross-national differences in the propensity to take action to remedy an unjust situation. See also Barnes, Kaase, et al. 1979 for data from several countries, including the United States, on change in subjective competence over time.

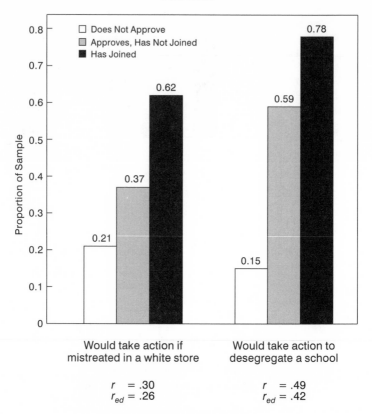

Would take action if   Would take action to
mistreated in a white store   desegregate a school

$r = .30$ $r = .49$
$r_{ed} = .26$ $r_{ed} = .42$

Source: Negro Political Participation Study, 1961–1962.

Note: All correlations are significant at the .01 level.

Figure 5-2   Civil rights involvement and local subjective competence

a school, compared with those who were not active in the movement and did not approve of sit-ins. Five times as many activists as nonsympathizers said they would take action to desegregate a school. Those who approved of the movement but were not personally involved in it are in between the other two groups on both measures.[6] Differences between activists and others in subjective competence remain significant and almost unchanged when education is controlled, suggesting that the civil rights movement's "school of war" was more powerful than formal learning when it comes to preparedness to take action against segregation or racially motivated mistreatment.

A third aspect of the curriculum of the civil rights movement "school" is

---

[6] Differences between all three groups are statistically significant, and those differences remain significant on both measures when education is controlled.

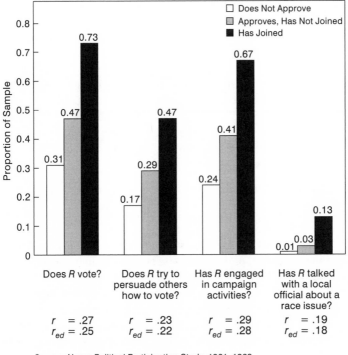

Source: Negro Political Participation Study, 1961–1962.
Note: All correlations are significant at the .01 level.

Figure 5-3   Civil rights involvement and political activity

participation in campaigns and elections. Figure 5-3 shows that movement activists are more likely than others to have voted, to have tried to persuade others how to vote, to have engaged in campaign activities, and to have spoken with a local official about an issue connected to race.[7]

Although these activities are typically analyzed as types of conventional political participation, it is worth remembering that for an African American in the South in 1961, voting and the other activities associated with electoral campaigns were anything but conventional and riskless. Contacting a local government official about a racial issue almost inevitably meant contacting a white official hostile to political participation by blacks, something that would require an unusual degree of assertiveness and even courage. The data show that those who approve of the movement but have not been involved in it participate in elections at lower rates than the activists and at higher rates

[7] Respondents were scored as having been active in a campaign if they have done *any* of the following: attended a campaign meeting or rally, given money to a candidate, or worked for a candidate.

than those who do not approve of sit-ins. Once again, controls for education diminish only fractionally the extent to which movement activists are distinctive in their use of a broad repertoire of political involvement.[8]

In sum, participation in the civil rights movement is associated with a high degree of political interest, subjective political competence, and political activity. These are the three elements that make up political engagement. They are indicative of desire and ability to participate in the collective life of the community. Even when activists are drawn from populations that have had little prior opportunity to be involved in politics, movement activism is associated with a high degree of political engagement.

SELF-SELECTION VERSUS LEARNING ON THE JOB

The data in figures 5-1, 5-2, and 5-3 demonstrate the association between movement participation and political engagement, but they cannot tell us which is a cause of which. Do activists learn to be politically involved in the course of their activism, or are those who are already highly politicized more likely to become involved in the movement?

The only way to examine the causal direction of the link between movement participation and the development of political engagement is by tracking movement activists for a period of time beginning before the initiation of their movement involvement. These data requirements are met by the research of Kent Jennings and Richard Niemi, who surveyed a national sample of high school seniors in 1965 and then followed the subsequent evolution of their political values over a period of seventeen years, with interviews in 1973 and 1982. Roughly half of the high school class of 1965 had graduated from college by 1973; and 29 percent of those who obtained a college degree also took part in a demonstration, protest march, or sit-in in that period.[9] The three-wave design of the Jennings-Niemi study, anchored in a first round of interviews carried out before respondents became involved in protest, offers the best possible evidence of the relationship between movement participation and political engagement.

In their own analyses of these data, Jennings and Niemi restrict their focus to those who became college graduates by 1973. This maximizes comparability between protesting and nonprotesting groups, since all can be assumed to have spent a substantial amount of time between 1965 and 1973 on a college campus. Figures 5-4 and 5-5 follow this Jennings-Niemi convention

---

[8] When education is controlled, differences between the approve-but-inactive group and the group that did not approve of sit-ins are not statistically significant for persuading others how to vote or talking with a local official.

[9] Two-thirds of these protests were related to the war in Vietnam; the second most common cause was "student issues," with 13 percent. In the context of the time, "student issues" would generally mean campus governance or admission policies for minorities.

in a comparison of political engagement, trust, and personality traits among protesters and nonprotesters. In these data, "protesters" are defined as anybody who took part in at least one demonstration, march, or sit-in between 1965 and 1973. It is likely that many of those included in this category had a relatively mild exposure to the student movement. The search for differences in political engagement based on participation in as little as a single campus protest poses a severe test of the hypothesis that movements foster high levels of political engagement among their activists. Yet the effects of protest participation are plainly visible even under these circumstances.

In some ways, participants in the student movement were already distinctive in their attitudes as high school seniors. Figure 5-4 shows that this is the case with both political knowledge and political efficacy. Prior to graduating from high school in 1965, future participants in campus protest had higher levels of factual political knowledge and were less likely to feel that politics is too complex for "a person like me" to understand. By 1973, though, differences between protesters and nonprotesters in knowledge and efficacy became more striking, and those enhanced differences endured with little change up to 1982.

In other respects, future protest participants were not distinctive prior to their involvement in protest, but they became temporarily distinctive in the wake of protest participation. This is the meaning of the inverted-V pattern found for readership of political news in newspaper and magazines. As long as the issues they had demonstrated about remained in the news, campus protesters were far more likely than other college graduates to read newspapers and magazines. With the Vietnam War concluded and pressure to increase minority admissions to colleges no longer considered newsworthy in 1982, the differences between protesters and nonprotesters in media consumption for political news were substantially attenuated.

In the immediate wake of campus protest, participants were also more likely to espouse active ideals of citizenship. The Jennings-Niemi study coded up to four mentions of "things about a person that are most important in showing that one is a good citizen." The answers clustered broadly into four categories: showing loyalty to the government and obedience to its laws, voting, getting involved in ways other than voting, and a miscellaneous group of private traits such as being honest, working hard at one's job, or being a good neighbor. In 1973, protest participants were strikingly less likely than nonparticipants to endorse loyalty and obedience as traits of a good citizen (data not shown). They were somewhat more likely to believe that a good citizen must participate in ways beyond voting to improve the political community. It is interesting to note that the nonprotesters also grew increasingly likely to endorse political action beyond voting as a means of remedying a problem; the culture of direct action reached beyond those who had actually been involved in protest. But this shift toward an activist con-

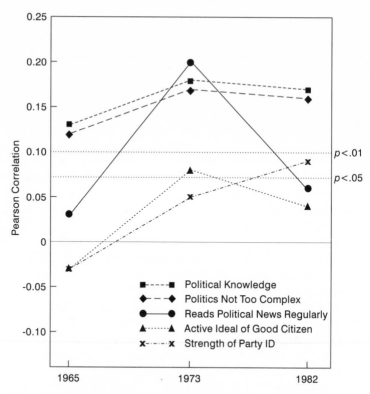

Source: Youth-Parent Socialization Study.

Figure 5-4   Effect of movement involvement on political engagement

cept of good citizenship among nonprotesters was dwarfed by the transformation among those who had been involved in the student movement (see figure 5-4). As Jennings and Niemi (1981: 342) summarize,

> Among the protesters in particular there was an increase in outright calls for direct citizen action if things are not going well, declarations that one cannot simply sit back, that the good citizen goes out and organizes and even protests and demonstrates to achieve desired goals. The ethos of vigorous activism was alive and well among the veterans of the movement.

These differences, too, were most striking in the immediate wake of the student protest movement. By 1982 the differences between protesters and nonprotesters in activist citizenship orientations had abated to levels below the threshold of statistical significance.

A final pattern of the effects of protest involvement on individuals occurs when an orientation is created by the experience of protest and is then reinforced by later life experiences. In this pattern, differences between pro-testers and nonprotesters increase in intensity as the generational cohort ages. This pattern is illustrated in figure 5-4 by party identification.

Party identification is different from the other traits and orientations in figure 5-4 because it is the only belief that is periodically reinforced by external events for the duration of one's life. Political knowledge, efficacy, citizenship ideals, and reading habits are essentially individual decisions and behaviors; they may show considerable stability over time but they are sub-ject to modification as one's interests and situations change. In a democracy, though, party identification is reinforced (or altered) through the external stimulus of regular elections in which rival parties and candidates profile their ideas. As Converse (1976) has demonstrated for the United States, and as others (e.g., Dalton 1988: 183) have demonstrated for other democracies, the effect of this external reinforcement is normally to increase the strength of partisan attachments as one gets older.

Of course, not all members of a given age cohort will have the same degree of party attachment. And it is logical to assume that experiences of political activism in early adulthood are among the factors that create differ-entiation within an age group in strength of party attachment. In the case of the student protesters, involvement in the campus movement led to relatively strong party attachments in 1973 even though the future protesters had had slightly *weaker* party attachments in 1965. Because of the regular reinforce-ment that occurs through the electoral calendar, these differences in partisan-ship were not only not diminished by 1982, but were in fact augmented. The experience of protest as college students created relatively intense (and pro-Democratic) feelings of partisanship early in life. These partisan feelings continued to grow at a rate slightly faster than usual between 1973 and 1982.

The effects of movement involvement go beyond the realm of political engagement and action. Figure 5-5 shows that movement participants have also developed a distinctive profile in their levels of political and personal trust, and in the strength of their opinions. The most dramatic changes oc-curred with respect to political trust. As high school seniors in 1965, future protesters were somewhat more trusting politically than those who would later choose not to protest while in college.[10] That was dramatically changed by 1973. The political trust of all respondents declined, but trust among protesters fell through the floor. The 1973 difference between protesters and nonprotesters in political trust was substantially reduced by 1982, though protesters remained less trusting.

[10] The elements of the political trust index are the six items that have become standard in the American National Election Studies: whether the government pays attention to what people think; whether it is run by a few big interests or for the benefit of all; and whether people in government are honest, waste a lot of money, can be trusted to do what is right, and know what they are doing.

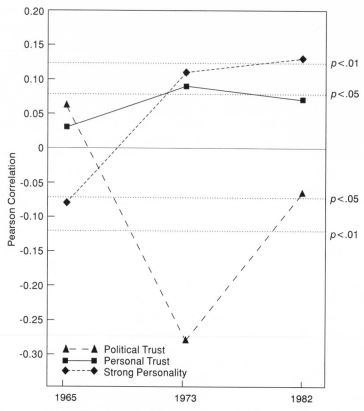

Source: Youth-Parent Socialization Study.

Figure 5-5   Effect of movement involvement on trust and opinion strength

At the same time that protesters were becoming less trusting of government, they became somewhat more trusting of other people, relative to non-protesters. Protesters also developed a sense of themselves as having firm opinions. The "strong personality index" combines questions on whether the respondent tends to have strong opinions and to stick by those opinions when others argue a different point of view. Future protesters answered these questions somewhat less confidently than other college-bound high school seniors in 1965. By 1973 the protesters were more likely to describe themselves as having firm opinions, and by 1982 the difference between protesters and nonprotesters had widened still further.

The data in figure 5-4 show that the elements of political engagement—skills and resources—are enhanced in the wake of involvement in a protest movement. It is important to be clear that these are not all direct effects of the actual protest involvement. To some extent, protest was a politicizing agent that worked in later years to engage people in a wide variety of political activities. In 1973 the former student protesters were more likely to be politically active by every available measure of participation, including election campaigns, contacting officials, and getting involved in community organizations.[11] Those activities, in turn, helped to maintain or even heighten the other elements of political engagement among protesters.

The Jennings-Niemi study provides substantial support for the view that it takes a certain level of political engagement in order to become active in a movement, but that movement activism also produces a further leap in political engagement. Relative to the nonprotesters, those who participated in campus protest acquired more political information and felt more able to understand politics, had a more activist approach to citizenship and were more engaged in political life, had firmer opinions and stronger party attachments, and had more trust in other people and less trust in government. As respondents in the Jennings-Niemi study approached middle age in the 1980s, a great deal of their cumulated history of political orientations and involvement can be traced back to the schism between young adults on college campuses who decided to join in the protest and those who did not. As Jennings (1987: 370) summarizes, "Protestors were somewhat different prior to the protest era but dramatically different afterwards." Given the many experiences that intervene between gathering with others in a campus demonstration and celebrating one's thirty-fifth birthday, it is striking how clearly protest involvement continued to differentiate political beliefs and activities among members of the high school class of 1965.[12]

These findings dovetail perfectly with those of Verba, Schlozman, and Brady (1995), whose Civic Voluntarism Model proposes that people learn communication and organizing skills in a variety of settings. They conclude (1995: 352) that "the exercise of a single skill in each of the three nonpolitical domains leads to an increase in political activity of roughly a third

[11] The measures of participation include attending a campaign meeting, working for a candidate, displaying a campaign button or sticker, donating money to a campaign, working with others to solve a community problem, writing a political letter to a newspaper editor, contacting an official about some issue, and talking with others to influence their votes. The protesters were substantially more likely than the nonprotesters to take part in all of these activities both in 1973 (Pearson $r = .42$ for the cumulated activity index) and in 1982 (Pearson $r = .19$).

[12] A variety of follow-up studies of student activists affirm the durability of political liberalism and active participation among former campus activists. See Hoge and Ankney 1982; Fendrich and Turner 1989; and Whalen and Flacks 1989. On continuity in political beliefs among student activists in the civil rights movement, see Fendrich 1977 and Marwell, Aiken, and Demerath 1987. Braungart and Braungart (1991) find comparable degrees of continuity among former members of SDS and the conservative student group Young Americans for Freedom. What distinguishes the Jennings-Niemi data from these studies is the possibility of examining the extent of political engagement *before* participation in the student movement, as well as the durability of attitudes in later life.

of a political act (in a population which engages in an average of 2.1 political acts)." Of course, movement activists develop civic skills in the context of a political organization, and so we would expect the translation of skill development into political activity to be even more striking than that found by Verba et al. in their examination of the effects of activity on the job, in churches, and in nonpolitical voluntary organizations.

A comparison of the effects of participation in the civil rights movement (figures 5-1, 5-2, 5-3) and the student movement (figures 5-4 and 5-5) suggests a great deal of consistency in the lessons activists learn even from movements whose general orientations to politics are distinct. The civil rights movement sought the political and social inclusion of African Americans. The student movement, to a greater degree than other movements of the 1960s and 1970s, embraced an angry rejection of the political system. Particularly after the failure of efforts to elect a peace candidate in the 1968 presidential elections, much of the student movement became confrontational, moving from protest to resistance. This led at one extreme to the endorsement of terrorism and at the other extreme to a decision to drop out of American society.[13]

Despite these differences between the civil rights and student movements, participants in each learned the same lessons. Both the civil rights movement and the student movement created a generation of politically engaged activists whose desire and ability to get involved in politics stand out in significant excess of the American norm.

RIPPLE EFFECTS OF MOVEMENT INVOLVEMENT

We have seen that mobilization into a movement increases the level of political engagement among activists. A full measure of the individual-level impacts of movement activity must, however, include its effects on the political attitudes of outside observers. The very existence of a movement that articulates a new group identity is bound to attract the attention even of those who do not choose to become active. We saw earlier in this chapter that African Americans who were not active in the civil rights movement, but approved of the sit-ins, had significantly higher levels of political engagement than those who did not approve of the movement. This suggests that sympathetic spectators of a movement may also respond to the movement by increasing their levels of political attentiveness and activity. However, cross-sectional data cannot tell us whether sympathetic observers of the movement were affected by the movement itself or whether they already had relatively high levels of political engagement. To determine whether movements have ripple

[13] Similar ideas gained strength in the civil rights movement only after 1961, the year in which the data reported in figures 5-1, 5-2, 5-3 were gathered.

effects beyond the circle of activists, we must know whether the political values and actions of nonmobilized group members were changed by the existence of the movement.

If there are movement ripple effects, they should be most pronounced among those who have direct contact with movement activists. Ripple effects may, for example, be found among family members and close friends of activists. We can examine this hypothesis by taking advantage of the fact that the Jennings-Niemi panel study incorporated interviews with one parent of each respondent from the high school class of 1965. Parents were interviewed in all three waves, enabling us to compare the parents of student protesters with those whose children went to college but did not engage in protest activity. The issue of whether movements have ripple effects on the political engagement of nonactivists, then, can be interpreted in this case as whether the activities of student demonstrators led to changes in the political values and behaviors of their parents.

The evidence from figure 5-6 is that they did. In fact, the figure suggests both the influence that parents have on the political values of their children and the reciprocal influence of young adults on their parents. Parental influence on student activists is suggested in a study conducted by Richard Flacks (1967), which showed that, compared with the parents of other college students, the parents of activists were politically more liberal and had a less "interventionist" approach to child rearing.[14] To this profile, we can add that the parents of future student demonstrators were more likely than other parents of college-bound children to read political news regularly and to be active in electoral campaigns (see figure 5-6). They also had notably higher levels of political trust—that is, faith that the government is capable, represents the people, and generally does the right thing.

By 1973 the parents of student protesters had become more distinctive in a number of ways. They had increased their relative levels of political engagement, reflected in high rates of reading newspapers and magazines and in high levels of conventional political activity. On the other hand, the elevated levels of political trust among the parents of student protesters disappeared, to be replaced by a slightly greater degree of *distrust* in politics. Although the influence of their children's protest participation on newspaper readership and political activity appears to have been confined to the Vietnam era itself, the effects on political trust proved to be more enduring. In an era when political trust in the American population as a whole was plunging, trust among the parents of protesters fell particularly rapidly.

Although there is evidence that student protesters influenced the political

---

[14] Flacks determined level of interventionism by asking parents in his sample what they would do if their child dropped out of college, and what they would do if their child moved in with a member of the opposite sex without being married.

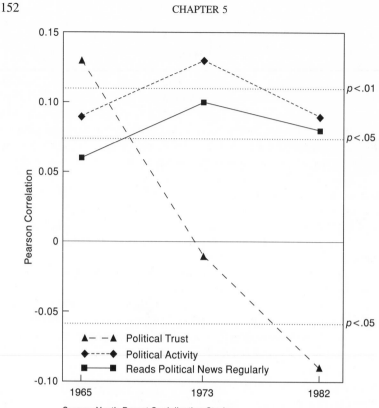

Source: Youth-Parent Socialization Study.

Figure 5-6   Effect of movement involvement on parent attitudes and activity

development of their parents between 1965 and 1973, it is important to note as well the personal and political values that are *not* represented in figure 5-6. The parents of student protesters did not become different from other parents in their degree of political efficacy, interpersonal trust, and strength of opinions. Changes in these areas were confined to the student protesters themselves. There are some benefits that can be had only through personal experience of movement involvement.

Changes in political engagement and trust among the parents of student protesters are probably not simply a reaction to their children's political experiences. For one thing, 8 percent of these parents had themselves participated in a demonstration in the past eight years, compared to only 1 percent of the parents of nonprotesters.[15] Nonetheless, the evidence from the three

[15] In order to isolate the ripple effect of offspring movement participation as clearly as possible, those parents who have themselves participated in a demonstration are excluded from figure 5-6.

TABLE 5-1
Parent-Child Correlations on Political Trust

	1965	1973	1982
All college edu- cated	.23*	.07	.10**
Protesters	.19*	.19*	.14
Nonprotesters	.24*	.01	.07

Source: Youth-Parent Socialization Study.
Note: * $p < .01$, ** $p < .05$.

waves of parent interviews suggests that the parents of student protesters internalized lessons from their children's involvement in protest politics—including the negative lesson of not trusting government and politicians.

The most suggestive evidence of the political influence of young adults on their parents comes from examination of the correlation in political trust between parent and child. When the future protesters and nonprotesters were high school seniors, their levels of political trust conformed to that of their parents (see table 5-1). These correlations suggest a strong parental influence on the trust levels of high school students who had as yet little or no personal experience of the political world.

By 1973, members of the student generation were in their early twenties. They had spent the intervening years on campus in a very politicized atmosphere; they had had the opportunity to vote in their first presidential elections. Among nonprotesters, the parent-child correlation in political trust had all but disappeared by 1973, as the young adults graduated from college, moved away from home, and began developing an independent political outlook. Among those who protested between 1965 and 1973, though, the parent–young adult correlation remained steady. Even though the level of political trust changed more dramatically among the protesters than among the nonprotesters, a parallel evolution among the parents of protesters maintained the parent-child correlation between 1965 and 1973. Although the 1965 correlation was almost certainly due to the influence of parents on their children, it is reasonable to suppose that by 1973 there was a two-way flow of influence. Knowing that their children were involved in campus protests (and no doubt being involved in discussions with their children on that subject) apparently caused parents to increase their own levels of political engagement, and to reduce the high degree of political trust they had felt to that point.

The parent-child bond is, of course, unique. All important undertakings by a child will elicit parental interest and all have the potential to result in some degree of responsive learning by parents. We have seen that participation in a movement is one of the activities that can leave an impact on family members. The existence of ripple effects that affect political engagement and trust among the family members of movement participants is part of the total effect of movements on cultural change.

The existence of ripple effects within the families of movement participants leaves open the question of whether there are similar effects in circles further removed from the activists themselves. Beyond the family, the most likely people to be influenced by ripple effects of movement protest are the members of any group whose interests a movement claims to champion. Particularly when movements demand group rights and develop an ideology of group solidarity and pride, it is likely that group members not active in the movement will nonetheless be touched by movement ideas.

We can examine these more distant ripple effects of movement activity by tracing changes in the levels of political engagement and participation of the African American population beginning in 1952. We have already seen that activists in the civil rights movement were exceptionally high in their level of political engagement and participation (figures 5-1, 5-2, 5-3). To what extent did other African Americans, watching the movement without playing a role in it, also become more involved in politics?

Figures 5-7 and 5-8 are constructed as a comparison between blacks and whites in levels of voter turnout and political efficacy.[16] White efficacy and turnout is in each case represented by the horizontal line running across the figure. While the "white standard" is arbitrary, and other standards for measuring attitudinal change among African Americans are certainly possible, using whites as a comparison group has the useful trait of controlling for general trends in society, which over this period saw declines in both efficacy and turnout.[17] Whites serve in effect as a control group in order to measure changes in black political attitudes net of general trends in American culture.

Figures 5-7 and 5-8 depict dramatic changes in turnout and efficacy among African Americans, changes that altered the political landscape in the span of a single generation. Starting from an extremely low point in 1952, black efficacy levels and voting rates rose very close to those of whites by 1964. These increases are concentrated geographically in the South and temporally in the late 1950s and early 1960s, suggesting in both instances the influence of the civil rights movement. When differences in education and

[16] These figures are derived from previous work done with Ikuo Kabashima of Tsukuba University, reported in Rochon and Kabashima 1998. My thanks to Professor Kabashima for his collaboration in this research.

[17] Turnout and efficacy both underwent substantial declines among the American public as a whole in the period covered by these figures. Any impact of the civil rights movement on the political attitudes of African Americans occurs in conjunction with these other period effects.

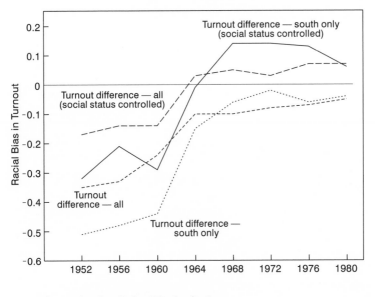

Source: American National Election Studies.

Figure 5-7   Gains in voting turnout among African Americans

social status are controlled, black levels of turnout and efficacy actually sur-
passed those of whites beginning in 1964.

It is significant that these increases in turnout and efficacy occurred before
passage of the 1964 Civil Rights Act and the 1965 Voting Rights Act. The
barriers to black registration and voting in the South were reduced to some
extent in the late 1950s and early 1960s, but this occurred without assistance
from the federal government until after 1964. The impact of the Voting
Rights Act, which applied only to the South, is visible in the increase in
Southern black turnout (but not national black turnout) between 1964 and
1968. As important as the Voting Rights Act was in some areas of the country, though, the greatest gains in turnout among African Americans had already been recorded by 1964. Three-fourths of the increase in turnout among
African Americans between 1952 and 1968 occurred during the voting rights
campaigns of the civil rights movement, and not as a result of the federal
response to that campaign. The civil rights movement, whose voter registration activities were also focused largely on the South, had by 1964 brought
voting rates among African Americans in the South up nearly to the level of
African Americans in the North. The Voting Rights Act nudged turnout
among African Americans in the South higher than in the North, and higher
than for whites when educational differences are controlled.

There was little in the actions of the federal or state governments prior to

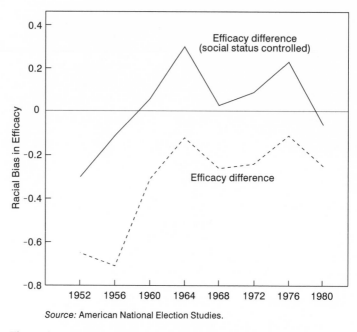

Source: American National Election Studies.

Figure 5-8   Gains in efficacy among African Americans

1964 that could account for the large observed changes in levels of efficacy and turnout among African Americans. To the extent that it became easier for blacks to register to vote prior to 1964, and to the extent that political events gave cause for increased feelings of efficacy, these changes were due to the efforts of the civil rights movement. In their study of *Participation in America*, Verba and Nie (1972) also find that blacks on the whole had higher rates of political participation than whites, controlling for socio-economic status. They find that these high rates of participation are confined to African Americans who exhibit relatively high rates of "black consciousness" (assessed by the propensity to use racial issues as a point of reference in talking about politics). Richard Shingles's (1981) analysis of data on black participation from the same era shows that highly participant blacks are most likely to be high in efficacy but low in political trust. This contrasts with the participation profile among whites, which involves high levels of efficacy and trust. As we have seen, high efficacy–low trust is precisely the attitudinal profile characteristic of those who are involved in a protest movement.

These studies converge on the same conclusion—that participation among blacks was higher than that of whites during the 1960s and into the 1970s, with social status controlled. And each of these studies explains this high rate of participation by pointing to attitudes, such as black consciousness and high efficacy–low trust, that are unambiguous fingerprints of movement influence. Because relatively few African Americans were active in the civil rights movement, the bulk of the increase in black levels of participation and efficacy is due to ripple effects on those who observed the movement but were not active in it.

In some respects, the effects of the movement on the African American population have proved to be enduring. A return to the low rates of voting turnout and efficacy characteristic of the early 1950s is all but unimaginable. But the specific influence of the civil rights movement in motivating participation through group consciousness and by creating the high efficacy–low trust syndrome appears to have been temporary. Turnout differences between blacks and whites have remained stable since 1972, but as of 1980 levels of efficacy among blacks were once again lower than those of whites, with socioeconomic status controlled (see figure 5-8). Verba et al. (1995: 355–356) found in the late 1980s that racial consciousness was no longer associated with higher levels of political participation (controlling for education, skills, and other resources). In a more detailed analysis of the 1984 and 1988 elections, Katherine Tate (1991) finds that short-term effects now account for interelection changes in voting turnout among blacks. Jesse Jackson's presidential candidacy in 1984 stimulated turnout among African Americans in both the primary and general elections, but Jackson's renewed candidacy in 1988 did not have the same effect and the absence of President Reagan from the 1988 race removed another incentive for blacks to vote. Using 1987 data from the General Social Survey, Bobo and Gilliam (1990) have shown that African American participation is much higher in cities where blacks have been relatively successful in winning election to office. The declining relevance of group consciousness as analyzed by Verba et al., and the growing importance of election-specific factors analyzed by Tate and context-specific factors analyzed by Bobo and Gilliam in accounting for voting turnout among African Americans all attest to the end of the era in which the struggles of the civil rights movement created a generalized impulse toward high rates of electoral participation within the black community.

Nevertheless, the civil rights movement inspired a general shift upward in political efficacy and electoral participation among African Americans. One of the major themes of the civil rights movement was to stress the importance of the vote as a means of expressing political demands, and by 1964 this message was being translated into action by unprecedented numbers of black voters. Increases in political engagement were particularly concentrated among those who actually took part in the movement, as we saw in figures 5-1, 5-2, 5-3. But substantial increases in efficacy and participation took place in the black population as a whole, and particularly among those for whom racial issues had become a salient criterion of political judgments.[18] As effective as the civil rights movement ultimately proved to be in the political arena, it is clear that the movement also had a powerful social arena impact on the political engagement of African Americans.

IMPLICATIONS FOR MOVEMENT STRATEGY

Solidarity provides the motivation to participate in movements. Participation fosters the skills and habits of thought that are essential to maintaining participation. Successful movements must be concerned to cultivate both group solidarity and political engagement among those they seek to recruit into demanding forms of participation. In the preceding chapter and this one, we have seen that movement participants do indeed possess strong group solidarities as well as high levels of political engagement. Before movements can ever bring change in cultural values to the wider society, they first alter the culture of solidarity and engagement among activists.

The presence of virtuous circles involving solidarity, engagement, and activism suggests that the optimal strategy for movements is to make the initial costs of entry as low as possible in the expectation that people will later develop both the desire and the capacity for more demanding forms of involvement. The importance of prior protest experience in motivating continued movement activism is suggested by Opp (1988: 858–859), whose study of two waves of antinuclear protest shows that hostility to nuclear energy was the most important factor in mobilizing people in the first wave, but that prior experience of protest was more important in mobilizing people for the second wave. As Gamson (1991: 50) put it, "movements that take seriously the goal of enhancing the capacity of people for collective action must make sure that their practices do in fact promote and encourage participants to be active and collaborative."

The importance of getting people involved demands that movement organizers fashion protest activities that may be incomprehensible from the standpoint of achieving policy goals, but quite effective in strengthening ties of group solidarity or in developing participatory orientations and skills among activists. For example, the fate of nearly all petitions to government is to be discarded after desultory debate thanking the petitioners for their involvement and dismissing their demands. The entire exercise would be an extraordinary waste of time were it not for the fact that a petition campaign presents an opportunity to go door-to-door and talk with people about movement goals. This was perhaps never more apparent than when a House of Representatives ban on considering petitions related to slavery spurred aboli-

---

[18] As reflected in the measurement of "black consciousness" by Verba and Nie (1972).

tionists to *increase* their signature-gathering efforts. Canvassers were instructed to "Neglect no one. Follow the farmer to his field, the wood-chopper to the forest. Hail the shop keeper behind his counter; call the clerk from his desk; stop the waggoner with his team; forget not the matron, ask for her daughter. Let no frown deter, no repulse baffle. Explain, discuss, argue, persuade" (cited in Dillon 1974: 102).

In the year after this gag rule was passed in the House, abolitionist organizations sent an unprecedented number of petitions to Congress, gaining the signatures of between 20 and 40 percent of the voters in many New England towns.[19] Abolitionist zeal in sending petitions to authorities who have legally bound themselves not to read them suggests that the real targets of a petition campaign are not the authorities at all, but rather the activists gathering signatures (whose commitments are reinforced by being given a task to do) and those who are approached to sign the petition (who become aware of the cause and who may also come to feel a stake in its success by virtue of having lent their signatures to its demands).

Movement strategists are fully aware that at least some of their tactics must widen the pool of activists and develop their solidarities, rather than "merely" having an impact on politicians. Mailings of preprinted postcards with a political message are, for example, notoriously ineffective among legislators. But Staggenborg (1991: 100, 101) quotes a director of the National Abortion Rights Action League (NARAL) as saying "the best thing about the postcards was that they gave us new contacts. . . . We also got names for a mailing list." Even such tactics as lobbying may be more about building the organization than about political influence.

> We do some lobbying as part of our electoral work—we do it for the benefit of our members, not for its impact on legislators. Like sometimes we will get a member to visit a person who we know is completely intractable. They're so upset after the visit they can't wait to get into campaign work! You know, they think, "This person is representing me?"

Large demonstrations that have the quality of a festival are another form of movement activity with dubious political benefits but with the potential to engage large numbers of people by minimizing the threshold of participation. As Verba et al. (1995: chap. 11) point out, participation in a demonstration does not require a great deal of civic skill. All that is asked of people is that they show up at the appointed time and then listen to the program of speeches and entertainment. Being present at such a demonstration may not expose people to new thinking on the issue, but the very act of standing among thousands of people who care about the same issue makes people

[19] See Magdol 1986 for an analysis of the spatial, occupational, and religious distribution of the signers of abolitionist petitions.

aware of belonging to an ideologically defined group. According to a strategist in NARAL, "Politically things like pickets have zero effectiveness, but
volunteers like them. So occasionally we'd do them for the volunteers, to rev
people up when they need a boost" (Staggenborg 1991: 100). A low level of
initial commitment will, for some fraction of those present, begin the spiral
of mobilization based on increasing solidarity, skills, and engagement.

The lesson for the study of movements is that we must often look beyond
the manifest goal of a movement activity (e.g., political influence) to consider its impact on the development of solidarity and skill. Movement organizations may undertake a wide variety of activities in order to involve people with varying levels of commitment. The key for movement mobilization
is to get people in the door and to get them involved in some kind of activity. What happens after that might best be described by a student from Howard University who joined an antisegregation sit-in. "[We] all rejoiced, and
we all felt the opportunity was here; and the fact that college students were
doing it is one of the powerful reasons for participating ourselves . . . we all
realized we had been *wanting to do something* and now was the time."[20]
Similarly, a student involved in a 1966 occupation of the administration
building at the University of Chicago reported "such feelings of ecstasy,
such feelings of being able to make the new world right there; this was our
building, we were setting up the institutions governing this building, they
were going to be fair and just and generous and democratic" (cited in Evans
1979: 172). A leader of the Mexican American Youth Organization (MAYO)
in Texas experienced "A loss of fear. [Getting involved] means that we
stopped being afraid of the gringo" (cited in Navarro 1995: 238). A formerly
homeless man who joined the Tent City in Portland, Maine, concluded that
"Being involved has really made me proud to call myself homeless. Even
though I have a place now, I still think of myself that way" (cited in Wagner
and Cohen 1991: 551).

"Rejoicing" in the opportunity to do something about segregation of public facilities; "ecstasy" in the belief that the occupiers of a campus building
are making a new world; a loss of fear; "proud" to call oneself homeless.
Movement organizations are viable, once started, because of these reactions
to the experience of activism.

CONCLUSION

The two preceding chapters lead us to three major conclusions about the
microfoundations of movement mobilization:

---

[20] Cited in Fishman and Solomon 1970: 145, emphasis in the original.

Group solidarity assists in movement mobilization by connecting individual interests to group interests, leading to a calculus of action based on collective
rationality.

Movement mobilization is maintained as a function of the participation of
others, success in achieving objectives, and a steady flow of the rewards that
are associated with movement activism.

Movement mobilization expands in part through the ripple effects of protest
activity that lead to increased engagement among those who have contact with
movement activists (e.g., family and friends) and among those who are members of the group whose interests the movement represents.

The exploration of movement mobilization in these chapters also helps us
better understand the connections between critical communities and movements. It is of course true that issues defined in a critical community help
mobilize people who share the ideals behind the issue. The civil rights
movement would never have begun had not millions of people believed pas-
sionately in the vision of racial integration and equality articulated by the
movement. Verba et al. (1995: chap. 14) show that those who have deep
feelings about an issue are more likely to participate in politics, even when
education and other background factors are controlled. Critical communities
affect patterns of mobilization by defining the issues about which people
may come to feel strongly. As Swidler (1986: 275) points out, "To adopt a
line of conduct, one needs an image of the kind of world in which one is
trying to act."

But commitment to an issue is not enough to overcome the barriers to
collective action. The ideas of the critical community assist mobilization not
only by defining an issue, but also by placing the issue in the context of
specific claims about groups. Of particular relevance here are beliefs embedded in a critical community perspective about group boundaries, the causes
of group oppression, and the special traits shared by members of the group.
Critical communities connect local, tangible experience to more global, abstract causes. Their ideas help determine the possibilities for group solidarity
and mobilization. By placing the issue in a larger context, the ideas of the
critical community help define the friends and enemies of the cause, and
suggest possible lines of action. A person is more likely to become active in
a movement if she thinks of herself as a victim of racism or sexism, than if
she simply thinks of herself as a victim. In short, the critical community
creates a map of the social and political world. Movement mobilization occurs when large numbers of people are able to locate themselves on that
map.

However, movement organizations and activists do not simply use the
ideas of the critical community as off-the-shelf, finished products. Instead,

these ideas are modified in the course of movement struggle. The virtues of the group are confirmed through collective action. Expectations of political authority and of allies and opponents are also developed and altered through experiences of assistance and repression. Tarrow (1992: 197) has pointed out that "new frames of meaning result from the struggles over meaning within social movements and from their clash with their opponents. They are elaborated not intellectually but through struggle, which is always a struggle over meaning as well as over resources." As the movement develops, then, it makes its own intellectual and emotional contributions to the system of thought developed in the critical community.

The effects of movement protest on the solidarity and engagement of movement activists, their families, and other group members are significant in the near term because they widen the circle of those who are psychologically prepared for mobilization. In the longer term, these effects are an important means by which a movement fosters cultural transformation. Even after mobilization has ended, the movement leaves behind a society that is permanently changed by the development of new group solidarities and by the growth of political engagement. The microfoundations of movement mobilization thus create new patterns of social thought and action, contributing to the breadth and pace of change in cultural values.

The cultural tides generated by movements begin with the profound changes in thought and behavior that occur among their activists. The ripple effects of movement activism also have an impact on family, friends, and fellow members of a group. But cultural change and political reform do not take place solely through the internal processes of movement mobilization. Rapid social and political change instead occurs through shifts in strategic interactions and alliances between political and social institutions. It is to those macroconsiderations that we now turn.

PART THREE

Social and Political Structures

Chapter 6

DIFFUSION OF CHANGE IN SOCIETY

WE HAVE seen that critical communities are the carriers of new social values, which they elaborate into an integrated ideology through the processes of value conversion, creation, and connection. Movements aid in the spread of these critical ideologies by creating a cadre of activists who are both willing (because of group solidarity) and able (because of political engagement) to mobilize for collective action. The issue that remains for us to examine is how the ideas of critical communities, as embodied in social and political movements, break out of the movement community and become part of the wider society. To address these questions, we move from a microlevel focus on movement activists to a macrolevel focus on the structural features of society and polity.

The specific patterns by which movement ideas are disseminated to the society, and by which the political system adopts, co-opts, or ignores these ideas, are heavily dependent on social and political institutions and processes. The opportunities to form critical communities, the standing of such communities in the wider society, and the receptivity of the political system to groups mobilized around new policy demands are among the structural elements that affect the potential for the conceptual innovations of critical communities to have an impact on cultural values and public policies. Taken together, these institutional features constitute the social and political opportunity structures within which critical communities must operate.[1]

In this chapter and the next we will look at the aspects of social and political structures in liberal democracies that influence the ease with which critical communities form, spread their ideas in society, and contribute to reform of the polity. Our concern here is with the societal conditions that enable critical communities to form, movements to mobilize, and publics to receive their messages. When we compare contemporary social conditions to the situation even a hundred years ago, it is clear that there has been what Huntington refers to as "The Change to Change." "At the intellectual level, modern society is characterized by the tremendous accumulation of knowledge about man's environment and by the diffusion of this knowledge

---

[1] Movement scholars have used the idea of a political opportunity structure to examine the institutional aspects of politics that give movements an opportunity to arise and that structure their strategic choices (see, e.g., Tarrow 1989, Kitschelt 1986). The social and political opportunity structures referred to here represent a broadening of that same concept.

through society by means of literacy, mass communications, and education" (Huntington 1971: 287).

Among the keys to this change to change are expansion of the change-acceptant strata of society, of channels for the diffusion of ideas, and of the speed with which ideas are communicated and incorporated into a new pattern of cultural values. During the eighteenth-century Enlightenment, the relevant actors came from the most privileged segment of society, ideas were communicated through channels we would today identify as high culture, and the rate of diffusion of critical ideas can only be characterized as slow. In twentieth-century democracies, by comparison, critical communities and their audiences are found in many organized niches in society and the diffusion of new ideas occurs much more rapidly through a wide variety of communications media.

In this chapter we will focus on three traits of contemporary American society that encourage the formation and influence of critical communities and movement organizations. These are the cultural traits that encourage critical thinking in the first place, the institutional niches that nurture the development of critical communities, and the media channels that foster diffusion of new ideas.

BEING CRITICAL

Studies of different cultures have revealed a wide range of orientations toward change and the potential for change to bring progress. Although the idea that there is a single dimension of cultures running from traditional to modern does not stand up under empirical scrutiny, there is nonetheless a set of cultural beliefs characteristic of modern societies, many of which originated with the Enlightenment. As Black (1967: 7) points out, the creative impulse for change "stems initially from an attitude, a belief that society can and should be transformed, that change is desirable." In a culture that features the belief that problems can be solved and that the path to progress lies through change, the ideas of critical communities have an increased likelihood of meeting with a positive reception.

No society is monolithic in its attitudes toward change. The Matthews-Prothro survey of black and white Southerners in the early 1960s disclosed a deep ambivalence toward change among both groups (see figure 6-1). Despite their clear group interest in changing virtually everything about the political, economic, and social institutions of the South, blacks in this sample were somewhat more skeptical of change than whites. Fewer than half of African Americans in the segregated South disagreed with the proposition that "If you start trying to change things very much, you usually make them worse." This is testimony to the fact that the desire for change cannot be

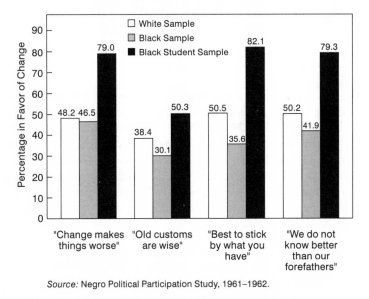

Figure 6-1   Acceptance of change in the American South

reduced to a function of one's objective status in society. At the same time, there was a much greater acceptance of change among African American college students than was found among adult respondents of either race.[2] This generational difference suggests that while there are cultural differences in acceptance of change, those differences are not immutable with the passage of time.

No matter what the traditional heritage of values in a society, there has been a powerful shift toward the embrace of change as a result of the process Deutsch (1961) called social mobilization—particularly education, urban residence, and exposure to information. In his study of the global cultural changes associated with urbanization, Inkeles (1969) found that increased education and exposure to the mass media, along with the experience of factory life, led to dramatic increases in degree of political interest,

---

[2] The full question wording is:

a. If you start trying to change things very much, you usually make them worse.

b. If something grows up over a long time, there will always be much wisdom in it.

c. It's better to stick by what you know than to be trying new things you do not really know about.

d. We must respect the work of our forefathers and not think that we know better than they did.

information, civic participation, and active citizenship orientation.[3] Inkeles concluded that "the feeling that the society and the economy need a 'total and immediate change' is more common precisely among the groups who . . . have experienced influences such as the school, the factory and the mass media."[4]

These same elements of life experience are powerful in shaping attitudes toward change in the United States. Table 6-1 shows the large effect of education on acceptance of change. In fact, the greater acceptance of change among Southern whites than among Southern blacks can be attributed solely to the effects of their higher average education levels. With education controlled in table 6-1, each group of African Americans was slightly more likely to embrace change than whites (though none of these differences are statistically significant). The high level of acceptance of change among black

TABLE 6-1
Education and the Acceptance of Change

	Index of Change Acceptance Among	
	African Americans	White Americans
Elementary education	6.1	5.0
Intermediate education	8.5	8.1
Completed high school	11.1	10.1
Beyond high school	13.1	14.7
All	8.6	10.4
(Number of cases)	(547)	(575)
Pearson's *r* with		
Education	.43	.52
Urbanization	.29	.21
Number of newpapers or magazines read	.41	.33

Source: Negro Political Participation Study, 1961–1962.

Note: The index in this table is an additive index composed of the four attitudes toward change listed in figure 6–1. The scale runs from 0 to 20, with 20 the most favorable to change. The correlations reported above with urbanization and media usage are diminished slightly when education is controlled, but they remain significant at the .01 level.

[3] Inkeles and his team of researchers studied Argentina, Chile, India, Israel, Nigeria, and Pakistan. They found that urbanization itself does not affect attitudes toward change, controlling for the influences of education, media exposure, and factory experience.

[4] Inkeles 1969: 1134. The attitude toward change was measured only in Chile and Argentina.

college students is also an artifact of their education. Those from the adult sample of African Americans with some college experience are statistically indistinguishable from the sample of college students in their acceptance of change. These data demonstrate that attitudes toward change do vary between cultures, but cultures are highly mutable in this respect. And education is a primary source of cultural mutation in the acceptance of change.

Where there is relatively little agreement that change is possible and desirable, a critical community seeking to become a social movement will find it difficult to gain an audience for its ideas. Where there is widespread education, urbanization, and exposure to the mass media, the social acceptance of change will be greater and the task of propagandizing on behalf of a specific change of cultural values is made easier. The philosophes were forced to aim their message at a tiny fraction of the French population, but some version of their ideas was accepted by much of the French citizenry before the Enlightenment century was over.

The change to change has been even more abrupt in America in the second half of the twentieth century; it would perhaps be impossible to find today any group as resistant to change as were uneducated Southerners in 1961. Optimism in the limitless possibilities of progress has undergone substantial peaks and valleys in the course of the twentieth century, and some observers believe we are now in the midst of a crisis of confidence about progress.[5] If we conceive of the acceptance of change, however, as the belief that human agency can and should be employed to improve the quality and fairness of social life, then this is a view shared by virtually the entire society. As Sztompka (1990: 249) put it, "Not the achievement but achieving, not the attainment but striving, not the finding but quest—are the marks of progress." The substantive messages coming from movement organizations may be controversial, but their underlying assumption that societies should strive for betterment through collective action is not.

Finding Societal Niches

The belief that society can be changed for the better becomes potent in fostering cultural change only when it is coupled with a social structure in which critical communities can flourish. Just as with attitudes toward change, societies vary in the extent to which they contain institutional niches that nurture critical communities.

Once again, the contrast between prerevolutionary France and contempo-

---

[5] See, e.g., Alexander and Sztompka (1990). That crisis of confidence is often described as part of the postmodern condition, though there is little evidence that the postmodern mentality has spread beyond academic circles to the wider public culture.

rary liberal democracies is instructive. It was difficult under French absolutism to be a propagator of any ideas other than those approved by the court
and the church. This was due both to restrictions on the publication of ideas
and the difficulties of earning a living as a dissident intellectual. The situation is very different today. In a contemporary democratic society the opportunity to earn a living by the production of ideas and knowledge is vastly
improved over the situation in absolutist France. Black (1967: 12) points out
"that in the most advanced countries as much as a quarter of all human and
material resources is devoted to the production and distribution of knowledge in all its forms, . . . about triple the proportion at the turn of the [twen-
tieth] century."

Contemporary societies are relatively hospitable to critical communities
because of the proliferation of institutional settings devoted to the generation
of knowledge and ideas. Institutions of higher education, charitable foundations, and, to a lesser extent, governmental support of research have in this
country all created a supportive infrastructure for critical thinking that is
without precedent in human history. Universities have been centers of critical discourse for centuries, albeit on a much smaller scale than today. Foundations have, however, only recently become significantly involved in the
production of ideas for change. They have become in essence "venture capitalists" to critical communities. The 1950 statement of principles adopted by
the Ford Foundation, described by Richard Magat (1979: 18–19) as the blue-
print for everything the foundation has since done, lists five areas for action:
world peace, economic well-being, improved education, "knowledge of factors that influence or determine human conduct," and "solution of the insis-
tent problems of an ever-changing society." Each of these provisions, but
particularly the latter one, justify foundation support for critical communities
and movement organizations.

This change-oriented agenda was not limited to the Ford Foundation. J.
Craig Jenkins (1989) reports that the proportion of foundation spending
going to social movement organizations peaked in the late 1970s at a bit
less than 1 percent. But even this shift of resources meant an increase from
less than one million dollars per year in the early 1960s to a peak of just
over $25 million in 1977. According to Jenkins (1989: 296), organizations
representing African Americans received $57 million from foundations in
this period, and another $60 million was shared among Mexican American
organizations, environmental groups, consumer organizations, public interest groups, prisoners' rights groups, and peace groups. As significant as
these amounts are, they represent only the level of foundation funding
going directly to social movement organizations. Using a broader definition
of community organizations oriented to social and political change, Alan
Rabinowitz (1990) has estimated that foundations have devoted between

one-third and one-half of their total operating revenue to change-oriented purposes.[6]

In a study of the ideologies of foundation officers, Nagai, Lerner, and Rothman (1994) found a great deal of variation in beliefs on nearly all social and political issues. Both liberal and conservative foundation officers were united by one common viewpoint, however: the conviction that desirable social change can best be achieved by fostering critical communities. According to Nagai et al. (1994: 27),

> We attribute much of sixties philanthropy to a vision that combines two ideas. The first is an expansion of the notion of a "social problem." In the 1960s, cultural deprivation, bad education, widespread disease, and war were added to poverty as social problems looking for solutions rather than situations endemic to the human condition. The second belief shaping sixties philanthropy . . . was the belief that the government had a tremendous capacity for doing good, internationally as well as domestically.

The involvement of foundations in social change has provided the seed money not only for social movement organizations but also for change-oriented research in universities, nonprofit think tanks, and for-profit research organizations. Ricci's (1993) study of think tanks—institutes dedicated to research on issues related to public policy—shows that their number expanded during the 1970s from just a few to over one hundred. Increases in research budgets at the largest think tanks were of a comparable order of magnitude. In addition to the expansion of foundation funding for policy research, Ricci points out that the growth of government programs directed at an ever-widening array of social problems has created a publicly funded demand for policy advice and program evaluation. As Weiss (1992) points out, "helping government think" has been a twentieth-century growth industry.

Think tanks are only the most politically focused part of a private sector (both for profit and nonprofit) research infrastructure that has grown significantly over the last generation. The number of for-profit research organizations engaged in product testing, market research, policy research, and forecasting expanded by 87 percent in just the five years from 1982 to 1987.[7]

The greatest expansion of research capabilities has occurred within the American universities. There were just 563 colleges in 1870, including technical and vocational schools. One hundred years later there were 2,525 colleges and universities, with an aggregate faculty that had also grown from

---

[6] Rabinowitz (1990) defines social change philanthropy as giving designed to help redress grievances or to empower citizens in autonomous organizations.

[7] *Research Services Directory* (Detroit: Gale Research Inc.) editions from 1982 and 1987.

just over 5,000 in 1870 to 729,000 in 1970.[8] As they have grown, universities have also become more research-oriented in their activities. From 1930 to 1970 research expenditures in institutions of higher education increased 120-fold, a rate well above the expansion of the total budget. Research activities accounted for only 3.5 percent of university budgets in 1930, a proportion that by 1970 had risen to 10.2 percent. If library expenditures are counted as part of the research effort of universities, then the percentage of their total budget going to research has risen from 5 to 13 percent.[9]

The growth of foundation support, the government demand for policy knowledge, and university expansion all come together in the establishment of university-based research centers that specialize in social and political issues. These research centers are subsidized by universities, typically through the provision of facilities and other infrastructure. Actual research activities, however, are carried out with the aid of grants from the government and from foundations. As the pool of research dollars from these sources has expanded over the past generation, so have the number of university research institutes.

Not all university research institutes house critical communities working on ideas for social change. Even so, they are an exceptionally benign environment for such communities. If we restrict our focus to research institutes dedicated to the study of government and policy, law, international studies, labor and industrial relations, education, and behavioral and social sciences, then the number of such institutes has grown from 412 in 1960 to 2,738 in 1994—more than a sixfold increase in just thirty-five years.[10]

The expansion of research centers connected to universities is particularly significant because their funding sources make them relatively (though not absolutely) independent of market demands. To a far greater extent than for-profit research firms, institutes connected to universities are free to explore topics at the cynosure of public concern, regardless of whether there is a profit generating potential in the results of the research. Thus, rapid growth of women's studies programs and research institutes followed mobilization of the women's movement (Davis 1991), and there was an upsurge of research programs on nuclear weapons and war during and after the nuclear freeze movement (Joseph 1993: 166–167). Table 6-2 expands these examples by showing some of the most spectacular growth areas in nonprofit research centers, most of are based in universities.

Table 6-2 shows that the total number of nonprofit research institutes grew more than fourfold between 1965 and 1977. Within this nonprofit sector,

---

[8] *Historical Statistics of the United States* (Washington, DC: U.S. Department of Commerce, Bureau of the Census, 1975), part 1, series H 689–699.

[9] *Historical Statistics of the United States*, part 2, series H 728–738, 1975.

[10] These numbers are from the *Research Centers Directory* (Detroit: Gale Research Inc., various years).

TABLE 6-2
Growth in Research Institutes

	University and Nonprofit Research Centers		For Profit Research Centers
	1965	1997	1995
	784	3,443	na
or and industrial relations	35	224	14
e, race relations, racism, prejudice, anti-Semitism	3	130	2
men, feminism[2]	0	259	7
ce, disarmament	7	98	0
vironment, ecology, pollution, recycling	54	1,237	985
d raid	0	64	4
enhouse effect	0	22	0

ource: Data on nonprofit institutes come from *Research Centers Directory* (Detroit: Gale Research, 1965,
7); for-profit institutes are listed in *Research Services Directory*, 6th ed. (Detroit: Gale Research, 1995).
'All" includes only research institutes in the areas of government, education, labor relations, law, regional
area studies, and the social sciences.
ncludes institutes dedicated to specific themes such as women in business, law, politics, religion, literature,

the most dramatic growth areas are linked to those issues on which critical communities and social movements have been most active. In areas such as race relations, women's studies, the environment and peace research, a substantial university-based research infrastructure has been created virtually from scratch. The areas of most rapid growth in the development of new institutes have been in precisely those fields where cultural change has been concentrated.

Dependence on research grants means that establishment of an institute is not likely to occur at the very beginning of the development of a critical community, but rather only when there has been some progress toward putting a particular issue on the social and political agenda. For example, McCrea and Markle (1989: 117) find that foundation funding of issues related to the prevention of nuclear war rose threefold (from $16 million to $52 million) between 1982 and 1984—after the nuclear freeze movement demonstrated its mobilizing capacity. And yet, the existence by 1997 of eighty-six institutes dedicated to study of the greenhouse effect and to acid rain suggests that the period of critical community incubation required to establish university research institutes may be relatively short. Although the theoretical possibility of a greenhouse effect was first broached in 1827 by the French mathematician Baron Fourier, the contemporary research agenda dates only from 1975, when V. Ramanathan of the National Center for Atmospheric Research produced the first research paper incorporating the effects of methane and chloroflurocarbons (CFCs) into existing models of atmospheric warming.[11] The research agenda on acid rain is of about the same vintage, having been called to scientific attention in a paper presented at the United Nations Conference on the Human Environment in 1972 (Regens and Rycroft, 1988). Within a decade, research efforts on both acid rain and the greenhouse effect had yielded most of the basic data that shape our current understanding of these processes. These two cases, then, demonstrate how quickly a research program can be created around a new concept or a theorized physical process. The government-foundation-university research nexus is capable of rapid response to the emergence of new concerns.[12]

A similar analysis of for-profit research institutes shows that they do not follow new social trends to the same degree, with the significant exception of research on the environment. The private firms enumerated in table 6-2 are focused on themes unlikely to further social change. The for-profit research firms connected to race and gender, for example, typically generate studies that enable them to recommend marketing strategies for selling products to women and various minorities.[13] Only in the case of the environment has a significant private market for research emerged—testimony to the power of Environmental Protection Agency (EPA) regulations to force firms to seek the assistance of environmental consultants for information on regulatory requirements and compliance strategies The for-profit environmental sector continues to expand, with a tripling in the number of firms between 1987 and 1995. However, the exigencies of profitability inevitably structure the kinds of topics that are addressed within the broad category of environmentalism. The problem of acid rain, for example, which affects the commercial value of forested lands, is the focus of a small number of for-profit firms. No firm has yet found a way to make a profit from the study of global climate change.

That seductive curmudgeon William F. Buckley (1993: 99) once asked,

---

[11] Prior models dating from the late nineteenth century had considered only the effects of carbon dioxide (Arrhenius 1896). The addition of methane and chlorofluorocarbons to those models made a dramatic difference in projections of the rate of accumulation of greenhouse gases, according to Oppenheimer and Boyle (1990: 34).

[12] Congressional attention also lagged the first research reports on acid rain and the greenhouse effect by just ten years. The first congressional hearings on acid rain took place in 1983, and continued at an average of twenty hearings per year through 1990. The first hearings on the greenhouse effect took place in 1984, and there was an average of thirty hearings per year between 1989 and 1992.

[13] There are exceptions to this rule. One for-profit research firm listed under "women and feminism" in table 6-2 focuses on sexual harassment, as do eight of the nonprofit research firms.

"Have you noticed the anomaly? If there is a dumb thing to be done or said, it will almost always be done or said in a college or university." The comment is on target, but it misses the positive social value attached to saying and doing dumb things.[14] The defining trait of intellectuals, according to Lewis Coser, is that they "never seem satisfied with things as they are" (cited in Eyerman, Svensson, and Söderqvist 1987: 5), and it is precisely that relentless dissatisfaction that is so productive of new ideas. Dissatisfied people oriented to the development of new ways of looking at the world have an unprecedented number of career opportunities in America today, from which they can do the conceptual and empirical work necessary to define their sources of discontent. The research apparatus that universities have developed over the past generation stands at the center of a government- and foundation-funded nexus that has greatly expanded the capacity of American society to develop, explore, and test competing claims about social and political problems. It is here that critical communities are able to go beyond the realm of speculation and to develop their ideas in the form of arguments and evidence likely to be persuasive to the academic and political communities.

The net result of these changes has been an expansion in the number of social institutions within which one can live comfortably while developing new perspectives on emerging social and political issues. The significance of this expansion can be seen from a simple thought experiment. Imagine the life of Jean-Jacques Rousseau were he to have lived in the latter half of the twentieth century. Rousseau became a literary and philosophical sensation in Paris in 1750 with the publication of his *Discourse on the Arts and Sciences*. He was a prolific writer for the rest of his life, the author of philosophical tracts such as *The Social Contract* and philosophically driven novels such as *The New Heloïse*, which was the eighteenth century's number one best seller. Even while he was alive, Rousseau was lauded as one of the leading intellects of the century. He was someone to whom people wrote for advice on a wide variety of topics and concerns, much the way people wrote to Einstein in the twentieth century.

Despite his fame and intellectual influence, Rousseau's life was always marked by concern over material survival. He lived from the patronage of others, usually withdrawn when he became estranged from his patron. His success as an author brought him little relief from reliance on others. The lifelong experience of dependence on others may have contributed to Rousseau's paranoia in later life, which robbed him of his friends. Rousseau died a celebrated figure, but alone and in poverty. It takes little imagination to picture the very different life he would have led as a social critic and celebrity intellectual in the twentieth century.

---

[14] Or, at any rate, novel things, which have a better than average chance of striking many people as dumb.

REACHING AN AUDIENCE

The development of cultural attitudes linking change to progress has led to high levels of societal demand for the change-oriented ideas that critical communities espouse. The social structure of contemporary American society, particularly the expansion of universities and research institutes funded by prochange foundations and an activist government, makes it easier for intellectual communities to supply these critical ideas. The result is an enhanced rate of social change that is driven both by a growing number of critical communities and by an increasingly receptive society.

This tale of the change to change has thus far left unanswered the question of how the ideas of critical communities reach the wider society. How do small critical communities become large social movements; how are the supply of ideas and the demand for ideas connected to each other? It is at this point that the issues of movement mobilization described in chapters 4 and 5 become significant for the process of cultural change. The existence of mass mobilization attracts public attention to an issue area. As movement organizations get involved with the issue, they activate their formal and informal networks of communication. Through their newsletters and community-based organizations, movements help spread the ideas of the critical community.

Movements are the driving force behind the spread of (suitably adapted) critical community ideas, but they cannot succeed if they restrict themselves to their own networks. To reach a wider audience, movement organizations must also conform to the opportunities for wider communication of ideas that exist in a given time and place. As Hilgartner and Bosk (1988) point out, public attention is a scarce resource for which there are many claimants. To get an issue recognized as a social problem, movement organizations must work with and compete against a variety of other social institutions that also participate in selecting, defining, packaging, and presenting issues for public discussion.

To get their ideas before the public, the philosophes relied on the *salons* and on novels and plays that expressed their themes. In nineteenth-century America, the common practice was to send movement-trained lecturers from town to town, bringing new ideas and perspectives to a populace that did not have the option of staying home and watching television. Thus the pre–Civil War labor movement was substantially fed by itinerant preachers who used the Christian gospel to condemn the wage exploitation of early capitalism (Lazerow 1993). This tactic was later expanded upon by the Knights of Labor, whose lecturers preached the nobility of toil and, as Fink (1983: xiii) put it, "helped sustain a national debate over the social implications of industrial capitalism." The abolitionist and temperance movements also trained their own lecturers to fan out across the country, delivering speeches on the evils of slavery and alcohol.[15] Some of their lecturers were women who later went on to become prominent in the suffrage movement.

If the practice of sending lecturers on a circuit of the cities and towns of America has fallen by the wayside, the arsenal of ways in which contemporary movements may spread their message is nonetheless significantly expanded. Of particular importance are the mass media. With the size of their audience and the sheer volume of ideas they can communicate, contemporary media networks magnify the rate of social change over anything conceivable prior to this century. They make it easier for movement organizations to project their ways of looking at the world beyond the boundaries of the movement itself.

One part of the expanded capacity to spread ideas comes from the growth of the print media. Indicative of the expansion of all forms of printed information is the growth in the number of published books. There were two thousand books published in the United States in 1880, compared to thirty-six thousand in 1970—a doubling in the volume of volumes every twenty years.[16] But sheer numbers tell only part of the story. A more detailed breakdown of the types of books published from 1950 to 1970 shows that traditional topics such as biography and fiction have not quite doubled in number during that period. Books in the areas of medicine, science, and technology increased in number by 340 percent. Books in the social sciences increased by 865 percent. These figures suggest that the expansion of technical information has outrun the overall expansion of book publication, and the expansion of information about society has in turn substantially outrun the expansion of information about the physical world.

To the traditional channels of books, essays, newspapers, and magazines, there has been added in the past one hundred years an entirely new range of nonprint media. The suddenness with which these alternative media of mass communications have been deployed is startling, beginning with magnetic tape recording and radio at the beginning of the twentieth century, and concluding with development of the Internet at the end of the century. These technologies increase the volume, speed, and types of information that can be disseminated to a population. They enable us to gather images and information about situations and conditions far removed from our immediate environment.

Would-be agents of cultural change must be centrally concerned with their relationship to the mass media. Although research shows that the mass media do not necessarily determine what we think, they are a powerful force in helping determine what subjects we think about and how we think about

---

[15] Abolitionist lecturers restricted their travels to the North, knowing that they would be killed if they ventured into the slave states.

[16] *Historical Statistics of the United States*, part 2, Series R 192-217.

them (McCombs and Shaw 1972; MacKuen and Coombs 1981; Winter and Eyal 1981; Iyengar, Peters, and Kinder 1982; Graber 1988). Specifically, the media determine the criteria of judgment deemed appropriate to thinking about the issue (Iyengar and Kinder 1987; Neuman, Just, and Crigler 1992: 17–19; Snow and Benford 1988). These are the media functions that Graber (1984) designates as agenda setting (determining what is important) and agenda building (supplying a context in which to think about an important issue). As we shall see, the means of influencing agenda setting are not the same as the means of influencing agenda building.

Agenda Setting: Gaining Media Attention

The first task in harnessing the power of the media to a particular subject is, logically enough, gaining media attention. Only after media gatekeepers have been persuaded that an issue is important enough to merit attention in the first place can the matter of *how* the issue is presented be given consideration.

In considering the factors that attract media attention to an issue, it is useful to distinguish between acute and chronic issues. Acute issues are marked by sudden changes in the environment caused by wars, natural disasters, or outbreaks of civil violence. Chronic issues are ongoing problems such as poverty, pollution, and crime. While acute issues (above a threshold) are automatically considered to be news and are covered as such in the media, chronic issues are treated as news only if there is some particular peg or angle that makes the issue newsworthy at a particular moment.

Studies of the correspondence between public concern about an issue and media attention to it show a high correlation in the case of acute issues (R^2 in the range of .5 to .7 for various issues, according to Neuman 1990). The correlation between media attention and public concern is not as high in the case of chronic issues (Neuman finds an R^2 ranging from .18 to .32). The implication of this finding is that both the public and representatives of the media have more discretion in deciding when an ongoing issue is worthy of media attention and public concern. External influence on media coverage of acute issues is likely to be negligible, as such coverage is overwhelmingly event-driven. But there is much greater ambiguity in the relationship between events and the coverage of chronic issues. Journalists and their editors must look for some clues other than events themselves to determine when to pay attention to chronic issues.

Critical communities and movement activists are highly likely to view their issues as chronic, though they may also recognize moments of acute crisis. The development of an ideological perspective on an issue, itself a central activity of the critical community, includes viewing the issue as connected to institutional structures and everyday behaviors in the polity and society. Critical communities do not define their issues as isolated problems. They develop a viewpoint that instead sees manifestations of the issue every-where—the very definition of a chronic problem.

The task of translating the chronic problem as described by the critical community into an acute problem that will attract media attention is the province of the social and political movement. The very existence of move-ment protest in either the social or the political arena signals that an issue is controversial, and controversy is one of the means by which a problem comes to be defined as acute rather than as chronic. As Gitlin (1980: 42) put it, "Editors take arrests as a sign that something significant has taken place." On matters ranging from slavery in the 1830s to alcohol-related traffic deaths in the 1980s, public clamor has generated news coverage of long-term problems that are suddenly seen as acute.

While movements are specialists at generating controversy, journalists are specialists at ferreting it out. Particularly when the survival of a news organi-zation depends on profitability (e.g., the number of subscribers or viewers), it will search for unusual events, new crises, or novel perspectives on issues. A competitive market for audience, whether an elevated market or one ap-pealing to least-common-denominator tastes, creates an almost insatiable de-mand for controversy (Goldenberg 1975).

Reporters who specialize in a subject area will routinely monitor trade journals and specialized publications, including those of the critical commu-nity and of movement organizations, to learn about new developments and controversies (Kielbowicz and Scherer 1986: 88). Analysis by Strodthoff et al. (1985) of more than three thousand articles on the environment in spe-cialized and general interest magazines between 1959 and 1979 showed that until the late 1960s the general interest magazines picked up stories first developed in the specialized magazines. By 1970, after development of a large movement, the general interest magazines actually led the specialist magazines in their treatment of such topics as energy conservation, appropri-ate technology, and management of natural resources. Critical communities and movements both supply goods that the mass media seek.

Of course, some controversies are more newsworthy than others. Those movements most successful in gaining media attention are able to portray their causes graphically and visually, rather than simply proclaiming their views. Frank Wilson (1993) reports on a natural experiment that testifies to the importance of designing protest tactics that will make a good news story. Fishermen in France and Britain decided in 1993 to protest the import to their countries of "cheap" fish from Russian trawlers. The French fishermen carried out their protest by confiscating the offending fish at the docks, dous-ing them with kerosene and setting fire to them. British fishermen decided to blockade the mouths of British harbors to prevent Russian fishing boats from entering. The British protest was, if anything, more extensive, better organized, and more effective in keeping Russian fish off the market than was the French protest. But fish bonfires photograph much better than do fishing boats lined across the mouth of a harbor, and the French protest received substantially more coverage than the British protest.

The symbiosis between movement tactics and the visual and narrative demands of the media may be the reason why movement organizers some-times count the media among their closest allies (Dalton 1994: 185–189). There is, however, an obvious drawback in portraying one's cause in a pro-test idiom attractive to the media. The need for colorful and dramatic pro-tests can easily make the movement appear to be extreme, unrealistic, or even something to be feared. The dilemma is that representatives of chal-lenging perspectives "must contend with other would-be claimants for [me-dia] attention at the back door, finding some gimmick or act of disorder to force their way in. But when they do so, they enter defined as upstarts. . . . Those who dress up in costume to be admitted to the media's party will not be allowed to change before being photographed."[17]

In more prosaic terms, the secret of movement access to the media is to engage in colorful protest, but that strategy also ensures that the colorful protest is what will be reported about the movement. The media hunger for dramatic events makes the movement appear to be more aggressive, destruc-tive, and perhaps even violent than it actually is. Even worse, as Gitlin (1980: chap. 5) points out, is the danger that the movement organization will become what the media portray it as being. A reputation for extremism may attract extremists. Media focus on a single leader will generate organiza-tional tensions about the role of that leader. Gitlin observes that few move-ment organizations are prepared for the acceleration of attention and activity that follows from being cast into the glare of the media spotlight. Organiza-tions such as SDS and SNCC were forced almost overnight to handle a vastly increased volume of inquiries, volunteers, and requests for position statements on a variety of national issues. This is one aspect of what Gitlin (1980: 241) refers to as "the contraction of time in a media-saturated soci-ety."

Although the effects of media attention may disrupt the developing rou-tines of a movement organization, it is worth noting that these disruptions at least mean that the movement is on the media agenda.[18] In fact, gaining

---

[17] Gamson and Wolfsfeld 1993: 122. Sometimes the costume required to enter the media party is a literal one. Jerry Rubin's wearing of an American Revolutionary costume to testify before the House Committee on Un-American Activities was an effective means of putting forward the argument that HUAC itself was un-American, a statement that Gitlin (1980: 171) labels an "act of devout derision." On media bias in the coverage of movement activities, see also McCarthy, McPhail, and Smith 1996.

[18] In an insightful book devoted to the problems of media attention for movement organiza-tions, Gitlin (1980: 242–243) makes only a brief and almost apologetic note of the fact that

access to the media is in some ways the easiest part of the task of communicating with a wide audience. The mobilization of a protest movement is interpreted as evidence of controversy on some issue. But the interest of the media in dramatic instances of protest inevitably colors the way in which the movement is portrayed. Having gained media access through its protests, advocates of a new issue perspective must now confront the problem of conveying their ideas about how the problem should be defined and what its remedies are. The distinction between ideas and events creates a tension that brings us to the second problem facing advocates of new issue perspectives: agenda building.

Agenda Building: Conveying New Perspectives

Although it is to the advantage of advocates of new issue perspectives to have their issue certified as controversial, it is not necessarily to the advantage of those who actually raise the controversy. When policies become controversial, the "balance norm" of journalism is evoked. This norm requires journalists to go beyond official positions on controversial issues by including statements from critics of the official policy, in order to represent "the opposing viewpoint."

Having evoked the balance norm, journalists must then decide who will speak for the opposition viewpoint. By implication, they decide just what "the" opposition viewpoint is. The most common choice is to contrast the views of leaders in the Democratic and Republican parties, particularly when the source of the controversy is elite disagreement. This pattern of coverage is a consequence of the news gathering routines employed by journalists. As Leon Sigal (1973) makes clear through his study of the sources of news stories in the *New York Times* and the *Washington Post*, less than 20 percent of sources for national and international page one stories are nongovernmental. This reliance on governmental sources is in turn the result of the organizational routines of news gathering, in which nearly 60 percent of news sources come from official reports, press conferences, and press releases (Sigal 1973: 119–130; see also Tuchman 1973; Gans 1979; Behr and Iyengar 1985; Weaver and Elliot 1985).

In an organizational setting where the definition of news is largely the definition of what governmental officials are saying and doing, the surest way for others to be heard is to demonstrate that governmental actions (or inactions) are controversial beyond the confines of the government itself. In other words, if controversy is found in the social as well as the political

---

media attention is, in the end, helpful to the movement cause. "It [media attention] diffused some of the ideas, some of the concerns, some of the terms of the movement. It diffused them in an oversimplified and often distorted and debased form—in a diffuse form, one might say—but it did diffuse them."

arenas—if there is public protest on the matter—then the balance norm is likely to send journalists beyond governmental circles to find commentary and explanation. The most likely beneficiaries of this decision are not leaders of the movement organization that has created the protest, but rather leaders of the critical community. The journalist's rule is to choose "responsible critics" of the existing policy, people with positions or titles that justify the decision to quote their views (Tuchman 1974). The media may even make a point of contrasting the words of responsible critics with the actions of "irresponsible" or "naive" protesters (Rojecki 1997). As Gitlin (1980: 210–217) points out, the "moderation-as-alternative-to-militancy" image is a standard one in the media reporting of a social movement. Gamson (1988: 235) has summarized this tendency by noting "When demonstrators are arrested at Seabrook, phones ring at the Union of Concerned Scientists."

The predominance of governmental sources over nongovernmental sources and, among nongovernmental sources, the predominance of experts from critical communities over movement organizers are both reflected in a study by Entman and Rojecki (1993) of coverage of the nuclear freeze movement in the *New York Times*, *Washington Post*, *Newsweek*, and *Time*. They searched all stories about the freeze to see how often these media quoted leading movement spokespersons (Randall Forsberg, Randy Kehler, and Roger Molander) and government spokespersons (Alexander Haig, George Schultz, Caspar Weinberger, and Ronald Reagan). Just under 12 percent of the quotations were from the movement sources; the remaining 88 percent of quotations were by key members of the Reagan administration. Indeed, 87 percent of the stories about the freeze contained no citation of a movement spokesperson at all. As Entman and Rojecki (1993: 170) conclude, the media portrayal of the nuclear freeze movement "was largely an official record of elite views and reactions to a nearly invisible movement."

There was nonetheless, some commentary on the freeze proposal from a perspective critical of the Reagan administration. Entman and Rojecki (1993) found that the most commonly cited figure was Roger Molander, director of Ground Zero. Molander, a former nuclear strategy adviser on the National Security Council, clearly possessed expert credentials. Moreover, Ground Zero was an organization dedicated to grass-roots education on the destructive potential of nuclear war. The choice of Roger Molander to be the single most visible critic of the president's nuclear weapons policy must nonetheless have been painful to freeze organizers, for Molander was also opposed to the freeze.

The second most commonly cited critical figure was Dr. Helen Caldicott, leader of Physicians for Social Responsibility. Although Dr. Caldicott was in favor of the freeze proposal, her approach to the issue was not typical of the wider movement. Dr. Caldicott used the image of physician as healer to focus her critique on the human consequences of nuclear war rather than on proposals for limiting the nuclear arsenals of the superpowers. From the Nuclear Weapons Freeze Campaign itself, national coordinator Randy Kehler was quoted three times on front page articles, and Randall Forsberg, author of the freeze proposal and a prominent strategist in the movement, was never cited.

The peak of newsworthiness for the freeze movement was the New York demonstration of about 750,000 in June 1982. Both CBS News and the *New York Times* reports on the demonstration led with the Caldicott sound bite that "We're thinking of our babies. There are no Communist babies; there are no capitalist babies. A baby is a baby is a baby" (Meyer 1990: 129). More substantive discussions of the freeze proposal presented at the demonstration by Forsberg and Kehler were not cited by either CBS or the *New York Times*.

The pattern of press coverage of the nuclear freeze movement suggests that there is a division of labor in publicizing critical perspectives. Movement organizations demonstrate controversy and hence make an issue newsworthy. Credentialed members of the critical communities are then called on to interpret the controversy for a media-consuming public. The credibility to be cited as a critical expert comes from having a titled position in one of the recognized niches of social criticism, such as a professional organization or research institute.[19] While agenda setting generally requires the adoption of controversial tactics, agenda building requires expert credentials. Hence, those who raise the controversy are not the ones called on to explain it. Movement organizations typically specialize in being unruly, whereas critical communities specialize in being expert.

Maintaining Access

The orientation of the news media to acute issues brings with it a pattern of attention cycles. Today's controversy is replaced by another tomorrow; to each issue comes its fifteen minutes of fame. If gaining access to the media is difficult for critical communities, and if conveying a substantive critique is even more difficult, then maintaining media attention is the most difficult task of all. This is the problem that Downs (1972) has dubbed "the issue attention cycle."

The primary tool that movements have to prolong their media exposure is to escalate their tactics (Kielbowicz and Scherer 1986; Dalton 1994: 188). This escalation tendency was first described by Todd Gitlin (1980: 182) in connection with the 1960s student movement. "Where a picket line might have been news in 1965, it took tear gas and bloodied heads to make head-

---

[19] The media have of course other requirements as well, such as the ability to convey a point of view clearly, succinctly, and in an interesting way.

lines in 1968. If the last demonstration was counted at 100,000, the next would have to number 200,000; otherwise it would be downplayed or framed as a sign of the movement's waning."

Gitlin's observations echo precisely the pattern discovered by Funkhauser in his analysis of newspaper stories about urban riots in America in the late 1960s. Funkhauser found that the ratio of riots to stories was 4 to 1 in 1967, 12 to 1 in 1968, 16 to 1 in 1969, and 65 to 1 in 1970 (cited in Graber 1984: 78). Although urban riots peaked in frequency in 1968, the number of stories had already peaked in 1967, when the issue was fresh.

The increasing threshold of newsworthiness makes it difficult to sustain media attention without undertaking activities that will tend to put ever greater distance between the movement and the social mainstream. Even with movement radicalization, though, media interest generates at best a temporary spotlight on the movement and its issues. The brevity of media attention is not a great handicap to a movement campaigning for reform in the political arena, because its objectives may be met in the short term. The dilemma becomes more acute when the movement seeks the kind of change in cultural values that can only be obtained over the longer term. When movements seek to use the media to engage the wider society in a debate about values, the tendency to be portrayed in increasingly radical terms presents a serious handicap. This brings us back to the question with which this chapter began: how do critical communities and movement organizations convey their thinking to a wide audience within the society?

Transforming Issue Perspectives

The orientation to acute crises and the rules of expert access characteristic of the news media create a cycle of attention to social movements that overemphasizes the aggressiveness of their tactics, relies for commentary primarily on sources external to the movement, and is susceptible to rapid decay as the media turn to new issues. Movement activists often complain about the media treatment of their cause, a frustration that unites them with presidents, celebrities, and every other object of media scrutiny. The generality of these complaints suggests that patterns of media attention are not driven by ideological bias (as is generally alleged in movement circles) so much as they are by organizational routines and the nature of the market for news.[20]

---

[20] This does not mean that the media approach their topics and sources without bias. Entman and Rojecki (1993) find that the scrutiny of freeze movement organizations for their expertise on the issues, their representativeness of the broader public, and their internal unity was far more exacting than the scrutiny of Reagan administration officials on the same dimensions. Thus, for example, President Reagan's one-liners about the Soviet Union and arms control made him the Great Communicator; comparable slogans from the freeze movement were taken as a sign of being simplistic. Entman and Rojecki (1993) report further that administration officials

These general caveats, however, should not lead us to an overly bleak assessment of the potential for disseminating critical issue perspectives via the mass media. Although critical communities and movements are not likely to be portrayed fully or sympathetically, their issues may be. When an issue appears to be a matter of broad public concern (or when it has the potential to become so), the media will seek to report on the issue itself, as well as on the protest events that have pushed the issue onto the public agenda. Yet, because it is a new issue or perspective, journalists will be forced to draw upon critical community understandings of the issue to frame their own reporting of it. To borrow an example developed by William Gamson and his colleagues (1988; 1989; 1993), when nuclear power became controversial, media representatives had to learn new considerations that could be applied to nuclear energy. To the dominant existing image of faith in advanced technology were added considerations of cost effectiveness, holding the nuclear industry and electric utilities accountable for the public safety, and the merits of "soft energy paths," including energy conservation and development of energy sources that are safer, environmentally sound, and renewable.

We have already seen in the case of the Equal Rights Amendment a comparable expansion of the scope of media attention from governmental decisions to coverage of movement activities, and then still further to coverage of a wide range of related social activities and events (see chapter 2). Early in the 1970s ERA stories focused on the institutional process of passing the constitutional amendment, but the ERA later became a vehicle for media consideration of a wide variety of issues connected to the social, economic, and political equality of women.

These examples suggest the kind of media attention critical communities and movement organizations must seek. Once an issue is recognized as being controversial, it becomes a routine part of the news. The elements of controversy—the new claims being advanced by the critical community— are woven into a wide variety of news stories. Thus, Baumgartner and Jones (1993: 65) demonstrate that the number of news stories about nuclear energy rose fivefold between 1967 and 1973, during which time the percentage of positive stories about nuclear energy fell from over seventy to under five. Similarly, between 1978 and 1982 the number of articles connected to the ERA was maintained at almost the level of the period 1975–1977, despite the impending demise of the amendment itself. This occurred because the ERA had become embedded in a wide variety of controversies concerning

---

were said to "think" when they stated their positions, while statements from movement representatives were characterized in more emotional terms. Thus, "Paul Nitze thinks that an arms control agreement may be possible within two years," whereas "Roger Molander fears this will not be the case."

equality for women. When attention to a controversial issue becomes part of the routine news agenda, the media pattern is one of continuous coverage with regular spikes of increased attention.[21] It is a pattern generated by viewing an issue as chronic with periodic acute episodes: the chronic nature of the problem leads to continuous coverage of low intensity, and the acute crises produce peaks of attention.

In sum, the role of a movement and critical community in setting and building the media agenda is to accomplish three tasks. First, the issue must be shown to be controversial, a task that usually falls to movement organizations. Second, journalists must be able to identify periodic acute crises, a matter in which the movement and the critical community are both involved. Third, journalists must identify the underlying chronic crisis in terms compatible with the critical community–movement perspective on the issue. This is a task preeminently given to those members of the critical community with expert credentials and an ability to package ideas in the forms needed for media transmission.

These are the conditions that enable a new issue perspective to become part of the routine agenda of the mass media. If the issue were seen in acute terms only, it would disappear from the media agenda as soon as the acute phase is over. What is worse, even during the acute phase media attention will be trained more on the controversy surrounding the immediate issue than on the systemic critique applied to the issue in movement circles. Media channels contribute to the diffusion of a new issue perspective only if they accept a "chronic plus acute" view of the issue.

AGENDA SETTING AND BUILDING: THE CASE OF SEXUAL HARASSMENT

We saw in chapter 3 that sexual harassment was the subject of regulatory attention beginning in 1980, and that it became the focus of a wider social debate in October 1991. Because of the clear boundary in social awareness marked by the Clarence Thomas confirmation hearings, sexual harassment is a particularly good case for examining the ways in which media coverage changes when an issue comes to be seen as chronic plus acute.

As we have seen, the key problem facing advocates of any new issue perspective is how to get the issue accepted as a problem that has both acute and chronic features. It cannot be taken for granted that a major acute episode, such as the Thomas-Hill hearings, will cause this to happen. The first question we must answer, then, is whether the Thomas-Hill hearings, which generated so much publicity in October 1991, also resulted in sexual harassment being placed on the routine agenda of the news media. Accusations of

---

[21] For nuclear energy, see the data in Baumgartner and Jones 1993: 65; for the ERA, see table 2-2 and figure 2-2.

sleaze in high places are guaranteed to obtain an audience, and so such accusations are covered with substantial consistency in different media outlets. Did media attention to this episode also mark a longer-term shift in coverage of sexual harassment?

Figure 6-2 maps the series of peaks and valleys of attention given to sexual harassment in the *New York Times* between January 1990 and December 1993.[22] The eye-catching spike in the middle of the graph is composed almost exclusively of stories about the Clarence Thomas–Anita Hill hearings held by the Senate Judiciary Committee in October 1991. Other spikes in the figure correspond to particular events of a lesser magnitude, including the Mike Tyson rape case in the spring of 1990, harassment of a female reporter in the New England Patriots' locker room in the autumn of 1990, harassment of military and civilian women at the Navy's Tailhook convention, and the charges of sexual harassment against Senator Packwood beginning in 1992 and continuing throughout 1993.

This pattern of attention spikes is the result of coverage of sexual harassment as a series of acute episodes. The frequency of the acute phases is the same before and after the Hill-Thomas watershed, occurring with remarkable regularity three times per year. There are nonetheless two important changes in media attention after the Hill-Thomas hearings. Each media spike is higher than was the case before October 1991, indicating an increased level of media attention given to the issue in each acute phase. This does not by itself indicate a watershed in media coverage of sexual harassment, since it could be argued that the specific issues arising after the Hill-Thomas hearings simply happened to be more newsworthy than those arising in 1990 and 1991.[23]

The second way in which media attention to sexual harassment changed after 1991 is that coverage became a constant, even between acute phases. Media attention to the issue returned essentially to zero between each episode during 1990 and 1991. Beginning in 1992, media attention to sexual harassment between acute phases remained at a level comparable with the attention given to each acute crisis prior to October 1991. The nonacute rate

[22] Of course, an analysis of the *New York Times* cannot stand in for a wider analysis of all the mass media forms that shape popular culture. The *Times* seeks an elite audience, and it places journalistic values above entertainment values to a relatively great extent. However, wider tracings of media attention patterns, for example, through the *Reader's Guide to Periodical Literature*, show patterns of attention to sexual harassment closely parallel to that of the *New York Times*.

[23] The increase in attention paid to each acute episode may be due to the tendency for the focus of the pre–Thomas hearings stories to be on sports figures, whereas after the Thomas hearings it was more likely to be on military officers or politicians. Since formal complaints of sexual harassment number in the thousands, journalists have a great deal of choice in which cases to publicize. It is possible that journalists came to believe as a result of the Hill-Thomas hearings that stories of sexual harassment in government would command popular interest.

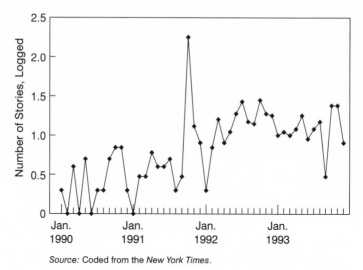

Source: Coded from the *New York Times*.

Figure 6-2   *New York Times* attention to sexual harassment, 1990–1993

of media coverage settled in at between nine and twelve stories per month beginning in 1992, compared with the rate of one to two stories per month prior to Hill-Thomas.[24] This increase in the "low intensity" rate of coverage suggests that the issue has come to be seen as a chronic problem—a point that is central to the critical community's own analysis of sexual harassment.[25]

The final bit of evidence from figure 6-2 on the transformation of sexual harassment in the media concerns the attention spike in October 1992. This is the "Thomas echo," a burst of stories occasioned by the anniversary of the Hill-Thomas hearings. It was the first attention spike that was largely unrelated to a current claim of sexual harassment. Nor were the stories that composed this spike simply a rehash of the hearings themselves, or an update on the lives of Justice Thomas and Professor Hill. The anniversary spike (the largest of 1992) was instead devoted to more general issues concerning sexual harassment, and to the question of whether conditions for working women were improving as a result of the attention given to the Hill-Thomas case.

The existence of the anniversary spike suggests that the Hill-Thomas hear-

[24] There were 61 articles on 34 different news stories in the twenty-one months prior to the Hill-Thomas hearings. In the fourteen months after the Hill-Thomas hearings, there were 222 articles on 103 different news stories. (These figures are for news stories only; that is, they exclude feature stories, editorials, and the like). These numbers suggest that the Hill-Thomas hearings encouraged more people to make public accusations of sexual harassment, and that those accusations were in turn more likely to be considered newsworthy.

[25] Rubin (1994) finds that attention to environmental problems in the *New York Times* made a comparable transition from isolated episodes to continuous (chronic) coverage beginning in 1965.

ings have become what Bennett and Lawrence (1994) call a "news icon": "a powerful condensational image, arising out of a news event, which is introduced into coverage of other events and which evokes primary cultural themes . . . contradictions and tensions." As Bennett and Lawrence observe, news icons are historical markers of an acute crisis that first introduces some theme or problem to the public. The news icon becomes a symbol of that wider theme, serving as a shorthand for the specific issue as well as a nest of related ideas and claims associated with the issue.[26]

The Hill-Thomas hearings served just this function for the issue of sexual harassment. News articles at the time were not restricted to accounts of the hearings, but included features and background on the concept itself. Public opinion polls and person-on-the-street interviews were used to convey the range of experience with sexual harassment as well as reactions to the Hill-Thomas hearings. There was also coverage of related issues such as problems of protecting the privacy and the rights of both accuser and accused. Some stories even delved into the question of how the word "harassment" should be pronounced.

This broadening of coverage is shown in table 6-3, which rests on a tripartite distinction between news reports (accounts of events that took place on the prior day), feature articles (essays that discuss linkages between events or give the historical background of a current event), and opinion articles (in the form of editorials, op-ed pieces, and letters to the editor). Compared with the periods preceding or following it, the Hill-Thomas hearings drew an unprecedented amount of feature article and opinion attention, including fifty-four editorials, op-ed essays, and letters, more than half of all such pieces printed during the 1990–1993 period. The greater significance of the hearings, though, lies in the fact that coverage of sexual harassment issues never returned fully to the patterns prior to those hearings. The intensity of media coverage of sexual harassment created by the Hill-Thomas hearings declined after October 1991, but there were permanent alterations in the type of newspaper stories on the subject.

Table 6-3 shows that the number of feature articles and the number of opinion pieces both increased in the total proportion of stories covered after the Hill-Thomas hearings, compared with numbers before the hearings. The *Times* was in effect engaged in a wider analysis of sexual harassment in society, with articles on its legal history, its conceptual scope, its causes, efforts in particular communities or organizations to reduce the problem, and so forth. This transition from news issue to feature material made possible a more systemic analysis of sexual harassment.

---

[26] The example developed by Bennett and Lawrence is the *Mobro*, a garbage scow from Long Island that wandered the seas for three months in 1987 looking for a port that would accept its cargo.

TABLE 6-3
Types of Press Coverage of Sexual Harassment, 1990–1993 (in percent)

Story Type (Number)	January 1990 to September 1991	October 1991	November 1991 to December 1993
News: reporting of daily events (397)	87.2	60.1	64.9
Analysis: feature essay, review of events or issue (109)	7.7	11.2	21.6
Opinion: editorial, op-ed, letter to editor (103)	5.1	28.6	13.4
Total (609)	100.0	99.9	99.9
Number of stories	79	188	342

Source: Content analysis of all articles in the New York Times indexed under sexual harassment, January 1990 through December 1993.

Coverage of sexual harassment as a series of acute crises brought on by the inappropriate behavior of individuals had created in the pre-Thomas era a pattern of peaks of attention focused on events, with no coverage between crises. Adoption of the systemic view of sexual harassment has not only generated more continuous coverage but has also led to a different kind of coverage. Systemic problems demand some sort of larger perspective, the elements of a causal explanation. For the New York Times to reflect a causal analysis of sexual harassment, it was necessary to broaden coverage of the issue from accounts of particular instances to an integrated (even stylized or synthetic) narrative that articulates a chronic, structural perspective on the issue.

In other words, the shift of emphasis from news to analysis brought with it a shift in the most prominent aspects of sexual harassment cases. When covering sexual harassment as a news event, the focus tends to be on the dispute between a plaintiff and an accused person. The shift to analysis and opinion brings with it more attention to such issues as the scope and boundaries of sexual harassment, and why sexual harassment appears to be more prevalent in some institutions than others (universities, sports, political life, and the military have come under particular scrutiny).

Figure 6-3 shows that these shifts of attention are reflected in the types of people who are quoted in stories on sexual harassment. Prior to the Hill-Thomas hearings, the focus on sexual harassment as discrete episodes of wrongdoing led to a high rate of citations of judges or others charged with

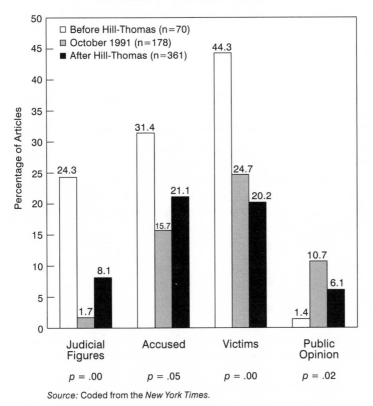

Figure 6-3   Citation trends in *New York Times* articles on sexual harassment, 1990–1993

arbitrating the case.[27] The proportion of articles that quoted an arbitrator fell from one-quarter of all articles to less than 2 percent of articles in the Hill-Thomas month.[28] Articles written after the Hill-Thomas case did not return to the earlier rate of quoting judicial authorities. The same principle also applies to the other major figures in a courtroom drama: the accuser and the accused. Alleged perpetrators were cited in 31 percent of articles prior to

[27] This category includes judges when the case is in the criminal justice system. When the case is being handled within some private organization such as a university or corporation, this category refers to the person in charge of investigating an accusation and making a recommendation on punishment.

[28] Members of the Senate Judiciary Committee are not included in these figures, for they were charged with investigating Judge Thomas's fitness for the Supreme Court rather than with determining his guilt or innocence in the charge of sexual harassment. Judiciary Committee members were quoted in 43 percent of Hill-Thomas articles.

the Hill-Thomas hearings but only 21 percent of articles after. The change was even greater for the alleged victims, who were quoted less than half as often after the Hill-Thomas hearings than before. Increasingly, lawyers spoke for the plaintiff's point of view, with victims making only brief statements for the public record. One of the cultural lessons of the Hill-Thomas hearings may have been that it is not a good idea for victims of sexual harassment to take a high public profile on their complaint.

The judicial confrontation involved in specific charges of sexual harassment continued to receive a great deal of attention in the news, but this attention was now supplemented by articles that examined the issue as a general social problem. Public opinion, in the form of surveys and person-on-the-street interviews, was featured more prominently in the posthearings coverage. Public opinion was typically cited to demonstrate that sexual harassment is of concern to the average person, but that people have sharply divergent viewpoints on its scope and incidence.

Routinization and Cultural Acceptance

We have seen thus far that the combined efforts of movements and critical communities are able to put a new issue on the media agenda (by shaping perceptions of an acute crisis) and to keep it there (by conveying the perspective of chronic crisis as developed within the critical community). Despite the heavy reliance that journalists place on routine categories of news and official sources of information, there is room for new issues to be taken up if a movement can demonstrate the existence of controversy, and if credentialed experts from the critical community can offer a systemic interpretation of the issue.

To put an issue on the routine media agenda is to enlist the resources of an institution skilled in information gathering and packaging. Reporters on a variety of beats develop stories from their own particular angles about the implications of the new issue. Business section writers who had never previously reported charges of sexual harassment in the corporate world begin to write of the problem from the perspective of its costs in worker morale and productivity. Feature articles examine the issue in particular settings, such as between professors and students, between psychiatrists and patients, and between firefighters who spend twenty-four-hour shifts in a cohabitation setting in the firehouse. Columns are devoted to sexual harassment in the sports, education, social trends, and science sections of the paper.

One of the transitions that occurs as the issue becomes familiar in a widening array of contexts is that the phrase "sexual harassment" comes to be viewed as self-explanatory. Prior to the Hill-Thomas hearings, stories about sexual harassment frequently included explicit mention of at least one of the two situations that violate EEOC regulations: quid pro quo and conditions of

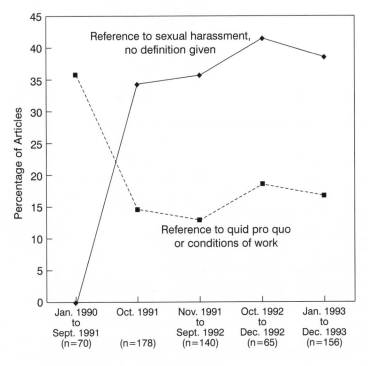

Source: Coded from the New York Times.

Figure 6-4   Conceptual evolution of sexual harassment, 1990–1993

work. After the hearings, however, sexual harassment was no longer used primarily as a technical term based on EEOC regulations. It came instead to have a more intuitive, and less clearly defined, cultural meaning. The consequences of the cultural acquisition of the concept are apparent in figure 6-4, which shows that articles in the *New York Times* were less likely after the Hill-Thomas hearings to refer explicitly to the two EEOC conditions, and were at the same time more likely to use the phrase "sexual harassment" without further elaboration.[29] These trends chart the transition in thinking about sexual harassment from its legal context of specifically defined situations to a term that is left undefined because it has developed a more broadly understood meaning in the culture.

The analysis presented here of media amplification of a new issue has so far been confined to the news media. But the entertainment industry may be

---

[29] The remaining articles coded did not use either the phrase "sexual harassment" or the two EEOC defining terms. Primarily news reports, these articles simply described the actions that were alleged to have taken place. There were no trends over time in the proportion of articles with the "action oriented" definitions.

an even more powerful vehicle for spreading new cultural values. Commercial television can be particularly powerful in this respect, since television weaves together entertainment and information into an almost seamless repertoire of program formats. The situations faced by television families may be recognized as fictional, but they are assumed to reflect problems that (with some license for comic or dramatic exaggeration) are potentially real. Summarizing their long-running study of television violence, George Gerbner and his colleagues conclude that television has blurred the line between fact and fiction: "commercial television, unlike other media, presents an organically composed total world of interrelated stories (both drama and news) produced to the same set of market specifications. . . . [T]elevision audiences (unlike those for other media) view largely non-selectively and by the clock rather than by the program" (cited in Hawkins and Pingree 1981: 359).

Studies of the world portrayed by television generally conclude that it is a world with a number of distortions, including a paucity of very young and very old people, of poor people and of minorities. It is a world of exaggerated successes and misfortunes, and above all a world with an extraordinarily high crime rate. To these ongoing biases, the peaks of concern about a particular issue add other, more temporary, biases. Nelson (1984: 56–57), for example, reports a spate of television dramas concerned with child abuse during the 1970s. In the case of sexual harassment, there were no television shows featuring the problem in 1990 or 1991, but in the year after the Hill-Thomas hearings it became the focus of individual episodes of *Family Matters*, *L.A. Law*, *Murphy Brown*, and *The Simpsons*, as well as being the subject of a made-for-television film and something called the *Sexual Harassment Quiz*.[30]

Ten years earlier, the nuclear freeze movement was responsible for one of the most-watched dramatic programs in American television history, a show about the consequences of a nuclear attack on Lawrence, Kansas, called *The Day After*. The broadcast had an audience of 100 million people, including more than half the adult American population. Many watched it in groups, meeting in church halls and on college campuses. The program itself was followed by a panel discussion on nuclear deterrence, further blurring the line between entertainment and information. The show and panel discussion became, in turn, a springboard for the nationwide organization of discussion groups.[31]

---

[30] According to entries in the *Review of the Arts: Film and Television* (New Canaan, CT: News Bank Inc., various years).

[31] The notoriety of *The Day After* spread beyond the United States. Within a few weeks the film was broadcast in Great Britain and shown to packed theater audiences in Germany, Austria, and Denmark. On the audience for *The Day After* and follow-up response to the film in the United States and abroad, see Robert Trumbull, "*Day After* Helps Foes of U.S. Bases"; and "Germans Fill City Theaters for War Film." Both articles are in the *New York Times*, December 11, 1983, p. A26.

The effect of this blending of fact and fiction in the television world is to make child abuse, sexual harassment, awareness of the consequences of nuclear war, or other such topics part of the everyday social and political landscape. The issue is no longer something remote, played out in hearings of the Senate Judiciary Committee or in arguments between government officials and the ideologues of some critical community. The concepts connected to the issue instead become a widely accepted tool for organizing observations of the world around us.

This is precisely the effect that the French philosophes hoped to create by holding forth in the *salons* and by writing novels and plays that incorporated their way of looking at the world. But the means available to the philosophes for showing the connections of their ideas to events in daily life were extraordinarily limited compared with the ability of electronic media, particularly television, to reach a vast public in a compressed span of time. The readiness of the mass media to integrate new issues and themes into their news and entertainment formats enables them, as an unintended side effect, to play a major role in the insinuation of new cultural values in daily life. This role goes well beyond the mere conveyance of information. The potential of the mass media to amplify an issue and to get people talking about it creates opportunities for critical communities of which the philosophes could only have dreamed.

Cultural Acceptance and Loss of Ownership

We have seen that movement protest combined with the expertise of a critical community creates conditions that put a new issue perspective on the routine agenda of the mass media. When the explosion of societal attentiveness to an issue is sufficiently great, the issue is explored from every conceivable angle by virtue of its incorporation into a wide variety of news and entertainment formats. In the case of sexual harassment, media treatment expanded from coverage on the crime beat to analyses of sexual harassment as a general social problem with implications for all working people.

This expanded understanding of an issue represents the ultimate success of the critical community, for it means that a wide audience is now securely in possession of the new concept. Ironically, though, it is at precisely this point that the influence of the critical community in shaping understandings of the issue begins to wane. As the culture takes hold of a new idea, adaptation occurs to make the concept fit with existing cultural beliefs. Although the culture may generally condemn sexual harassment, there will be differences of opinion over whether particular actions constitute harassment or not. A culture that promotes belief in individual responsibility, for example, will inevitably downplay the structural analysis of sexual harassment that figures so prominently within the feminist critical community. People will consult their own lifetime of experience to answer questions such as whether a woman can often end sexual teasing simply by making clear that it is not welcomed, or whether the taunts of preadolescents on the school bus and in the playground should be litigated by the same codes as those applied to adults. Although critical communities are never united on such issues, as the wider culture takes possession of the concept there will develop an even wider spread of opinion.

In effect, the critical community loses exclusive ownership of the issue—precisely because the new concepts are now part of the wider culture. As a consequence of this expanding interest, people outside of the critical community begin to portray themselves (and to be accepted by the media) as "experts" on the issue. Because experts from the critical community are understood to be advocates, journalists will expand their network of commentators.

Figure 6-5 shows the loss of critical community ownership of sexual harassment during and after the Hill-Thomas hearings. Prior to the hearings, citations of expert opinion, used typically to explain the definition of sexual harassment or to comment on a court decision, were confined almost exclusively to people identified as feminists. Feminists were cited in just over 10 percent of all articles on sexual harassment, including 30 percent of all feature articles.

The feminist monopoly in expert commentary was lost with the Hill-Thomas hearings. The Hill-Thomas case inspired journalists to cast the net widely, and many "new" experts, usually with backgrounds in law or psychology, were called upon to comment on the case.[32] In the year after the Hill-Thomas hearings, these experts (a majority of whom were women, though not identified as feminists in any way) maintained an advantage of about three citations on the subject for every two by feminist experts.

The first anniversary of the hearings created a sharp, albeit temporary, reversal of the nonfeminist advantage in citations. In that period of thoughtful retrospective, feminist experts were sought out to an unprecedented degree to comment on the legal and social changes that had taken place in the intervening year. Within a few months, however, experts other than those identified as feminists were once again being cited in the same relative proportions of three to two over experts explicitly identified as feminists.

It would take a more nuanced analysis than the one presented here to determine the degree to which the feminist and nonfeminist experts quoted in these articles have offered systematically differing views of sexual harass-

---

[32] "Citations of feminists" refer to any direct quotation of an individual identified with reference to a feminist organization (e.g., president of the NOW Legal Defense and Education Fund, or of Federally Employed Women), or of an individual prominent as an advocate of feminist causes, such as Catherine MacKinnon, Barbara Ehrenreich, or Susan Estrich. Women in the latter category are often identified explicitly as feminists *and* as experts on violence toward women when they are quoted. The coding rule in figure 6-5 is that everyone identified as a feminist is coded as a feminist, while any expert not referred to as a feminist (or some clear synonym) is coded as a nonfeminist expert.

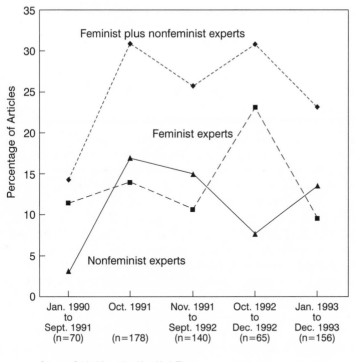

Source: Coded from the *New York Times.*

Figure 6-5   Citation of feminists on sexual harassment, 1990–1993

ment. My own reading of the articles persuades me that there are few or no differences between types of experts in commentary on current events, such as major court cases that have just been decided. There are greater differences when it comes to a vision of what should happen next: whether the standards of proof of sexual harassment should be further relaxed, whether school districts should be held accountable for the behavior of elementary and junior high school students, whether penalties should be made more severe. Although feminist experts are by no means agreed on these matters, the broadening of the debate to include experts not identified as feminists has increased the range of opinion. For that matter, the enormous increase in editorials, op-ed columns, and letters to the editor that began with the Hill-Thomas hearings (see table 6-3) has had the same effect of widening the range of publicly expressed opinions.

CONCLUSION

The evolution in both quantity and content of coverage of sexual harassment in the *New York Times* demonstrates that the Hill-Thomas hearings did indeed mark passage of the issue from acute to chronic. At the same time, ownership of the issue passed from the feminist critical community to a wider range of experts, and from movement organizations to the culture at large.

When a story is covered in the acute crisis mode, the central theme is to describe the problem and to report how officials intend to respond to it. When an issue is covered as a chronic condition, journalists are no longer limited to reporting particular cases, but instead assemble accounts on the history of the problem, the rate at which the problem is growing, its wider social and political implications, the kinds of efforts that have been made to deal with it, and what sort of future efforts appear to be most promising. These are all issues on which the critical community is prepared to engage, and some representatives of the critical community consequently become valuable media personalities in connection with an issue newly defined as chronic. Far from needing to put on a costume to join the media's party (as Gamson and Wolfsfeld put it), critical communities are now welcomed precisely for their perspective on the issue.

The critical community's approach to sexual harassment has remained in force through regulations of the EEOC and supportive judgments of the courts. Outside of the political arena, though, a wide range of voices now seeks to influence the way we think about the scope, causes, and best remedies for sexual harassment. For example, interviews of working women suggest a widespread belief that a woman can generally shame a harasser into better behavior by telling the perpetrator in clear language that he must stop. This view is not widely shared within the feminist critical community, but it is a view that has come to be more commonly expressed as the idea of sexual harassment becomes common property. More fundamentally, the view of sexual harassment as abuse of power has taken hold only to a partial extent, supplementing but not supplanting the view of harassment as sexual misconduct (Scheppele 1995). As long as members of the feminist critical community were talking primarily to themselves (through specialized journals) and to the courts (through *amicus curiae* briefs), they retained a great deal of control over the definition of sexual harassment. In the years since the Hill-Thomas hearings, critical community control has been lost. But it is in precisely that loss of control that we recognize success in persuading the culture to adopt a new concept.

Social acceptance of change, the creation of institutional niches in which critical communities can form, and the development of a dense media network reaching the entire population with a mixture of information and entertainment all shape the impact that movements and critical communities can have on the rate and direction of cultural change. Success of the concept sexual harassment in breaking out from critical community and movement organizations to the wider society is only a single case study, but it is one that suggests a number of lessons on the conditions for rapid cultural change. Movement protest helps give a concept visibility and suggests to media representatives that a particular problem is newsworthy. When the media are searching for an interpretive context, and sometimes even a label, with which to discuss an acute problem, the critical community stands in a position of great potential power. Merely naming the phenomenon gives the critical community significant influence over the way a problem is viewed. Supplying a label and an analysis enables the critical community to give society a firm push down a new avenue of cultural thought. While movement protest suggests that a problem is acute, the critical community analysis also identifies the problem as chronic. That combination of acute plus chronic is a powerful spur to sustained media coverage that goes beyond the use of official sources to comment on current events, engaging instead the full scope of a problem, its underlying causes, and possible avenues for remedy.

The various gateways and obstacles presented by existing cultural values and by the nature of the mass media make it obvious that the translation of critical community ideas into new cultural values is neither mechanical nor automatic. The values and structures of society are important in creating possibilities for critical communities to form, for movement organizations to mobilize, and for new values to break out into the wider society. These social institutions create a pattern of opportunity and constraint with respect to rapid cultural change.

We have examined the societal opportunity structure for critical communities and movements in this chapter. Alongside these elements of societal opportunity and constraint, there are also political structures that affect the potential for critical community influence and movement mobilization. In the next chapter, we will look at the impact of political arrangements in shaping the opportunities for change.

Chapter 7

POLITICAL AND SOCIAL ALLIANCES

SOCIAL VALUES and institutions shape the possibilities for critical communities and movements to form. Cultural acceptance of the idea that human intervention (governmental or private) can remedy social problems has created a society amenable to proposals for change. The development of institutional niches for independent research and thought has made it easier for critical communities to form. The proliferation of mass media of communication, and the organizational traits of the media that structure decisions about what is newsworthy, have created opportunities for movements to spread their messages widely.

This account of the social opportunity structure has so far left out of consideration a concept more familiar to movement scholars, namely the political opportunity structure. The political opportunity structure is shaped by the institutions, processes, and alliance possibilities that encourage and channel movement activity. Movement organizations develop strategies for change that are predicated on assumptions about how they will be received by political authorities. This chapter will examine the elements of the political opportunity structure and the effects of political opportunities on movement tactics and success. These political opportunities are in some measure institutional, and therefore are relatively fixed over time. But political opportunity is also structured to a significant degree by the relative balance of progressive and conservative political forces and by the political alliances open to a particular movement organization. These elements of the political opportunity structure vary over time, and they are also different for different movement organizations at a single point in time.

The importance of political institutions in shaping the potential for cultural change is clearly illustrated in the case of sexual harassment by the role of Senate Judicial Committee hearings in bringing Professor Hill's charges against Judge Thomas before the American public. Without those hearings, Anita Hill's testimony would not have been heard. And without the rigors of periodic election campaigns, senators on the committee would not in turn have heard so clearly the extent of public dismay at the conduct of the hearings. "You just don't get it" was a telling accusation to which senators responded with determined efforts to prove their sensitivity on the issue of sexual harassment. The American political process was responsible both for the public confrontation between Anita Hill and Clarence Thomas and for the fact that U.S. senators monitored public reactions so closely, and tried to be responsive to them.

ELEMENTS OF THE POLITICAL OPPORTUNITY STRUCTURE

Definitions of movements sometimes stress their role as opponents of the state. Francesco Alberoni (1984) reflects this perspective with his claim that movements are a kind of nascent state, a countercommunity with alternative structures of authority and bases of legitimacy. Such definitions are useful in that they highlight the depth of the movement critique of the political and social system. But an emphasis on opposition risks losing sight of the strategic interaction that also goes on between movements and states. Total opposition between movement and state exists only under the restricted circumstances of a revolutionary movement that seeks to replace the government. Most movements are not revolutionary, and none of the movements that have had a major impact on American politics and culture in the last 150 years could be considered implacable opponents of the state.[1]

When movements are defined as the form of collective action that has ultimate ends in both the political and social arenas (see chapter 2), the assumption of implacable opposition between movements and states disappears. Movements and states each control resources the other needs. Movements attempt to harness the power of the state, and political leaders attempt to incorporate for their own purposes the political energies that movements mobilize. In order to accomplish their objectives, movements and states engage each other in a complicated dance that mingles conflict and cooperation.

In order to go beyond the general statement that the relationship between movements and states mingles cooperation and conflict, we must acknowledge that both movements and states are composed of multiple agencies. The state is, of course, composed of majority and minority parties, courts, and a large number of bureaucratic agencies. Movements are also composed of a wide array of organizations, each of which has its own prescriptions for what the movement's primary goals and appropriate tactics should be.[2] As Dalton

---

[1] The last such movement was the Garrisonian wing of the abolition movement, which (at times) embraced dissolution of the Union in order to separate citizens in the free states from complicity with slavery. More recent movements opposed to the state, such as the portion of the student movement that in 1970 embraced resistance and revolution, lost influence as a result of their stance.

[2] Klandermans 1992: 94–99. As Jack Walker (1991: chap. 10) notes, interest groups make a comparable assessment of their resources in determining whether to adopt what Walker calls an insider strategy or an outsider strategy. The logic is much like that of movement organizations, except that movement organizations are more likely than interest groups to conclude they have

(1994: 112) put it, "This diversity in methods and goals enables environmental groups to mobilize a variety of supporters and to utilize a variety of tactics in influencing the policy process."

The movement-state relationship, then, is a composite of many different relationships that exist between particular movement organizations and state organizations. From the perspective of the movement organization, strategists must canvass the set of powerful state institutions and ask in each instance whether that institution is likely to be responsive to movement demands. The decision to focus on particular institutions commits a movement organization to emphasizing whatever resources, ideas, and tactics are most effective in influencing the institutions that have been singled out. Legal expertise is the key to an effective judicial strategy, policy expertise and connections to public officials are vital to a regulatory strategy, and widespread public support is the basis of an electoral strategy.

The distribution of institutional powers and the established system of political alliances determine what has come to be known as the political opportunity structure within which movement organizations operate. Democratic states are frequently characterized as open or closed to societal influence, depending on the extent to which state institutions engage with or stand aloof from social organizations. These political opportunity structures do not lead to monolithic movement strategies. At least in a democracy, opportunities are sufficiently diverse to preclude the existence of a dominant strategy to which all movement organizations will gravitate. Rather, organizational strategies stem from an assessment of the resources available to organizations and from the ideological culture of the organization itself (Rucht 1990, 1996; Dalton 1994). It would cost a great deal of member support for the National Organization for Women to endorse a campaign of civil disobedience, just as it cost member support for the leaders of the Clamshell Alliance to drop civil disobedience in favor of symbolic demonstrations (Downey 1986). Diversity in resources available to different movement organizations thus results in diversity of strategies pursued within the movement as a whole. Studies of the range of organizations within a single movement typically conclude that every conceivable strategy is represented to at least some degree.[3] The movement for the abolition of slavery had the Liberty League operating in the political arena and Garrison's American Anti-Slavery Society in the social arena. Those two organizations maintained an unwavering commitment to immediate abolition of slavery throughout the United States and its territories. Such organizations as the Free Soil Party

---

little hope of establishing close cooperative relationships with bureaucratic departments and legislative committees.

[3] See, for example, Freeman 1975, on the American women's movement, and Rochon 1988, on the European peace movements.

and the American and Foreign Anti-Slavery Society, by contrast, were read-
ier to compromise on the timing and scope of abolition. Their flexibility
made them more adept at finding allies for their position than those advocating an immediate end to slavery. Between them, then, leading abolitionist
organizations focused on both the political and social arenas, and within
each arena some took a hard-line approach while others were more moderate. Dalton (1994) finds the same eclecticism among contemporary European
environmental organizations, concluding that together they constitute a
"Green Rainbow."

Political opportunity structures are, in short, a system of permissive incentives rather than of firm constraints. They increase the costs of some types of
action while raising expectations that other forms of action may succeed.
Governmental institutions and alliance opportunities constitute a political
setting to which movement strategists must be attentive, but that does not
create one set of strategic rules binding on all.

Movement scholars have produced a number of closely related but distinct
specifications of the elements of political opportunity structures (Eisinger
1973; Jenkins 1985; Kitschelt 1986; Tarrow 1988, 1989, and 1994; Gelb
1989). Despite differences of emphasis, they all have in common several
core observations about how political institutions set a context for the activity of movements in the political arena. Three dimensions of political opportunity are particularly relevant to movements: institutional pluralism, institutional porousness, and alliance opportunities.

Institutional Pluralism

The degree of institutional access that movements enjoy is in the first instance a function of institutional pluralism, or the number of formally constituted decision nodes that exist in government. The greater the number of loci
where authoritative decisions are made, the more opportunities enjoyed by
movement (and other) organizations seeking to influence political decisions.
Such institutional features as federalism, a strong legislature vis-à-vis the
executive branch, and well-developed channels of judicial appeal all increase
institutional access. Because each institution is likely to respond to different
types of political resources, the multiplication of institutional decision
makers improves the chances of a movement organization to find a political
channel whose demands fit the organization's own resource profile.

All democracies have some degree of institutional pluralism. There is a
striking tendency for governmental interests to be divided, even in unitary
parliamentary systems with cohesive party majorities and weak judiciaries.
Divisions between executive agencies and between national and local government generally create conflicting political perspectives and lead to a de
facto pluralism of institutional powers.

Political authority in Great Britain, for example, is so concentrated that Lijphart (1984) considers it the paradigm case of unitary government, which he refers to as "the Westminster model." Yet even in Britain, a movement organization like the Greenham Common Women's Peace Camp was able to profit from divisions of authority. For nearly a decade, the Greenham Common women maintained an illegal encampment outside a missile base. Their lengthy stay was due to their own tenacity and to the fact that the land was owned by three public agencies that could not coordinate their eviction efforts. When the Ministry of Transport went to court to get an eviction notice, the campers simply moved to Ministry of Defense land or to ground owned by the local town of Newbury (Rochon 1988). Although British government is highly centralized, and was in the 1980s under the control of an exceptionally strong prime minister, institutional pluralism created political niches that even a small organization with few political allies could exploit.

If the Greenham Common women could survive in the institutional cracks in the British state, then it is fair to conclude that every democratic country contains divisions of authority and institutional perspectives significant enough to permit manipulation by a movement organization. Even so, there is great variation between democracies in the extent of institutional pluralism. And on that spectrum the United States ranks as having a particularly large number and diverse range of powerful political institutions. Federalism and the separation of powers create multiple targets for movement organizations to aim at.

The diffusion of authority in American government is reflected in the wide variety of institutional strategies adopted by American movements. The civil rights movement found the Supreme Court to be its earliest sympathizer in the federal government, followed only later by the executive and legislative branches. The early women's movement had its greatest success lobbying within the executive branch. The environmental movement relied on legislative access to create an environmental agency in the bureaucracy; that agency then built a regulatory structure for environmental protection; those regulations are now defended through the courts. The nuclear freeze movement established beachheads of local and statewide influence in order to persuade members of Congress to consider a freeze resolution.

Phrased in general terms, the institutional arrangements that most facilitate movement access to the political arena are those dubbed the consensus model of democracy by Arend Lijphart (1984). Separation of powers between the executive and legislative branches, strong bicameralism that permits the representation of regional or other minorities, a multiparty system, and federalism are among the constitutional and political arrangements that create multiple centers of authority. The diffusion of political authority gives mobilized movements an excellent chance of being heard through the political system.

We cannot, however, take for granted that gaining access to institutions is equivalent to exerting influence on them. The same dispersion of political authority that makes access possible may also make it difficult for the political system to marshal authority for major departures in policy. Kitschelt's (1986) comparative study of movements against nuclear energy demonstrates that multiple centers of institutional power can be a siren song that lures movements into participating in established institutions without giving them a realistic prospect of influencing policy. This tension between access and influence creates intractable strategic dilemmas for movements, and leads many American movement organizations to embark on a political arena strategy that ultimately ends in co-optation and failure (McCarthy and Wolfson 1992). This is an issue we shall examine more closely later in this chapter.

Institutional Porousness

A second aspect of the political opportunity structure is institutional porousness: the potential for a movement organization to become part of the decision-making system. At stake here is the matter of how difficult it may be to establish a new political party in the legislature, to become a key player in an existing party, to obtain standing in the courts, or to develop a continuous relationship with a relevant department in the executive bureaucracy.

One of the best-known determinants of porousness is the effect of electoral systems on the potential to form new political parties. Under proportional representation, a movement whose values are considered politically important by as few as 2 to 3 percent of the public can gain access to the national legislature. Such small parties may be unlikely to become key members of a governing coalition, but membership in the legislature is itself sufficient to give voice to the party program. The German Greens are a good example of this. Their vote totals typically hover between 5 and 10 percent, enough to be elected to state and federal legislatures. The Greens have participated in a number of state-level governments, often controlling the environmental ministry. They have not participated in a federal government, but even at that level their success has induced other parties to adopt many of their issues and organizational practices.[4] The mere presence of the Greens in the federal legislature forces the major parties to deal with Green policy perspectives. In the 1987–1990 *Bundestag* term, for example, the Greens put more than twelve thousand written questions before governmental ministers.

[4] All German parties have a substantially more proenvironmental outlook than was the case when the Greens first organized. And all German parties have followed the Greens in adopting quotas of women candidates for office. This practice was long anathema to many German political leaders, but has been accepted because of the popular attention the Greens received for their success in implementing a 50 percent quota of women on their electoral lists.

Despite the fact that the Greens were the smallest opposition party, this represented over 80 percent of the total number of written questions put to the government from the back benches (Schindler 1994).

The United States does not have proportional representation, and no new political party has entered its federal legislature with more than a few seats since the end of the nineteenth century. The American party system exhibits a different kind of porousness, however, in its ability to absorb newly mobilized interests. Thus, for example, when the People's Party (Populists) mounted its third-party challenge on the basis of relaxing the currency restrictions inherent in the gold standard, the Democratic Party responded by giving the 1896 presidential nomination to its leading champion of free silver, William Jennings Bryan. Grudgingly, the Populists accepted Bryan as their own nominee as well, effectively putting an end to their status as an independent third-party force.

The absorptive capacity of American political institutions is generally very great. The rules for judicial standing, though made stricter in recent years, remain unusually permissive of class action suits by groups of citizens.[5] The practice of allowing a new president to make approximately five thousand appointments to the top administrative ranks creates opportunities for new ideas to gain currency in the executive branch, sometimes with startling swiftness. Margaret Weir (1989) has demonstrated that the appointment of new economic advisers by the Roosevelt administration in 1933 made possible the rapid adoption of Keynesian approaches to combating unemployment during the Great Depression.[6] In Great Britain the closed ranks of the bureaucracy, whose department heads are ministry careerists, prevented Keynesian thought from gaining adherence within the Treasury Department for over a decade.[7]

This contrast between the porous American bureaucracy and the (relatively) impermeable British bureaucracy once again points up the difference between access and influence. American adherence to Keynesianism proved to be relatively ephemeral, substantially weakened after World War II as Roosevelt's economic advisers were replaced by those of Presidents Truman and Eisenhower. And British economic policy makers, once they adopted Keynesian stabilization policies in the late 1940s, stayed with them through several changes of party control until the Thatcher revolution of 1979.

---

[5] On the rules of standing in environmental litigation, see Plater, Adams, and Goldfarb 1992: 561–566.

[6] See also Tesh 1993, for development of the same point in the context of environmentalism. Environmental advocates joined bureaucratic agencies and congressional staffs in large numbers beginning in the 1970s, demonstrating yet again the porousness of the U.S. government to mobilized interests.

[7] This despite that fact that John Maynard Keynes actually had an office in the British Treasury Department.

Alliance Opportunities

Institutional porousness creates opportunities for movement advocates of a new policy perspective—and even for members of a critical community—to become part of the governing structure. Alliances with political elites may also bring new ideas into the political arena, but they do so by influencing existing elites rather than by having movement adherents actually become elites.

Alliance opportunities depend on the extent to which incumbent political leaders feel they must deepen their ties to groups currently supporting them, or that they must develop support among new groups. Forming and maintaining supportive coalitions is a foundational activity among political leaders, one that never ceases. However, the search for allies among social groups reaches a peak of intensity under conditions of finely balanced competition between rival parties, or when political alignments among key social groups appear to be in flux.

The situation most favorable to a new movement occurs when political leaders know their coalition is close to the margin between winning and losing (Tarrow 1994). There was a relatively close balance in political partisanship in the United States for much of the twentieth century, leading frequently to divided government. Elected legislators have generally enjoyed personal security in office, but their aspirations to be part of the majority have almost always forced them to engage in an active search for means of mobilizing new groups of voters to their cause. Contests for the presidency have been marked in recent decades not only by a close partisan balance but also by great variability between elections. With narrow margins *and* a weakening of the stability of party loyalties, shrewd presidential candidates realize that almost any addition to a personal or partisan coalition could make the difference between victory and defeat. Accordingly, every successful presidential candidate has had to be an energetic entrepreneur in creating a coalition supportive of his primary and general election campaigns (Wattenberg 1991, 1994).

For President Kennedy, this strategy meant courting the votes of women, who were in the early 1960s voting in increasing numbers. Since there was at that time no movement that could articulate women's issues or deliver their votes, Kennedy decided to help create one. Early in his presidency Kennedy set up a national Commission on the Status of Women, with Eleanor Roosevelt as honorary chair and Esther Peterson, head of the Women's Bureau in the Department of Labor, as vice-chair. This commission's report, published in 1963, created momentum for the Equal Pay Act passed that year, for inclusion of "sex" in the definition of employment discrimination in Title VII of the 1964 Civil Rights Act, and for the organization of a White House Conference on Equal Opportunity in 1965.

These were landmark events in putting labor force sex discrimination on the political agenda. But as Ferree and Hess (1985: 53) point out, "the most important legacy of the Commission on the Status of Women was not in the area of legislation at all, but in the mandate to convene commissions on the status of women at the state level." Ferree and Hess note that these state commissions and their staffs brought together politically active women, encouraged other women to think in terms of their distinctive political interests, created an unprecedented level of media attention to women in politics, and generated an expectation that something would be done about women's issues. The role of these commissions in the formative period of the women's movement is best exemplified by the fact that the National Organization for Women was established in June 1966 by a group that had gathered for an annual conference of representatives of the state commissions. Within five years, what had begun as an effort to mobilize women's votes for a presidential reelection campaign had blossomed into the first organizational manifestation of the modern women's movement.

The establishment of women's commissions illustrates both the porousness and the alliance possibilities in American government. Both the president and the Congress have the resources to bring advisory bodies into existence when they want to highlight some issue area or engage a particular community. The motivation to create such bodies, with their attendant effects in mobilizing new interests, exists because of the exceptional flexibility of political alliances in American politics. Partisan traditions create only the loosest of ideological constraints, and coalitions are forged anew by every politician seeking a national base of support.

Variation between Movements in Political Opportunities

Movement organizations engage with the state by responding to the strategic opportunities offered them. The more open the political opportunity structure, the greater the prospects for a movement organization to gain political influence by working through established political institutions, rather than by protesting against them.

The extent of political opportunities enjoyed by a movement organization does not depend solely on the degree of institutional pluralism and elite competition, however; traits of the movement itself influence the extent of opportunity for participation in the political arena. No institutions are neutral with respect to all comers. Consider the different political receptions accorded the temperance movement and the labor movement in the nineteenth century, or the civil rights movement and the gay rights movement in the twentieth century. Different movements enjoy different political opportunities, even when they are operating in the same institutional setting.

Organizations within movements also vary in the political opportunities open to them, depending on their own resources and their ability to form alliances with resourceful political and social actors. The root of this differentiation between organizations lies in the choice of a specific ideological identity within the broader movement. Militant or radical organizational identities, for example, are most likely to draw the committed support of a relatively small number of people, but will not lead to powerful social or political alliances. An organization with an ideological identity closer to the mainstream is likely to enjoy more resources and greater alliance possibilities. These resources, in turn, condition the possibilities for organizational activities. A large pool of highly committed activists dictates a decentralized and participatory organizational structure operating in the social arena; connections to political influentials suggest the development of a centralized membership organization suited to win policy reforms in the political arena.[8] Attempting to use committed activists to do the alliance-building work of the political arena can result in failure. As Mansbridge (1986: 3) has pointed out in the context of the ERA, "Volunteers always have mixed motives, but most are trying to do good and promote justice. As a result, most would rather lose fighting for a cause they believe in than win fighting for a cause they feel is morally compromised."

In short, the strategic orientation of a movement organization depends on two factors: the resource base of the organization and whether it seeks influence in the political arena or in the social arena. Table 7-1 summarizes the relationship between the resources of a movement organization, the arena in which its efforts are focused, and the strategy an organization is likely to adopt. When the movement's resources match the resource needs of a powerful political actor, movement organizations are likely to be offered an opportunity to work for their goals within established political institutions. I shall refer to this strategy as the "Campaign," a commitment by a movement organization to take advantage of participatory opportunities offered through such political institutions and processes as elections, referenda, legislative and regulatory hearings, and informal negotiations with governmental officials.

The Campaign strategy is similar to that used by conventional interest groups. The greatest difference between campaigns by movement organizations and interest groups lies in the types of resources a movement organization brings to such activities. Whereas interest groups are powerful primarily because of their expertise and economic resources, the effectiveness of movement campaigns generally rests on their base of mobilizable support. Examples of movement campaigns include the drive to pass an Equal Rights Amendment in the women's movement and the NAACP's effort to abolish segregation through legal challenges.

---

[8] See Walker 1991: chap. 7 and Dalton 1994: chap. 4, for further development of the links between organizational structure, activities, and membership roles.

TABLE 7-1
Arena Resources and Movement Strategies

	Goal Orientation	
	Political Arena	Social Arena
Alliances with powerful actors		
Resourceful: insider strategy	Campaign	Cause
Resourceless: outsider strategy	Confrontation	Critique

The social arena version of an insider strategy is the "Cause." To mount a Cause, a movement organization must be able to count on the support of leading social institutions and actors, and on access to the mass media. Many social institutions, especially churches and labor unions that were once movements themselves, have proved willing to further a Cause by placing movement goals on their own agendas. Movement organizations that seek to increase the level of attention and resources devoted to their goals find the Cause strategy especially useful. The strategy requires an organization to engage in activities that will generate publicity and make known the movement's support among prestigious elements of society. Such activities may include concerts, benefits, and large-scale rallies.

The purpose of the Cause strategy is not to publicize a specific political agenda, but rather to create and make visible widespread social concern about a general issue area. Politics is therefore a relatively peripheral part of the Cause strategy; political ideas will be phrased only in broad, unexceptionable terms such as "Stop the arms race," "Equal rights for all," or "Say no to drugs." The outcome of a successful Cause strategy may be to heighten awareness of a problem, to increase the amount of resources devoted to the problem (e.g., AIDS research), or to increase community pressure on some particular group (such as drug users or drunk drivers).

The Campaign and Cause are both resource-demanding strategies, and so are not available to all movement organizations. Relatively resourceless organizations must instead adopt one of the outsider strategies of "Confrontation" or "Critique." Both of these strategies involve protest, for as Lipsky (1968) has pointed out, protest is the resource used by groups that do not have other resources. Andrew Young, veteran of both movement and establishment politics, notes that "You don't have to demonstrate when you can pick up the phone and call someone" (cited in Sitkoff 1981: 230).

The strategy of Confrontation involves the tactics for which movements are best known, including demonstrations, occupations, blockades, and strikes. The primary resource required by the Confrontation strategy is that of activist commitment. Confrontation is a ubiquitous movement strategy because activist commitment is a relatively abundant resource in most movement organizations.

It is important, though, to understand that the element of confrontation in Confrontation strategies is generally more symbolic than real. Confrontation may be adopted by a revolutionary organization that seeks to coerce political responsiveness. But in contemporary democracies Confrontation is nearly always a strategy to create political pressure by appealing to the hearts and minds of the (societal) audience. Demonstrators may seek to block traffic and police may try to stop them, but both sides in this confrontation are likely to be professionals trained in means of keeping their conflict within mutually understood bounds (Rochon 1988; Dalton, Kuechler, and Bürklin 1990). The Confrontation strategy, then, must be understood as a *strategy* rather than as a literal reality.

The distinction between working through existing institutions and working in opposition to them is most familiar to us in the context of the political arena alternatives of Campaign and Confrontation. But the same principles may also be applied to the social arena, where the Critique strategy is adopted by movement organizations without the resources to mount a Cause. The Critique involves development of a network of activists who maintain as much debate as possible on the ideas that underlie the movement. The purpose of the Critique is to spread those ideas by applying them to local settings. Specific activities that might be undertaken as part of a Critique strategy include organizing debates, film showings, street theater, and a variety of symbolic protests such as sit-ins or teach-ins.

Critique has been an important activity within the women's movement in many countries, including the United States. Local feminist groups have established discussion groups, crisis centers, hotlines, and shelters. These programs raise local awareness of a problem, increase activist solidarity, and provide assistance to victims (Ferree 1987; Knafla and Kulke 1987; Davis 1991). Localism and smallness of scale mean that the Critique strategy can be employed without large amounts of money, coordination over a wide area, participation by well-known individuals and groups, or even cooperation by the mass media.

The two outsider strategies of political arena Confrontation and social arena Critique are, in the eyes of many people, defining of movement activity. Imagining Confrontation and Critique to be ends in themselves, however, movement observers sometimes view these strategies as symbolic acts of defiance, or even as irrational acts of frustration. Our perspective on such actions is altered if we instead view them as strategies adopted of necessity by groups without links to powerful social or political actors. These strategies may also be employed by resourceful movement organizations, but only at the risk of endangering their existing access to powerful political and

social institutions (Mansbridge 1986: 118–148). When the resourceful strategies of Campaign and Cause are available to a movement, it is powerfully
tempting to employ them.

RESOURCES, STRATEGIES, AND OUTCOMES

Distinctions between Campaigns, Causes, Confrontations, and Critiques are
useful only to the extent that they enable us to understand the relationship
between the resources of movement organizations, the strategies they use,
and the outcomes they achieve.

The importance of resources in shaping strategic choice is suggested by a
comparison of organizations within the same movement that have different
kinds of resources. The American women's movement, and particularly such
national organizations as NOW, has been resource-rich from its inception
(Boles 1991). NOW is led by women with professional skills, media savvy,
and extensive contacts in the political and social arena (Davis 1991: 106–
120). NOW's early press releases were designed by public relations professionals and printed on mimeograph machines owned by the U.S. Congress
(Tuchman 1978: 137). With the support of presidents, members of Congress,
and a number of executive department heads, NOW and its sister organizations led the women's movement on a series of Campaigns that relied on
access to political decision makers. The Women's Campaign Fund and the
National Women's Political Caucus are both engaged in helping women get
the information, skills, and contacts needed to run for elective office. These
efforts have so far yielded the greatest increases in the number of women in
municipal and state government, with more modest results at the federal
level (Clark 1991). Yet there are signs that the expanded base of women in
state politics is creating a pool that will soon yield dramatic increases in the
number of women elected at the federal level. In recent years, about
50 percent of presidential convention delegates have been women. These
women represent both political parties and a wide range of ideologies, but
nearly all have some connections to women's organizations and have devoted considerable thought to issues put on the agenda by the women's
movement.

How might the American women's movement have developed had its
leading organizations not enjoyed such a high level of access to powerful
political institutions? Joyce Gelb's (1989) study of *Feminism and Politics*
answers this question by contrasting the American women's movement with
the women's movement in Great Britain. British women's movement organizations have been resource poor, compared with their American counterparts. They have responded by focusing on the social arena and by giving
greater prominence to the Critique strategy. The British women's movement
is organized in small groups that emphasize local activity to provide a net-

work of social services and self-help projects. These efforts sometimes draw on social services grants from local government, but they are otherwise independent from any involvement with political institutions or processes. Women's organizations have had little involvement in parliamentary elections and have not tried to develop viable candidates for national office. The ironic result is that although there is a greater percentage of women in the British House of Commons than there is in the American House of Representatives, female MPs do not typically consider themselves to be feminists or to have any connection to the women's movement. Nor does the British judicial system offer any means of challenging legislation. As a result, British feminists have generally remained aloof from the political arena, apart from the occasional Confrontation.

A social and political movement is a multifaceted phenomenon that is likely to employ all possible strategies at one time or another. The American women's movement has at times employed the Campaign (for the ERA), the Confrontation (over abortion), the Critique (on rape), and the Cause (on both the ERA and domestic violence). But, as Gelb (1989: 185) points out, "the most visible manifestation of American feminism is the traditional interest group . . . even non-traditional groups with grass-roots origins are pulled toward political engagement and greater professionalization." By contrast, "the most active part of the British feminist movement emphasizes expressiveness, personal transformation, consciousness, and changed belief systems" (Gelb 1989: 180). These are striking differences, but those differences should not mask the fact that both the American and the British women's movements have developed their strategies in response to the social and political resources available to them.

The strategic constraints posed by resource limitations suggest the question of whether movement organizations forced to adopt the strategies of Confrontation or Critique have any hope of success. What outcomes can movement organizations expect to see, once they have decided on a particular strategy?

If the goal of a movement organization is to influence governmental policy by becoming a participant in the policy process, it is clear that the alliance-building strategy of the Campaign is the optimal choice. William Gamson's (1990) analysis of fifty-three "challenging groups" operating in America between 1800 and 1945 shows that 80 percent of organizations that established themselves as participants in the political process won changes in policy, compared with only 21 percent of those that did not participate in the political process.

One might infer from these results that all movement organizations should seek involvement in the political process. But the Campaign strategy may not be optimal, at least not by itself, for movement organizations that seek fundamental political reforms. Comparison of peace movements in different

European countries in the 1980s showed that those countries whose dominant peace organizations were centered on parliamentary influence tended to crowd out the possibility of grass-roots action oriented to long-term change in social values (Rochon 1988: chap. 9). The problem is partly one of longevity. At the peak of a Campaign, a movement may dominate a legislative agenda as few interest groups can. But movement mobilization is inherently short-lived, and that makes its political influence relatively brief as well. Conventional interest groups, by contrast, develop long-term relationships with politicians and bureaucrats; they will be around when the movement Campaign is over. As a result, well-entrenched interest groups are unlikely to be dislodged by a movement organization entering the political arena to campaign for a policy change. The Campaign strategy must lead to a quick-strike policy victory if it is to lead to anything at all. As the religious right discovered after the election of President Reagan in 1980, and as the nuclear freeze movement found out a few years after that, a Campaign may result in a brief flurry of largely symbolic activity, with few sustained results.

A second limitation of the Campaign strategy is that not all movement organizations are able to gain access as participants in the political process. Gamson's data show that the assistance of established interest groups, political parties, or government agencies helps a movement organization win participation in the political process. Figure 7-1 shows that 34 percent of Gamson's challenging groups were given assistance by established political groups or institutions, 11 percent were actively opposed by established groups, and the rest had neither allies nor enemies in the political establishment. Of those groups that enjoyed active political assistance, 61 percent gained acceptance in the political process, compared with just under half of the groups without active assistance and *none* of the groups that faced active political opposition.

Figure 7-1 depicts a stark reality for movement organizations: alliance with established political forces is necessary to gain entrance into the political system, but not all groups enjoy those alliances. There are obvious ideological biases in which groups are offered political assistance. As figure 7-2 shows, groups that use a critique of the system to justify change in institutions or authorities are not only denied political alliance, but are likely to face political hindrances such as censorship, arrests, violence, or changed rules concerning collective action. Only groups with a clearly reformist bent are likely to be offered alliance opportunities or other political assistance.

When the absence of political alliances eliminates the possibility of a successful Campaign, a movement organization may nonetheless fashion a social arena Cause by drawing on connections with socially prestigious patrons.[9] As table 7-2 shows (see page 217), alliances in the social arena are closely but

---

[9] Political alliances are measured by the presence or absence of assistance to the challenging group from established interest groups, political parties, or government agencies, other than

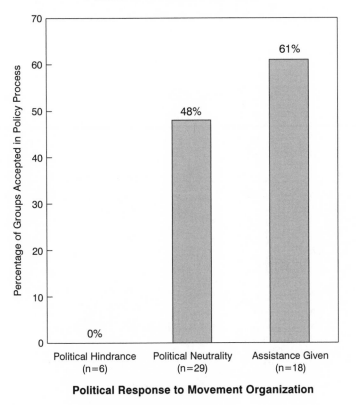

Political Response to Movement Organization

Source: Gamson data on challenging groups.

Note: Pearson correlation between alliance status and political acceptance is $r = .32$ ($p < .01$).

Figure 7-1   Political alliances and political acceptance

imperfectly related to political arena alliances.[10] Movement organizations that are resourceful in one arena are substantially more likely to be resourceful in the other, but 40 percent of Gamson's challenging groups that did not have a political arena alliance were nonetheless connected to a social arena sponsor. And 29 percent of groups that faced active political opposition still

---

those targeted for influence by the group (Gamson 1990: 314, col. 59). Social alliances are measured by the presence or absence of a nongovernmental sponsor whose wealth, prestige, or reputation is put in the service of the group (Gamson 1990: 315–316, col. 63).

[10] Gamson's coding of the resources of challenging groups offers only a single value in each arena, even for groups that existed for more than thirty years. The coding scheme appears to have been to assign the highest resource level that a group ever achieved. Thus, the resourcelessness of challenging groups at any one point in time may be even higher than the 51 percent rate found in Gamson's data.

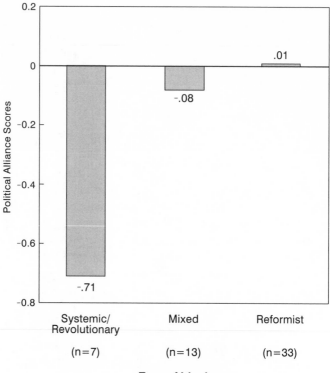

Source: Gamson data on challenging groups.

Note: F test for differences between type of ideology is significant
at the .05 level. Pearson correlation is $r = .29$ ($p < .05$).

Figure 7-2   Movement ideology and political alliances

had a social arena sponsor.[11] Social arena resources are sufficiently independent of political arena resources to create a separate niche for the Cause
strategy.

Successful outcomes in the social arena are a matter of changing people's
thoughts and behaviors on an issue. These outcomes are harder to evaluate
than outcomes in the political arena, and the Gamson data collection has no
measures of social arena success. We can, however, examine the impact of
social and political alliances on success in the *political* arena, defined as

[11] By contrast, only 7 percent of movements without a resourceful social alliance enjoyed a
powerful political alliance. The tendency for political resources to flow to movements with
social resources is stronger than the reverse tendency.

TABLE 7-2
The Relationship between Political and Social Alliances (in percent)

| | Political Arena Response | | | |
	Hindrance	Neutrality	Assistance	All
Social arena alliances				
None	70.6	60.0	18.2	54.7
Present	29.4	40.0	81.8	45.3
All	32.1	47.2	20.8	
Number of cases	17	25	11	53

Source: Gamson data on challenging groups.
Note: Pearson's r = .35 ($p < .01$).

gaining a voice in the policy process and seeing movement demands turned into policy reforms.[12]

Table 7-3 shows that political alliances are important for success in the political arena, but that social arena alliances with resource-rich institutions offer few advantages in gaining participation in the pollitical process or the reform of policy. Although political alliances and social alliances are related to each other, comparison of the first and third columns of table 7-3 shows that controlling for the presence of social alliances does not diminish the significant relationship between political alliances and political arena success. The far right column of table 7-3, on the other hand, demonstrates that

TABLE 7-3
Alliance Types and Political Outcomes

	Political Alliance	Social Alliance	Political Alliance, Social Controlled	Social Alliance, Political Controlled
Outcome:				
Gaining acceptance	.25*	.13	.23*	.04
Policy reform	.39*	.05	.40	− .10
Acceptance plus reform	.36**	.12	.35**	− .01

Source: Gamson data on challenging groups.
Note: Entries are Pearson's r, number of cases is 53 (* $p < .05$, ** $p < .01$).

[12] For operationalizations of these definitions of political arena success, see Gamson (1990: chap. 3.

TABLE 7-4

Political Alliances and Ideology as Determinants of Policy Outcomes

	Pearson's Correlation	Partial Correlation	OLS Beta
Political alliance	.35**	.23*	.24*
Ideology	−.59**	−.55**	−.54**
R^2			.38

Source: Gamson data on challenging groups.

Note: "Policy outcome" is coded as no response, partial response, full response (Gamson: column 21). "Political alliance" is coded as hindrance, neutrality, help (Gamson: column 59). "Ideology" is coded as reformist, mixed, systemic/revolutionary (Gamson: columns 32 and 37). * $p < .05$, ** $p < .01$.

social alliances make no independent contribution to success in the political arena. Political arena influence requires political arena resources.

One may ask whether alliances help even radical organizations achieve success in the political arena. Of course, radical groups—those that seek replacement of existing leaders or institutions and that champion a critique of the political system itself—are less likely to enjoy political alliances in the first place.[13] But political alliances contribute to political success regardless of the ideology of a movement organization. Table 7-4 shows that the relationship between political alliances and policy success is diminished but still significant when controls for the ideology of the movement organization are applied.

These data, and particularly table 7-3, are a reminder that the two arenas of collective action are distinct from each other, and that resources in one arena do not guarantee influence in the other. At the same time, the evidence in table 7-3 presents a misleading image of an impermeable barrier between the two arenas, because the data present a static view of the resource base of any given movement organization. Although movement organizations lacking political arena resources are unlikely to enjoy political success, it is nonetheless possible that an organization with social alliances may develop support for a Cause, which would attract the interest of potential political allies. Those political alliances could then aid the organization in achieving its political arena goals. In other words, resources in one arena may be fungible for resources in the other over a period of time. To understand those cross-arena developments, we must follow the career of particular movement organizations as they employ their resources in different ways. This is a theme to which we shall return later in this chapter.

[13] See figure 7-2.

STRATEGIC COMBINATIONS

The four strategies of Campaign, Cause, Critique, and Confrontation are not mutually exclusive; they may be used in combination. There are fifteen possible combinations of the four strategies, ranging from the use of one strategy in isolation to the simultaneous pursuit of all four. But this maze of combinations is greatly reduced if we begin with a few simplifying assumptions that are likely to account for the bulk of strategic situations. First, since movements (and, by extension, movement organizations) have ultimate ends in both the political and social arenas, we can assume that they generally choose at least one strategy of political influence and one strategy of social influence. Second, if we assume that organizations are reluctant to allow resources to lie fallow, then they will always select the most resource-demanding strategy available to them. Finally, the use of more than one strategy in a particular arena often leads to worse results than the use of either strategy separately: the militancy of a Confrontation can undermine a Campaign, and the compromises required for a Campaign can demoralize those involved in a Confrontation. We can therefore make a third assumption, that movement organizations will generally use only one strategy in each arena.

These assumptions will not account for the strategic choices of all movement organizations.[14] But even if the assumptions prove to hold only a majority of the time, they have the merit of defining for us four primary strategic combinations, as shown in table 7-5.

When movement organizations have connections to both social and political institutions, they are in a position depicted in the lower right-hand cell of table 7-5, and their optimal strategy is to combine a social arena Cause with a political arena Campaign. The organizations behind the Equal Rights Amendment enjoyed this status, at least before mobilization of the STOP-

TABLE 7-5
Alliance Types and Strategic Combinations

	Social Alliance	
	No	*Yes*
Political alliance		
No	Critique—Confrontation	Cause—Confrontation
Yes	Critique—Campaign	Cause—Campaign

[14] Dalton (1994: 180–181) notes that Greenpeace of Great Britain has employed direct action, court challenges, parliamentary lobbying, direct mail solicitations, and advertising campaigns—a mixture of resourceful and resourceless strategies in both arenas.

ERA countermovement. Mothers Against Drunk Driving has been consistently resourceful in both the political and social arenas. The temperance movement was politically and socially resourceful throughout the second half of the nineteenth century, when it was perhaps the single issue that brought together Progressives and Populists, middle-class reformers and labor organizers.

In each of these instances, movement organizations adopted the Cause-Campaign strategic combination. And in each case, the outcome was significant change in both social values and public policy. Although the ERA was defeated, many of the specific inequities the amendment was intended to address were repealed by legislatures or overturned in the courts (Mansbridge 1986: 189–191). MADD raised public awareness of the hazards of drunk driving and obtained tougher laws against driving under the influence in all fifty states between 1981 and 1985 (Reinarman 1988). The Women's Christian Temperance Union and the Anti-Saloon League generated extensive social pressure against drinking, while at the same time shepherding passage of laws in every state that mandated temperance lessons in the public schools (Gusfield 1970: 86; Kyvig 1979: chap. 1). Table 7-6 uses Gamson's data to generalize these examples, showing that fully 78 percent of the challenging groups between 1800 and 1945 that enjoyed both social and political alliances met with "unequivocal" policy success.

Many movement organizations are not so fortunate. Table 7-6 shows that half of Gamson's sample of challenging groups were resourceless in both the social and political arenas. This situation, depicted in the upper left-hand corner of tables 7-5 and 7-6, indicates a strategic combination of Critique-Confrontation. In its politically and socially resourceless infancy, the labor movement generally employed this strategy by developing a network of

TABLE 7-6
Strategic Combinations and Policy Success

	Social Alliance		
	No	*Yes*	*Total*
Political alliance resources			
No	51% of cases	28% of cases	$n = 42$
	41% success	40% success	40% success
Yes	4% of cases	17% of cases	$n = 11$
	100% success	78% success	82% success
Totals	$n = 29$	$n = 24$	$n = 53$
	45% success	54% success	

Source: Gamson data on challenging groups.

working-class mutual aid organizations (Critique) and by organizing illegal and often violent strikes (Confrontation). Policy reforms in the group's favor occurred in 41 percent of cases where the group was without resourceful political or social alliances.

Two-thirds of all movements are congruent in their political and social resources: either they develop alliances in both arenas or they do not develop alliances at all. But one-third of Gamson's challenging groups were resourceful in only one of the two arenas; they are found on the off-diagonal of tables 7-5 and 7-6.

When a movement is socially resourceful but politically resourceless, we should expect the combination of Cause and Confrontation. This situation occurs among 28 percent of Gamson's fifty-three challenging groups, but it is particularly common among the more recent groups in his sample.[15] The increase in the number of socially resourceful but politically resourceless groups is a consequence of the trend for prestigious (and wealthy) individuals and institutions to become increasingly willing to support critical communities and movement organizations.[16] Although there are no data comparable to Gamson's for the period since 1945, an unsystematic review of postwar movement organizations suggests that the opportunity for politically resourceless groups to develop social resources has continued to grow significantly, and that a peak was reached between the late 1960s and early 1970s (see, e.g., Jenkins 1989). Note, however, that social alliances without political alliances do not increase the chances of winning policy reforms. Two-fifths of groups without political alliances achieved significant policy reforms, regardless of the presence or absence of social alliances.

A final possible resource situation, illustrated in the lower left cell in tables 7-5 and 7-6, is that of a movement with alliances in the political arena but not in the social arena. This is the rarest condition among Gamson's challenging groups, occurring among only two of the fifty-three that he studied. Those two groups were the American Federation of Labor and the International Association of Machinists. Both were founded in the 1880s, both were part of the broad coalition that formed the People's (Populist) Party, and in both cases support in the political arena was limited to Populist politicians and their sympathizers within the Democratic Party. Both groups gained policy reforms, resulting in a gaudy but misleading 100 percent success rate.

The NAACP's legal challenge to school segregation represents a more recent example of the phenomenon of using political resources to gain policy reforms without (in its early years) prestigious social arena sponsors. In gen-

---

[15] Fifty percent of the groups formed between 1914 and 1945 were socially resourceful but politically resourceless, compared to just 17 percent of groups formed between 1800 and 1914.

[16] This trend is discussed in chapter 6.

eral, though, it is unlikely that political institutions and leaders will extend themselves for a movement organization that has not demonstrated support among resourceful groups in society. No third-party effort in the twentieth century achieved the success enjoyed by the Populists. The judicial system may be the only contemporary source of potential political support for a group that lacks alliances with prestigious, wealthy, or powerful social actors (Scheppele and Walker 1991).

Do movement organizations actually choose the strategies indicated by their resources in the two arenas? Gamson's data on challenging groups offer indications that they do. Figure 7-3 shows that movement organizations without social or political alliances are most likely to defend the use of violence, and violence belongs to the strategies of Critique and Confrontation. Becoming involved in elections, by contrast, is an important element of the Campaign strategy, and the data in figure 7-3 show that politically resourceful groups are more than twice as likely as other groups to work on election campaigns.[17] Figure 7-3 shows, then, that there is a link between the resources and strategies of movement organizations.

STRATEGIC SEQUENCES

Our consideration of strategic combinations has so far been premised on the assumption that the resources of a movement organization remain fixed. That is not, of course, the case: particular strategies may generate the resources needed to employ other strategies. Movement organizations may also need to adjust their strategies in response to a loss of resources. Useem and Zald (1982) offer the example of the growth of sentiment against nuclear energy, which led to development of a less resourceful pronuclear movement. Organizations on both sides of the abortion controversy have also adjusted tactics as their resources waxed and waned.[18]

We will conclude our examination of the relationship between organizational resources and strategic choice with consideration of how strategies generate new resources, leading to successor strategies. If movements select their strategies in conformity with their social and political resources, then changes in resources should motivate shifts in strategy.

A look back at table 7-6 reminds us that the most common situation faced by Gamson's challenging groups between 1800 and 1945 was one of resourcelessness in both the political and social arenas. In this situation, an organization's strategic options are limited to the Critique-Confrontation

---

[17] We have already seen that social arena resources do not increase political influence in the absence of political arena resources. Figure 7-3 helps us see why: social arena alliances do not make it more likely that movement organizations will participate in election campaigns.

[18] Staggenborg 1991: chap. 7. See also Gamson and Meyer 1996 and Tarrow 1996.

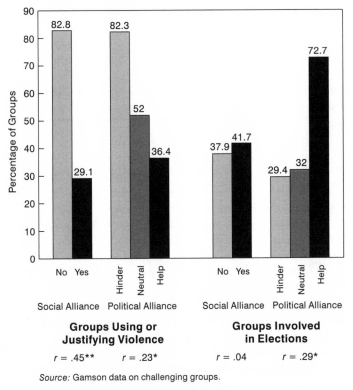

Figure 7-3   Resources and tactical choice

combination, and no change from that strategy is possible unless the organization develops resources in one of the two arenas.

Because political institutions (with the exception of the judiciary) are likely to incorporate new demands only in response to manifestations of popular support, the most promising place to search for initial resources is in the social arena. Resourceless movement organizations, then, are most likely to focus their efforts on the social arena.[19] Exposure to activities carried out as part of a Critique strategy may persuade prestigious social institutions to endorse the goals of a movement organization. If the movement develops

---

[19] The literature on new social movements claims that contemporary movement organizations adopt the social arena Critique strategy because of their desire to foster new identities and solidarities. But it is more likely their lack of resources that forces new movement organizations to develop distinctive and colorful versions of Critique, at least until they are able to cultivate alliances with resourceful social and political institutions. Until then, the strategic "choices" of new social movements are matters more of necessity than choice.

alliances with resourceful social actors, the infusion of resources enables the organization to promote its ideas in a social arena Cause. And, because the Cause is a strategy that raises social awareness of a problem, it is likely also to be an effective bridge to the political arena.[20] A successful Cause generates pressure to put the movement's concerns on the political agenda, and forces political leaders to respond to the movement's ideas. Gaining the support of some political leaders or institutions, finally, opens up the possibility of engaging in a Campaign.

The Abolition of Slavery

The history of any major movement contains distinct strategic phases that are interpretable in light of the movement's changing resources and of alterations in the political opportunity structure. The nineteenth-century movement for the abolition of slavery is illustrative. Although making slavery illegal would ultimately take an act of government, the abolition movement that formed in the early 1830s around the leadership of William Lloyd Garrison broke with the search for a political solution to the slavery issue. Garrison recognized that the abolitionist perspective had no access to political institutions. In the political arena, slavery was just one piece, albeit the most important piece, of the complex puzzle of sectional interests that had to be accommodated in order to hold the Union together.

The aim of the abolitionists was to dissociate the slavery question from the political context of balancing sectional interests, and to create instead a social climate in which the issue would be dealt with as a moral imperative. As Garrison put it, "Let us aim to abolitionize the consciences and hearts of the people, and we may trust them at the ballot box, or anywhere else" (cited in Walters 1976: 14). The Garrisonian abolitionist Wendell Phillips put the case for action in the social arena even more succinctly: "Insurrection of thought always precedes insurrection of action" (Walters 1976: 31).

The initial lack of interest in slavery was so great that it took Garrison several weeks in 1831 to find twelve people to become founding members of the New England Anti-Slavery Society (soon renamed the American Anti-Slavery Society, or AASS). The AASS innovated many of the tactics that we now associate with the social arena Critique. They put the issue of slavery before the Northern public by sending abolitionist lecturers to speak across New England and the Midwest, by publishing and distributing newspapers, tracts and autobiographical narratives portraying conditions of life in slavery, by opening stores in Northern cities that sold nothing made by slaves, and by

---

[20] At the same time, the vagueness of the political ideas associated with the Cause strategy means that political leaders are likely to enjoy a wide degree of latitude in deciding what their policy response will be.

sponsoring abolitionist fairs and picnics (which also served as effective fund
raisers). Ladies' Anti-Slavery Sewing Societies produced children's hand-
kerchiefs with abolitionist messages on them (Walters 1976: 24). The students of Lane Seminary in Cincinnati organized a nine-day teach-in on the
slavery issue, voted overwhelmingly to endorse immediate abolition, and
then went into Cincinnati's black community to organize churches, establish
a lending library, and conduct evening classes in reading and Bible study
(Dillon 1974: 62–63). The result of all these activities was to put the matter
of slavery as a moral issue before the public. Over time, this social arena
strategy made it increasingly difficult for Northerners to continue in the attitude that slavery was a distasteful subject that, however, did not concern
them.

That the movement had some success in these efforts may be inferred
from the steady growth of the AASS in the 1830s. Two years after its founding in 1833, the AASS had 225 local chapters; by 1837 the number had
grown to 1,600 (Walters 1976: 4). But there was also a great deal of institutional resistance to the effort to provoke a general social debate on the morality of slavery. Abolitionists had hoped that they could persuade church
leaders to take a stand in favor of immediate emancipation and to deny
fellowship to slaveholders. These efforts met with almost universal rejection
(McKivigan 1984: 13). Many denominations, as well as other associations
such as fraternal lodges and the YMCA, responded to abolitionist pressure
by passing rules prohibiting discussion of divisive topics like slavery. Compared with any major movement of the last half of the twentieth century,
abolitionists remained weak in alliances with prominent social institutions.

Despite the reluctance of social institutions to endorse abolition, the
movement received sufficient public attention and support to worry Southern
politicians and their Northern allies. The House of Representatives passed in
1836 a "gag rule" requiring that all petitions, resolutions, or propositions
relating to slavery must be tabled without being printed, debated, referred to
committee, or otherwise acted upon. This decision gave ammunition to the
abolitionists' claim that slavery creates an aristocratic mentality among
slaveholders and leads to the decay of democratic freedoms. Transformation
of the issue from slavery to free speech enabled the abolitionists to expand
their protest by giving it a new political significance. Northerners who believed that proposals for immediate abolition were unrealistic were nonetheless prepared to join in the agitation against the gag rule.

Abolitionist success in provoking debate on slavery as a moral issue was
reflected in the severity of the backlash the movement inspired. Abolitionist
conventions (always held in the North) were often broken up by mob violence, traveling lecturers were sometimes run out of town, and printing
presses were destroyed. The reaction was even more violent in the South, for
what was in the North an effort at value connection (getting slavery to be

seen as a moral issue requiring all citizens to take a stand) was in the South an effort at value conversion (getting white Southerners to abandon their attachment to slavery). An AASS campaign in the mid 1830s to blanket the South with abolitionist literature was met in Charleston, South Carolina, by a mob who broke into the Post Office, seized the mail sacks containing abolitionist tracts, and burned them. Vigilance committees were formed in Charleston and elsewhere to search the mail on incoming ships and confiscate abolitionist literature. Southern state legislatures sent resolutions to their Northern counterparts, demanding that antislavery societies be suppressed. A county grand jury in Virginia delivered an order to Massachusetts for extradition of the AASS executive committee to stand trial for sedition.[21]

The societal polarization generated by abolitionist activity crossed over to the political arena in the campaign of civil disobedience against the Fugitive Slave Act. The law, originally enacted in 1793 and then strengthened in the Compromise of 1850, required that citizens of the free states help apprehend any persons who might be escaped slaves, while denying to those captured the right to a trial by jury, to call witnesses on their behalf, or to habeus corpus. Abolitionists soon saw the potential utility of the Fugitive Slave Act in bringing awareness of the injustices of slavery into Northern communities. Theodore Weld urged in 1846 that escaped slaves remain in the Northern states rather than fleeing to Canada. Though this would make them subject to capture, Weld noted that their presence in the North "would make home the battle ground . . . and do more to abolitionize the free states than all other instrumentalities afoot" (cited in Dillon 1974: 178).

Black and white abolitionists alike organized vigilance committees to aid runaway slaves caught by federal marshals or bounty hunters. Some of the rescues attempted by these groups succeeded and some failed, but all made it clear that the option of ignoring the slavery issue was fast disappearing for Northern citizens. When members of a vigilance committee were caught and charged with violation of the Fugitive Slave Act, local juries sometimes failed to render a conviction despite overwhelming evidence of guilt. One slave rescue in Oberlin, Ohio, in 1859 led to the arrest of thirty-seven vigilance committee members, including college students, professors, and clergymen. A rally held in their support in Cleveland turned out ten thousand people who applauded speeches denouncing the Fugitive Slave Act. The trial itself became a nationally reported forum for abolitionists to denounce both the Fugitive Slave Act and slavery itself.

The Fugitive Slave Act was never in danger of breaking down completely. Enforcement generally occurred without Northern citizens even being aware that escaped slaves were being captured and returned from their communities. But, as Dillon (1974: 187–188) has observed, the extensive publicity

---

[21] Dillon 1974: 91. The Massachusetts authorities declined to carry out the extradition order.

given to rescue attempts led to a growing belief, particularly in the South, that the country was on a collision course over slavery. Despite their initial reluctance to engage the issue of slavery, church leaders became increasingly outspoken during the 1840s, resulting in a series of schisms within denominations as Northern and Southern churches broke away from each other (McKivigan 1984). These sectional schisms, in turn, freed Northern ministers to become even more outspoken advocates of abolition (Stange 1977).

The ultimate sign of this cultural conversion came with the publication of Harriet Beecher Stowe's *Uncle Tom's Cabin*, which appeared in serial form during 1851 and 1852 in the midst of agitation over the Fugitive Slave Act. Dillon (1974: 191) points out that "Mrs. Stowe's book was the literary sensation of the era. Sympathy for the slave as embodied in the 'Uncle Tom theme' soon became a part of popular culture. Within a few months, waltzes, dioramas, and stage plays based on the novel had been produced." Dillon cites a contemporary as reporting that (Northern) theatergoers cheered as escaping slaves turned and shot their pursuers.

During this period of social change, some "political abolitionists" came together to found the Liberty League and later the Free Soil Party in the 1840s. Garrisonian abolitionists continued to object to all entanglement with politics until a sufficient number of voters were prepared to endorse an immediate end to slavery everywhere in the United States. Garrison himself advocated dissolution of the Union in order to separate the North from any further association with slavery, and he borrowed the words of the Prophet Isaiah to denounce the slavery-condoning Constitution as "a covenant with death and an agreement with hell" (Walters 1976: 130).[22]

Ultimately, though, success in polarizing the slavery issue in the social arena meant that the political system had to find a response. As late as 1850 the Democrats and Whigs treated slavery as a pragmatic issue of regional difference, forging in that year the last of the great sectional compromises. But the polarization of the 1850s left no room for the center ground on slavery staked out by the Whigs, and beginning in 1856 electoral politics turned increasingly on the contest between proslavery Democrats and antislavery Republicans. The fledgling Republican Party surprised all observers—including its own leaders—with its electoral success in 1856, running on a platform declaring that "it is both the right and the imperative duty of Congress to prohibit in the Territories those twin relics of barbarism—Polygamy and Slavery" (Johnson and Porter 1973).

Three years after the Republican Party debut, church bells tolled and ral-

---

[22] Frederick Douglass broke with Garrison over this issue, pointing out that dissolution of the Union might keep the morality of Northerners unblemished but that it would do nothing for the Southern slave. Garrison's stance, illogical from the perspective of ending slavery, testifies to the importance he placed on the first step of creating a society both united and militant in its antislavery beliefs.

lies were held across the North to praise John Brown, leader of the failed slave insurrection at Harper's Ferry, as an American hero and martyr to justice (McKivigan 1984: 156). One year after that, in 1860, Abraham Lincoln's presidential candidacy carried every free state but three, running on a platform that was almost sure to provoke secession among the Southern states. These developments would have been inconceivable in a society that had not just undergone thirty years of abolitionist provocation, the early portions of which had taken the form of a great campaign of social education. A Northern opponent of abolition (as cited in Filler 1960: 276) provided a shrewd summation of these remarkable developments:

> Sewing parties have been turned into abolition clubs, while little children in the Sunday schools have been taught . . . from books illuminated with graphic insignia of terror and oppression; with pictorial chains, handcuffs and whips, in the act of application to naked and crouching slaves. . . . [Today] we see the influence around us in the millions of young men that now constitute the bulk of the republican party, who may trace their opinions upon the question of slavery to the early prejudices thus acquired.

Slavery was on the political agenda in 1830 and it was on the political agenda in 1860, but the nature of the issue was changed in that thirty-year interval. The abolitionist movement began without resources in either the political or social arenas. Through imaginative and consistent use of the strategic arsenal of Critique, the movement slowly won for itself the endorsement of Northern church denominations. These social resources made abolition a Cause, at least in the Northern states. Success of the Cause, in turn, attracted political resources in the form of a critical realignment of the party system, signified by the rise of the Republicans and the destruction of the Whigs. The abolitionists' social arena activities created a polarized climate of moral fervor in which the end of slavery went from a utopian dream to an achieved political objective.

Civil Rights

The civil rights movement offers a more recent example of the same strategic sequence: developing resources in the social arena and then using those resources to gain influence in the political arena. Throughout the 1950s different organizations within the movement engaged in a mix of the Campaign strategy (legal appeals) and the Confrontation strategy (marches, sit-ins). The charismatic leadership of Martin Luther King Jr. and Northern liberal outrage at the treatment of civil rights protesters helped the movement embark on a Cause strategy in the latter half of the 1950s. Although Confrontational elements persisted, they became more and more symbolic. The Montgomery bus boycott in 1955 was a literal Confrontation because its intent was to force desegregation of the local buses by putting economic pressure on the bus company. Six years later a socially resourceful movement undertook the Freedom Rides, a far more symbolic confrontation over interstate busing that had many elements of the Cause strategy in its design.

The success of the Cause strategy in the civil rights movement attracted the interest of Presidents Kennedy and Johnson, who—while remaining attentive to the range of anti–civil rights opinion within the Democratic Party—cautiously courted the movement by granting its leaders unprecedented access to decision making in the White House. Between 1962 and 1967 the Cause-Campaign strategic combination was dominant within the movement, with Confrontation relatively muted. Civil rights marches in this period may still have been part of a Confrontation strategy with respect to state governments, but they were also aimed at the federal government as an ongoing demonstration of the popularity of the Cause. It was in this period that Attorney General Robert Kennedy maintained close contact with Martin Luther King Jr., particularly before and during major civil rights actions. Both the interstate Freedom Rides in 1961 and the second voter registration march from Selma to Montgomery in 1965 were accomplished with the protection of federalized National Guard units (Sitkoff 1981).

The Cause-Campaign resulted in substantial policy reforms that provided federal enforcement of the civil and political rights of African Americans. But as the goals of the civil rights movement evolved to embrace new economic issues, the social and political alliances underpinning the Cause-Campaign began to weaken. Both Critique and Confrontation, the two strategies of resourceless protest, gained wider adherence within the movement. The social arena strategy of Critique took the form of the black power movement, championed by such groups as the Black Panthers. And leaders such as Malcolm X, who advocated political arena Confrontation, also gained an increasing audience.

A movement is a complex and variegated phenomenon. Currents of Critique, Cause, Confrontation, and Campaign may all be found in the civil rights movement at any time between 1950 and 1970. But the relative prominence of these strategies waxed and waned over time, corresponding to the political and social alliance resources of movement organizations. As resources accumulated, strategy shifted to take advantage of those resources. When partial success on some issues led to a broadening of demands, alliances began to melt away and movement organizations came once again to place greater emphasis on the strategies of a resourceless movement.

The United Farm Workers

The career of the United Farm Workers (UFW) offers another example of changing resources and strategic evolution. The UFW's predecessor organization, the Farm Workers' Association (FWA), was founded in the early 1960s to provide self-help services to Mexican immigrant farm workers by establishing credit unions, purchasing co-ops, and the like. This is a classic element of the Critique strategy, engaged in by groups without external social alliances in order to strengthen the bonds among group members and accumulate resources for collective action. As Jenkins (1985: 136–144) points out, FWA leader Cesar Chavez wanted to undertake a more outward oriented strategy of political advocacy, but was aware that he could not do so without the support of resourceful social and political groups.

In order to employ the professional staff needed to undertake a political Campaign, Chavez set about piecing together support from the Catholic Church, the AFL-CIO, the United Auto Workers, several private foundations, and the federal Office of Economic Opportunity (which was at that time operating similarly to a private foundation in its funding of social change organizations). The impact of these outside groups was especially great in the early years of the UFW, providing over 90 percent of income in the first year of operations.[23] These organizations provided cash contributions, volunteer work, and political and legal advice that enabled the UFW to undertake its first Confrontation in the form of a strike against the growers.

The growers retaliated with strikebreakers and had the picketers arrested for unlawful assembly. Chavez appears to have seen this Confrontation with the growers, which the UFW could never have won on its own, primarily as a means of increasing the movement's external support. On the day of the first arrests of UFW strikers, Cesar Chavez stood to denounce the growers' strikebreaking tactics and to call on his listeners for unwavering support. But Chavez was not speaking to UFW members in the fields of Delano; he was speaking to Berkeley students on the steps of Sproul Hall. The result was an outpouring of support not only at Berkeley but from college students across the country. This was the beginning of the national coalition of liberal groups whose support made possible the shift to a Cause strategy. The UFW slogan, *¡Viva la Causa!* could not have been more apt.

The UFW form of Confrontation had been the labor strike, which could be carried out by the workers themselves (albeit with the help of professional staff). With the support of organized labor, progressive foundations, university students, and many consumers, the UFW unveiled a new tactic that could only be carried out with extensive organization and the cooperation of a large segment of the public. This was the national boycott of California grapes. Jenkins's (1985) careful analysis suggests that the economic effects

---

[23] Growth in the number of members in the early 1970s reduced the proportion of external contributions to just 54 percent of the UFW budget. Even so, external support remained a significant source of UFW income, and one that remained more stable from year to year than did membership dues. See Jenkins 1985: 141, for a yearly accounting of the sources of UFW revenue.

of the boycott on grape growers were slow to take hold, due mainly to the common use of advance purchase contracts and to the fact that grapes are not labeled so as to make it possible to distinguish between union and non-union products. At the end of the first year of the national boycott (1968), wholesale grape deliveries were down just 12 percent. Only in the second year did wholesale prices drop below production costs, as grape shipments were reduced by 30 percent.[24]

Long before the growers were hurt by the boycott itself, though, the Cause strategy paid off by generating new political alliances. First on the band-wagon was Governor Edmund Brown, who was in 1966 involved in a stiff reelection battle against Ronald Reagan. Robert Kennedy's 1968 presidential campaign, engaged in a search for liberal votes nationally and for Mexican-American votes in California, also took note of the power of the Cause. Kennedy positioned himself at Cesar Chavez's side in March 1968, as Chavez ended the twenty-five-day fast with which he had launched the boycott.

The 1966 election in California produced a Republican governor and the 1968 national election brought in a Republican president, thereby aborting the budding political influence of the UFW. Even so, the tactical shifts of the United Farm Workers in this formative period can be understood only as a response to changing alliances and resources in the social and political arenas. Moreover, each strategy in this sequence appears to have been selected with an eye to its resource-generating potential to make possible the next move.

The Consequences of Strategic Error

Strategic shifts within movements are often seen as a response to changes in movement leadership, to the institutionalization of movement organizations, and/or to frustration with the lack of results gained by the existing strategy. The perspective developed here suggests that changes in the social and political resources of a movement are the underlying reason that frustration may grow, organizations may gain institutional access, or new leaders may become popular. When social and political resources are either growing or shrinking, movement organizations are impelled to undertake a shift in strategy. This may entail a transition in movement leadership—for example, if existing leaders remain wedded to their initial strategies, or if politicians, media, and public refuse to accept the new strategic posture of a movement leader who claims to have reformed (Walker 1963). Strategic shifts may also

[24] The decline in grape shipments would have been even steeper in 1969 had not President Nixon ordered the Department of Defense to increase its purchases of grapes fivefold, according to Jenkins (1985: 170).

be accompanied by changes in relative organizational strengths within a movement. Resources and alliances create pressure for strategic shifts, and those pressures are then reflected in shifts in the fortunes of different movement organizations and leaders.

The tendency for movement strategies to conform to social and political arena resources does not mean that strategic adjustment to new resource conditions is automatic. It is up to organization leaders to identify the opportunities created by the current state of social and political alliances. Having identified the optimal strategic mix, leaders must then persuade activists to orient themselves to that strategy, and the representatives of powerful social and political institutions must be prepared to perceive the movement as embarked on that strategy.

All of this means that there can be a number of possible causes of suboptimality in an organization's use of its strategic resources. Of these various problems, the one that appears most avoidable to an outside observer is misestimation of the alliance resources available to the movement organization.

Of course, any typology of movement organizations as resourceful and resourceless inevitably leaves fuzzy the dividing line between these two conditions. But there is a great deal riding on an accurate assessment of which side of the line a movement organization is on. If those who determine movement strategy do not accurately perceive the organization's alliance and resource position, they may select the wrong strategy. To ignore resources available to the movement is not only to miss the opportunity to employ a Cause or Campaign strategy, but also to risk alienating allies by undertaking the Critique or Confrontation strategy. On the other hand, to presume on resources that one does not have is to be frustrated by the lack of progress in efforts to execute a Campaign or a Cause.

Leaders of the student movement in the late 1960s consistently overestimated the amount of social support the movement enjoyed or could be expected to generate in the near term. When student radicals spoke of bringing about a political revolution, the range of disagreement appears to have been limited to whether it would occur in the coming year or within a few years (Kunen 1968; Sale 1973: chaps. 21–26). By the end of the 1960s, SDS had adopted the Cause-Confrontation strategic pair, presuming a high level of societal resources in the form of people rising up to support the movement and join in a revolution against the political system.[25] This was a disastrous

---

[25] The elements of the Cause were appeals to the working class, blacks, and other "marginal groups" to take action against their oppressors. The existence of Confrontation may be seen in the SDS role in organizing draft resistance and in distributing instructions for making bombs (Sale 1973: 456).

error for the organization and for the student movement as a whole. Although the anti–Vietnam War position at the center of the student movement enjoyed increasing public acceptance, there was little support for the wider goals of revolution against the political and economic system. Rather than arousing the populace in its support, SDS became increasingly isolated. Its infiltration by the Federal Bureau of Investigation (FBI) and suppression through the legal system was accomplished with public acceptance. The destruction of SDS brought with it a narrowing of the student movement to concerns centered exclusively on the Vietnam War.

To imagine social arena resources that do not exist is an unusual error, possible perhaps only in the overheated atmosphere of campus politics in the late 1960s. Overestimating a movement organization's resources for change may be more common in the political arena. American movements from the abolitionists onward have frequently enjoyed the support of some prominent individuals or groups within the political system. As a result, movement strategists may be seduced into the belief that political alliances can be parlayed into policy changes sought by the movement. The history of American movements is littered with the wreckage of failed Campaigns on the part of movement organizations that might have focused more profitably on emphasizing the need for change in cultural values. We can examine this phenomenon by considering one of the most recent victims of this tendency, the Nuclear Weapons Freeze Campaign.

The Nuclear Freeze

The nuclear freeze movement mobilized unprecedented numbers of people to protest against the cold war rhetoric characteristic of the first Reagan administration. The freeze proposal called for a verifiable halt by both superpowers to the development, testing, and deployment of nuclear weapons. With this simple formula, the freeze seemed a welcome alternative to the policies that many Americans believed ran the risk of leading to a nuclear war with the Soviet Union (Milburn, Watanabe, and Kramer 1986; Rochon and Wood 1997).

Strategically, the freeze movement can be characterized as having followed the common sequence that begins in the social arena with the Critique, blossoms into a Cause when resourceful social alliances are developed, and then jumps from the social arena to the political arena by undertaking a Campaign. The first freeze convention in March 1981 was explicit in proposing a strategic sequence in which activists would initially develop support throughout the country and would then take the plan to policy makers. The strategy paper approved at the conference (as cited in Feighan 1983) declared that

Past efforts at serious arms control . . . failed in part because they were not
preceded by active educational efforts among the general public by a sufficiently
broad spectrum of organizations. For this reason, the freeze effort is aimed, in
the first instance, not at Washington but at recruiting active organizational and
public support.

The strategy of local action combined with media attention did lead to
broad support for the freeze in the social arena. As a consequence of increased concern about deteriorating relations with the Soviet Union, the
freeze consistently garnered the support of about 70 percent of the American
population. The movement was able to gather somewhere between one-half
million and one million people for a demonstration in New York City in
June 1982.

In the political arena, the freeze movement organized itself as a Campaign, initially at the state and local levels. The tellingly named Nuclear
Weapons Freeze Campaign (NWFC) worked to put freeze language on the
ballot as an advisory referendum in eleven states in 1982. The referendum
passed in ten states representing 30 percent of the American population,
losing only in Arizona among states where it was on the ballot.

No grass-roots Campaign can attract so much support without drawing the
attention of national politicians. The social arena–political arena sequencing
envisaged by freeze strategists was sped along by Democratic Party leaders
who wanted to be identified with the movement's popularity. The decision to
introduce a freeze resolution into Congress was made by Senator Kennedy
(looking for an issue to propel a run for the presidency) and by Representative Edward Markey (looking for an issue to boost his aspirations for the
Senate).

Taken from the movement and handed to professional politicians and their
operatives, the freeze proposal became enmeshed in the broader political
game of congressional politics and of posturing between a Republican president and a Democratic Congress (Rochon 1997). Freeze resolutions were
passed in the House of Representatives in 1982 and 1983, but both pieces of
legislation were merely symbolic victories. The issues central to the freeze
proposal—arms control and superpower relations—are matters that have traditionally been controlled by the president. By going to the Congress, the
NWFC was placing its hopes in what would have been an unusual degree of
congressional meddling with presidential prerogatives.

The congressional resolution that was eventually passed reflected this hes-
itancy to get involved in international negotiations. The resolution stated that
a freeze treaty with the Soviet Union should be concluded only if the United
States and the Soviet Union had "essential equivalence in overall nuclear
capabilities," only to the extent that such an agreement would be mutual and
verifiable, only to the extent that such an agreement would be compatible

with NATO obligations, only to the extent that the credibility of the American nuclear deterrent would be maintained, and only to the extent that such an agreement would not jeopardize the ability of the United States to preserve freedom. Section 3b of the Act states that "Nothing in this resolution shall be construed to supersede the treatymaking powers of the President under the Constitution." The irrelevance of the freeze vote in the House is suggested by the fact that the same body went on later that year to approve funding for MX and Trident missile development, funding of the first segments of the Strategic Defense Initiative, as well as deployment of the cruise and Pershing II missiles in Europe. As it turned out, the freeze was never the basis of discussion in international negotiations.

The freeze movement was not a complete political failure. Social mobilization on behalf of the freeze persuaded President Reagan to modify his stance against arms control and to begin negotiations with the Soviet Union, albeit on terms that were unlikely ever to be accepted. More important, many of the arms control proposals discussed during the freeze mobilization were taken up again in 1986 and 1987, when Mikhail Gorbachev determined that a far-reaching accord with the United States was necessary to the survival of the Soviet Union (Joseph 1993: 170; Knopf 1997). Thus, the freeze movement had an influence on the terms in which arms control negotiations came to be phrased, albeit an indirect and delayed impact.

The direct political influence of the freeze movement was slight—it was able to stir up a tempest of debate within the political arena, but it achieved no concrete results. A large part of the blame for this failure must be laid to the adoption of a particularly difficult policy goal: altering the agenda of international arms control negotiations. To be successful, the freeze movement had to influence the foreign policies of both the U.S. president and the general secretary of the Communist Party of the Soviet Union. The task was formidable.

It was nonetheless a strategic failing that the freeze never articulated a goal compatible with the movement's resources. The goal of changing the president's arms control agenda would have required substantial support concentrated among the foreign policy institutions of the executive branch of government. The resources of the movement were chiefly in the social arena: the passive support of a preponderance of the American public and the committed support of a national network of activists. These resources were best employed in fostering an extensive social debate on superpower relations, nuclear deterrence, and security.[26] The movement, however, had no leverage on an electorally secure president or on the upper echelons of the Departments of State and Defense.

---

[26] That debate did take place between 1981 and 1983, but the shift of focus to the political arena caused the discussion to narrow to the task of getting Congress to pass a freeze resolution.

Although the freeze movement's attempt to influence foreign policy faced particularly grave difficulties, the experience of failing to be influential in an apparently welcoming political arena is common to many movement organizations. The same diffusion of political power that gives movement organizations entrée to the political arena also makes it nearly impossible to gain concerted support for policy reform among all relevant political institutions. It is easier to capture the attention of authorities within the federal government of the United States than it is to capture the attention of the national government of most democracies. But, once an issue has been placed on the political agenda, it is easier to obtain results in democracies where authority is relatively concentrated in institutions that work in close coordination.

A second dilemma illustrated by the freeze is that the strategic focus of a movement may shift to the political arena at the initiative of political leaders rather than movement leaders. Leaders of a movement organization engaged in a Campaign often develop the uncomfortable feeling that their blossoming relationship to the political authorities has robbed them of control over the movement itself. Randy Kehler of the Nuclear Weapons Freeze Campaign summarized this sentiment by telling reporters, "I feel like I'm on a comet, but I don't know whether I'm leading it or on its tail" (cited in Meyer 1990: 128).

To shift a movement's energy to the political arena meant, in the case of the freeze, relegating the network of activists to the role of fund raisers and letter writers. The decision in 1984 to relocate NWFC headquarters from St. Louis (chosen because it was in the middle of the country) to Washington, D.C., is symptomatic of this shift in attention. Even more telling is the plea sent to the NWFC office by an activist in New York, to "Just please let's have a simple, clear task for all of us to work on. . . . The five-hour-a-week volunteers want to know how to spend that time most effectively" (Solo 1988: 139).

Even the referendum campaigns lost much of their social change value as they became better funded and took on the characteristics of a media campaign rather than of a grass-roots contacting effort. Media campaigns are the best technology for generating votes, but not for changing cultural values. Door-to-door campaigns are labor-intensive and reach only one person at a time, but research on attitude formation shows that personal contacting on an issue is far more powerful than exposure to the same message through the print or electronic media (Eldersveld 1956; Oskamp 1991: 158, 167). When a state referendum drive becomes a direct mail and mass media campaign rather than an excuse to knock on doors, the social change potential of the referendum is diminished even as the prospect of winning the referendum goes up.

In short, the freeze movement's congressional and electoral strategy conflicted with the goal of changing cultural values. Advocates of a social arena emphasis in the movement knew they had suffered a strategic defeat when the NWFC shifted its efforts to Capitol Hill. As Roger Molander, director of the education-oriented group Ground Zero, concluded, "it was the [freeze] movement's failure to understand the role of education in movement development . . . that was the overriding cause of its failures and decline" (Molander and Molander 1990). A political arena strategy requires pragmatism, a narrowness of policy focus, and the concentration of organizational resources on a few targets. Each of these traits can be inimical to the maintenance of a movement for cultural change in the social arena.

CONCLUSION

Movements are responsible for bringing the message of a critical community before the public and the government. The American political system offers a number of exceptional opportunities for movement organizations, though it also places constraints on them. On the opportunities side, the American governmental system offers movement organizations an exceptionally wide array of institutions that may give access to the political arena. This leads movement organizations seeking political influence to engage in "venue shopping," a practice long used by interest groups. Baumgartner and Jones (1993: 233) explain that "Failure in one venue can lead to resignation, but it can just as easily lead to a search for a new venue. If the state [government] is unresponsive, what about the courts? Will a federal agency intervene on our behalf? Can we approach the school board as a potential ally?"

Although the American political system is unusually open to the claims put forward by mobilized movements, however, each choice of an institutional venue has its own costs. The price tag is denominated in the currency of resources that the organization must cultivate, ways in which movement demands must be formulated, and tactics that the organization must use to be influential with that institution. And, given the diffusion of political power in American politics, even a movement organization that earns the full support of the courts, the legislature, or an executive agency has no assurance that this support will yield effective governmental action.

The calculations of movement strategists are still further complicated by the fact that political opportunities change over time. This can be due to changes in party control of elected offices, altered alliances and changes in the degree of unity among elites, the mobilization of opposition to the movement, changes in the relative authority of different venues, or other factors. Movements must react to these exogenous changes in political opportunities, but they are also able to take an active hand in shaping their destinies by the accumulation of resources. We have seen examples of strategic adaptation to changing resources in the case of abolition, the civil rights movement, the United Farm Workers, and the freeze movement. In each case, shifts between the Confrontation and Campaign strategies in the political arena, and between the Critique and Cause strategies in the social arena, followed changes in resources.

The goals and resources of a movement organization combine with the range of institutional opportunities to delimit the organization's strategic options. The most significant constraint on movement strategy may come from inherent limitations on the political arena of action. Governmental policies are remedies to problems that have been defined and delimited. The systemic perspective on a problem as incubated within the critical community may not be amenable to policy solutions. There remains an unbridgeable chasm between the formulas in which political reforms can be phrased and the sweeping visions of critical communities and their movements. This is an issue we shall examine more fully in the concluding chapter.

Chapter 8

ADVANCING OUR UNDERSTANDING
OF CULTURAL CHANGE

It's a fact that people's everyday lives have changed from the
early 1960s to now, and certainly within my own life
[span]. And surely, that is not due to political parties but is
the result of many movements. These social movements
have really changed our whole lives, our mentality, our attitudes,
and the attitudes and mentality of other people, people who
do not belong to these movements.
—Michel Foucault

SWEEPING CHANGE in governmental policies and everyday behaviors is a
recurrent feature of American life. These changes occur in response to periodic shifts in cultural values related to the way we assess particular issue
areas. Deeply held beliefs may be given up through value conversion, new
considerations may be brought to bear on a particular subject through
value creation, and problems may come to be viewed in a new context
through value connection. Each of these kinds of change generates new
perspectives on what is right, what is fair, what is possible, what is necessary.

Our basic assumptions about the world may change so gradually that we
notice it only as we look back at the values that animated earlier generations.
But there are times when change occurs far more rapidly, less by generational turnover than by the wholesale adoption of new perspectives. This
process of rapid change in cultural values may sweep through the society,
resulting in the development of a new "common sense" that guides our
thoughts and behaviors. Such cultural changes may also flood the political
system like an irresistible tide, breaking up long-standing advocacy coalitions and forging new political alliances and policy networks.

We began this book by noting that although the forces of rapid cultural
change may be precipitated by new circumstances, technologies, information, or conditions of life, these effects of the physical world serve merely to
create possibilities for particular avenues of change. Human agency is necessary to turn disasters into crises, and crises into movements. Societies always
have degrees of freedom in formulating value-laden responses to new crises,

constraints, or possibilities. There are human agents—individual and institutional—engaged in the translation of ideas into cultural values.

Few (if any) social and political institutions stand completely outside of this process, for true cultural change reaches to the far corners of a society—even to fragrance ads in women's magazines. But two actors figure centrally in the process of defining and diffusing new cultural values. These are critical communities and movements.

The formulation of new ideas occurs within critical communities that knit together a contextual framework for thinking about a particular problem or issue. Although there is some overlap in organization and personnel between critical communities and movements, the most important distinction between them is that the issue exists in isolation for members of a critical community. Competing considerations, such as the need to accommodate other issues, to motivate activists, or to form alliances with other groups that have their own interests, matter little within the critical community. What does matter is the development of a set of claims about how the problem should be viewed and what changes in cultural values and public policies are needed.

Movements bring the issue and its value context to a wider public and to the political arena. One important part of this task is to organize demonstrations, discussion groups, petition signings, teach-ins, sit-ins, letter writing campaigns, self-help associations, and other types of collective action that draw attention to new values and show determination to act on them. While the critical community develops a language to express new values, the movement acts so as to create settings in which those values can be expressed.

There are, of course, other forms of collective action that may assist in the dissemination of new values. These include interest groups and political parties, both of which, however, are better suited to defending established interests than to creating new interests. Interest groups rely on resourceful constituents and on routine access to political decision makers. These traits make interest group action ill-suited to propagating new values, at least until those values have achieved a sufficiently wide currency to support lobbying efforts with the potential for success.

Political parties do respond to changing preferences among voters. But electoral laws, ideological traditions, and organizational inertia make it difficult for parties to address new issues or to incorporate new ways of thinking about an existing issue. When party system change does occur, it is through realignments involving a reconfiguration of the social bases of party support. A great deal of change in cultural values goes on beneath the threshold level necessary to trigger a party realignment, and such change is at best imperfectly captured by adaptations of major party platforms. It falls, then, to movements to demonstrate the mobilizing capacity of a new issue perspective. Since movements are "not constrained by election schedules, party lines, or problems of divided party control, they can be more versatile than parties" (Mayhew 1991: 163). Movements are the first public manifestation of an episode of rapid cultural change.

Of the primary forms of collective action, movements are most closely linked to critical communities and they are the best channel for the translation of critical values into topics of public discourse. Movements are also distinctive in their ability to connect ideas to group identities. By so doing, they infuse group identities with new political and social meanings, and they strengthen solidarity among group members. This enhanced degree of solidarity encourages mobilization by making people more willing to accept the costs and risks of collective action for a public good. The movement must have a strategy (or strategies) for connecting with existing group identities and networks, and for linking those identities to the movement cause. In forging that link, movements win acceptance of their core values, their specific goals, and the tactical means they have developed to reach those goals. Group identification is thus converted into solidarity and engagement among activists.

In the case of movements phrased as claims for group rights, the fit between critical community and group identity is usually clear. Indeed, the ease with which new ideas about group rights can be used to strengthen solidarity has resulted in these claims becoming the predominant basis of movement mobilization. In other instances, movement organizations must evoke solidarity based on more tenuous identifications and sympathies: for "the deserving poor," for endangered species, or (in the case of movements against violence and crime) for law-abiding citizens.

The need to establish a group identity for mobilization is an important constraint on the way movement organizations structure their goals. The environmental movement faces greater problems in connecting critical community ideas to group identities than do the women's movement, gay rights movement, or the student and civil rights movements of an earlier generation. As a result, a great deal of environmental movement activity is focused on threats to the public health of a community—an emphasis disproportionate to the range of environmental threats as identified by the critical community.[1] The range of movement mobilizations is thus shaped in part by the constraints of group identification and solidarity.

Movements bring the ideas of the critical community to a wider public, but the movement task is not simply to publicize critical community perspectives. These perspectives must also be formatted and adapted in a way that will make them suitable for influence in the social and political arenas.

---

[1] Examples of environmental threats on which movement mobilization has been weak relative to critical community assessments of threat include global climate change and the loss of biodiversity resulting from species extinctions.

In addition to refining the ideology of the critical community for the purposes of mobilization, a movement must also identify specific targets of action. This means in the first instance deciding on the allocation of effort to the social and political arenas. Within arenas, a movement organization must identify specific goals, potential alliances, and the range of tactics to be employed. These three elements of strategy within an arena—goals, alliances, and tactics—cannot be selected solely according to the tastes of organization leaders, but are constrained by amount and type of resources the organization controls or is able to acquire. Strategy must also help reinforce the group solidarity on which mobilization relies—it must conform to the group's image of itself. Finally, strategy must incorporate a gradient of roles for activists, ranging from the cheap and riskless to the costly and perilous.

The necessity of developing a wide network of social arena alliances in support of the Cause strategy mandates that the issue be phrased in the broadest possible terms: "Protect the environment." The Critique strategy rests on a more pointed version of the same values: "Trees have rights, too." In the political arena, translation of the ideas of the critical community into a Campaign for reform must be phrased as a specific policy proposal: "Preserve this stand of old growth forest." The Confrontation strategy, adopted by organizations outside of the policy process, may attack the process itself: "Take control of the forest from the logging companies and give it to the local community." Each of these claims derives from the same body of critical community thought, but each is shaped by the aspirations and resources characteristic of particular movement organizations.

These are the conceptual, organizational, and strategic developments that must occur in critical communities and movements in order to create the conditions for rapid cultural change. When the process of change begins to occur in a society, it is marked by broad discussion of new value perspectives. Critical community experts are joined by others who were not involved in development of the perspective. The debate that ensues may be highly polarized between passionate supporters and equally passionate resisters of the new concepts. Advocates of the new ideas claim that change to embody the new values is necessary to avoid severe injustices or dire consequences. Opponents reply that the ideas are utopian, that the dire consequences will not occur, or that the changes proposed would create other troubles greater than the problems they are supposed to remedy. Philosophers are likely to engage the issue, but so are radio and television talk show hosts. The process is not pretty, but it is highly consequential.

Handed over for action in the political arena, the new values fragment into specific policy claims. Policy proposals are formulated in terms that acknowledge the legitimacy of the problem and that propose symbolic and instrumental responses to it. Politicians and bureaucrats will dredge up their favorite ideas from what Kingdon (1984) calls "the policy primeval soup"—touting old medicines for new ailments.

The ability of a movement to stimulate societal debate and political response depends not only on its strategic choices, but also on the social and political institutions that encourage or inhibit reception of the movement's message. Within the society, the keys to effective transmission of movement values are the existence of supportive expert communities, social institutions that contribute prestige and resources, and mass media that view movement activities and ideas as newsworthy. The political reception of the movement depends on the presence of competing political elites, at least some of whom must see advantage in associating themselves with the ideas of the movement and in capitalizing on popular support for it. The stage of the policy process at which movements have their greatest impact is in the determination of important issues and of perspectives on those issues: agenda setting and agenda building. Studies of policy making on civil rights (Burstein 1985), women's issues (Costain and Costain 1985), urban problems (Baumgartner and Jones 1993), and poverty legislation (Imig 1992) show the existence of issue attention cycles initiated by movement protest, followed by media attention, and then by congressional attention.[2] Unlike the issue attention cycle as described by Downs (1972), however, the cycles generated by movements leave permanent effects on the policy process. If the coalition supportive of political change is large enough, the critical values may be enshrined in newly created institutions like the EPA and the EEOC, which develop and enforce a body of regulation responsive to the emerging value perspective.

Governmental attention can be heady stuff for the leaders of movement organizations. But as successive generations of movement leaders have discovered, movement influence declines sharply at the water's edge of agenda setting. Once policy proposals have been formulated, movement organizations become just one set of players competing against others—political parties, bureaucratic agencies, and interest groups—whose power resources are far greater. The movement may remain influential, but its moment of preeminence in the process of change is over.

It is a long voyage from the development of critical community perspectives to policy proposals that can survive the American governmental gauntlet. Policy ideas must address targets that are susceptible to legislative or regulatory remedy, and they must take into account the perspectives and

---

[2] The place of public opinion in this sequence appears to vary by issue. When public opinion is aroused in response to movement protest and media attention, it becomes part of the pressure for political action. On some issues, however, public opinion follows elite decision making in an area. See Page and Shapiro 1983 and Costain and Majstorovic 1994. One might hypothesize that the role of public opinion will depend on whether the movement places early emphasis on the political or social arenas, but that hypothesis will require further research.

routines of those institutions already involved in the policy area (Moore 1988). Deborah Stone (1989: 289) points out that the kinds of systemic thinking characteristic of academic disciplines (and of critical communities) "are not very useful in politics, precisely because they do not offer a single locus of control, a plausible candidate to take responsibility for a problem, or a point of leverage to fix a problem." Thus, for example, the ideas of environmentalism were ultimately translated into legislation requiring the use of technology to reduce pollution emissions, while ignoring more basic (but also more blurry) claims that we must live differently to live sustainably. Perspectives developed within the feminist critical community on the effects of patriarchal institutions on social priorities are translated into public actions that increase the opportunity for women to participate in otherwise unreformed social and political structures. Thus, for example, the portion of the feminist critical community focused on rape inspired the women's movement to efforts that led to reform of rape statutes, repeal of marital exclusion laws, and increased training of police officers to investigate rape cases. They did not get debates on patriarchy or on what Collins and Whalen (1989: 63) call "ending sexual terrorism against women."

The ideas of a critical community are, then, altered in the course of becoming common property of the society. Modification of the original ideas—and particularly the reduction of a broad perspective to a few specific policy initiatives—often leads to disavowal by the critical community and movement that initially sponsored them. Critical communities and their allied movements initiate the impulse for change. But it is governmental institutions that translate this impulse into legislation, and the whole of society that determines the content of altered norms of behavior.

Toward a Movement Society?

In the midst of the depression of the 1890s, an Ohio mineowner and horse breeder named Jacob Coxey issued a call for the unemployed to gather together and march on Washington. Their demand: that Congress issue "interest free bonds" to pay for a $500 million program of hiring laborers to build roads. Coxey's Army, as the marchers came to be known, set out for Washington in late February 1894. They were followed across the Ohio and Pennsylvania countryside by a smaller army of newspaper reporters who wired daily dispatches on the morale and experiences of Coxey's men, and on their reception by the people of the towns through which they passed.

Coxey's Army was one part of the late nineteenth-century challenge to orthodox theories of money and public finance, a challenge that also included the Farmer's Alliance, the Knights of Labor, and several third-party efforts including most notably the Populist Party with its free-silver program. Newspaper editors across the country followed the lead of classical economists in claiming that Coxey's Army was composed of tramps who could find work if they sought it, and that any government program requiring indebtedness through the issuance of bonds would be disastrous to monetary stability. One U.S. senator opined that "A *bona fide* offer of work would undoubtedly disperse the army faster than a cannonball" (*New York Times*, April 22, 1894). Editors of the *New York Times* were so hostile to the concept of a government program to put people to work paving roads that they equated paved roads with anarchism, claiming that nature intended roads to be unpaved and that man is happiest when traveling on a natural road.[3]

Although the newspaper-reading public was never given a careful account of the clash of economic theories at stake in Coxey's protest, it was given daily updates on the progress of the Army for the two months it took to march to Washington. In response to this publicity, other armies sprang up across the country and began commandeering trains to join Coxey. By the day of the parade to the Capitol to present the movement's demands to Congress, Coxey's Army (now thirty thousand strong) was front-page news across the country (Schwantes 1985).

The movement that spawned Coxey's Army contained in it all the elements that would grow into a standard sequence of social and political change over the next hundred years. A grass-roots social movement, headed by the rural Farmer's Alliance and the urban Knights of Labor, joined with a political movement—the Populist Party—to press for reform in both the political and social arenas. Within this broader movement, Coxey's Army fulfilled a need that was then just emerging, driven by developments in the mass media. This need is for the serial drama of a symbolic protest that combines a continuing storyline with fresh developments on a daily basis. Coxey's Army fit the bill perfectly, not least because of the maintenance of suspense about whether Congress would receive Coxey, and what his Army would do if Congress did not.

The sole element missing from the movement for monetary reform was the input of a critical community. The Populist plan to back the dollar with both gold and silver, the Farmer's Alliance proposal for a federal system of grain storage and rural credit,[4] and Coxey's demand for a road-building employment program all sprang directly from representatives of distressed occupations and regions. None were integrated into a broader theory of money and public finance, and none had the imprimatur of recognized experts, critical or otherwise. Even defection of the Democratic Party to the free-silver cause beginning in 1896, the monetary equivalent of Coxey's fiscal proposal, did not alter the expert consensus for budgetary orthodoxy. On the contrary,

[3] *New York Times*, May 1, 1894, p. 4 (editorial).
[4] C. W. Macune's subtreasury plan. For details see Hicks 1961: 187–188 and Goodwyn 1978: 109–113.

the elite press cited government officials and economists as ridiculing the very idea of deficit financing for a road-building program. It took the theories of John Maynard Keynes a generation later to legitimize the idea that involuntary unemployment exists, and that deficit spending and manipulation of the money supply by government are effective policy tools for generating economic activity and smoothing the business cycle.[5] It is difficult to imagine a more dramatic verification of the point made by Deborah Stone (1989: 294) that "science commands enormous cultural authority as the arbiter of empirical questions." The critical community is a vital element of the process of cultural change. Crane Brinton's (1952: 52) aphorism "No ideas, no revolution" might well be modified to read: "No expert-generated ideas, no reform."

Linkages between critical communities and movements, the communication of new value perspectives through the mass media, and the development of networks connecting movements to powerful social and political institutions all came into their own during the course of the twentieth century. It is common to observe that the pace of social and cultural change has greatly increased. Equally significant, though, is the *process* of change that has come to be dominant. The twentieth century was the century in which specialization, interdependence, mobility, and change came together to render obsolete the old utopia of a society steered from above according to a fixed set of principles. Totalitarianism was in this century invented, tried, and found wanting. A variety of political system types ranging from democracy to socialism to authoritarianism converged on an activist definition of government, in which the range of policy responsibilities has grown unprecedentedly wide. This kind of active-responsive government requires that the line between society and government be blurred in order to encourage widespread public participation in the determination of collective purposes and meanings, and in the negotiation of coordinated plans of action. At century's end, we continue to grope toward the development of organizational forms and public-private relationships that will link an activist government to a mobilized public.

At the heart of the active-responsive pattern of government is the exchange of information between public and private spheres that Jürgen Habermas (1984: esp. pp. 285–286) summarizes as "communicative action." It is rooted in a particular kind of linkage between knowledge and action in which purposes, processes, and outcomes are based on negotiated understandings. These understandings are recognized by all parties as tentative,

---

[5] Keynes's ideas were, of course, given greater credence by the experience of the Great Depression. However, the link between a tight money supply, expensive credit, price deflation, and widespread economic distress was obvious enough in the 1890s to anyone prepared to consider the matter with an open mind.

uncertain, and based on the temporary confluence of interests and needs. Change, or at least the possibility of change in response to continuous monitoring of present circumstances, is understood to be necessary and normal. As a result, the realm of unchallengeable authority (whether rooted in religious, scientific, or political dogma) has been reduced. In its place has grown the realm of communicative action, with its publicly contested meanings and contingent purposes.[6] In a society where change is thought to be necessary to efficiency, progress can be measured by the range of topics and institutional settings in which communicative action is the norm. The political process becomes increasingly fluid and politics itself becomes "a struggle over meaning" (Phillips 1994: 57). Legislative decisions are based on the provisional acceptance of a particular version of the problem, giving statute making "a speculative nature" (Jones 1995).

Application of these ideas to organizational forms and practices can be seen most clearly in changes in the theory and structure of the economic firm. The organizational demands of a shift from standardized mass production to adaptive flexible production has resulted in a partial intermingling of the role of managers and workers, who develop production strategies in collaboration with each other. The greatest change of all may be the increased reliance on interorganization coordination. Horizontal collaboration often replaces vertical integration in order to increase the speed with which a firm can incorporate new technologies and designs into its products (Piore and Sabel 1984).

There has been a parallel and equally significant revolution in government. Governance in America over the past decades has embraced an ever wider range of interest groups and movement organizations (Walker 1991). It has witnessed an opening of the legislative and regulatory processes that give these groups an expanded role in policy formulation, implementation, and oversight (Gormley 1989). It has seen the decline of programmatic party organizations and the rise of the political leader as policy entrepreneur, resulting in a reinterpretation of party ideologies with each presidential election (Wattenberg 1991, 1994). It has led to the adoption and abandonment of political agendas by would-be leaders according to the results of opinion polls and focus groups (Geer 1996).

The outcome of this political revolution is that the task of leadership becomes one of negotiating and coordinating decisions through policy networks. The difference between these policy networks and the "iron trian-

---

[6] Lindblom (1990) makes a similar point with his thesis of a transition from a scientific society (structured by expert knowledge) to a self-guiding society (in which large numbers of citizens contribute to social problem solving based on their own knowledge, experience, and ability to reason and communicate). See also Euchner 1996, whose concept of "extraordinary politics" incorporates the idea of ongoing contestation over issues, participants, institutions, and the public-private boundary.

gles" of an earlier generation is that policy networks are made of clay rather than iron: although normally stable, they are periodically reformed with new participants who bring novel perspectives to policy questions that are themselves no longer taken for granted. Constituted political leaders are today enmeshed in an ever closer relationship with a variety of political and social groups, whose influence may wax and wane with considerable rapidity.

The critical community-movement nexus contributes to the reshaping of policy networks in a number of ways. Most fundamentally, the ideas of the critical community place policy issues in a new value context. When these ideas are taken up by a movement, there is a growth of social and political pressure to reformulate the purposes of policy making, and possibly to change the policy process or the venue of decision making (Peters and Hogwood 1985; Baumgartner and Jones 1993). The mobilization of a movement may also carry new participants into the political process, participants who not only bring new voices to policy discussions but who also affect coalitional alignments among groups already represented (Press 1994). Finally, the existence of a movement may encourage a reevaluation of cultural images of the movement's constituency group. When a social group is viewed as increasingly powerful and purposive, different types of policies come to be seen as appropriate responses to group demands. Our images of who is poor and why they are poor, for example, affect our understanding of the kinds of policies best suited to fighting poverty (Baumgartner and Jones 1993; Schneider and Ingram 1993).

In the always provisional web of contemporary social and political communication, critical communities and movements combine to initiate the process of cultural change.[7] But movements have other impacts as well, beyond those directly associated with their immediate goals of cultural change. In the course of accomplishing their purposes, movements also:

> Create new group identities or reinforce the extent of solidarity attending existing group identities,
>
> Cultivate a cadre of activists who embrace active citizenship values and whose organizational skills may be applied to a succession of causes throughout their lives,
>
> Innovate new forms of protest and, more generally, new ways of communicating critical values through institutional and media channels,
>
> Expand the range of participants in the policy process and reduce the legitimacy of future attempts to restrict participation to already established groups,

---

[7] Habermas (1979: 125) assigns a more modest role to movements as being involved in social learning within existing cultural traditions, so that "latently available structures of rationality are transposed into social practice." This neglect of the possibility of creating and interpreting new cultural values may stem from a different definition of movements used by Habermas, which leaves out the role of critical communities.

> Add to the legacy of symbols and historical memories that embrace change as
> necessary to improvement of the community and that accept successful move-
> ments from the past as bearers of messages of justice and fairness.

There have been many interpretations of American politics that bemoan
the power of mobilized, entrenched interests. The perspective developed in
this book is far more optimistic. To the charge, for example, that "the media
generally reflect the views of the upper-class audience and influence the
views of the lower-class audience" (Ginsberg 1986: 147), we can reply that
movement activity is a lever that directs media attention to the ideas of
critical communities. When a lower-class audience appropriates a critical
community message and mobilizes in a movement, it is transformed from
audience to actor.

Even more significant for our understanding of the distribution of power is
the fact that although established interests are certainly influential, the identity of those established interests fluctuates over time. An account of politics
that focuses on the interests of already mobilized groups will miss these
elements of dynamism. Issues are not fixed, but have instead multiple elements that may receive more or less stress depending on who is involved.
The considerations brought to bear on an issue change over time, due both to
the mobilization of new groups and to the redefinition of interests on the part
of already mobilized groups. The definition of interests on an issue, of who
is a stakeholder and what the stakes are, will be altered when the issue
comes to be seen in a new context. An interest-based model of the policy
process is adequate to capture the statics of a well-specified issue conflict,
but only a model centered on the generation and diffusion of group solidarities and critical ideas can capture the flux over time in how an issue is
defined and who is mobilized on it.

We saw in chapter 1 that cultural change in a single value (like prohibition
or electing a woman as president) can move slowly as a function of population replacement or more rapidly as a function of widespread adoption of a
new cultural perspective. A number of scholars have found that periods of
quickening movement activity and cultural change tend to cluster together in
what Sidney Tarrow (1994) calls a cycle of protest.[8] When one movement is
successful in mobilizing large numbers of activists, innovating new forms of
collective action, and finding powerful social and political allies, opportunities for other movements are increased as well. Movement organizations
proliferate and develop links with each other. A cadre of activists with enhanced skills and solidarities is created, some of whom will shift their activity to other movements. Social and political coalitions mobilized for one
cause are at least partially transferable to other causes. The specific item of

---

[8] See also Downs 1972; Zolberg 1972; Hirschman 1982; Schlesinger 1986; Brand 1990;
McAdam 1995; Tarrow 1995.

value change championed by a movement develops a broader influence as people generalize to related phenomena. The result is what Tarrow calls the "movement society," one in which movements have become part of the normal political and social landscape. As Tarrow points out, this phenomenon is not limited to America or indeed to any national boundaries at all, since there has been an ever quickening spread of transnational movements as well.

At the heart of the idea of a movement society is the view that progressive change has come to be seen as possible and normal. Our confidence in the power of change is such that most projections of the future assume that new technologies will be developed, greater efficiencies will be found, and human organization and behavior will adapt to changed circumstances. It is not uncommon for legislators to set policy targets, such as pollution abatement requirements, that cannot be met with present technologies, population densities, and consumption patterns. The assumption is that the necessary technical innovations and behavioral adaptations will occur in order to meet these policy targets.

In a provocative essay on cultural understandings of political change, Harry Eckstein (1988: 795) has questioned whether the need in modern society for adaptability in cultural values means that such societies are "intrinsically acultural." There is a point, after all, where the adoption of new value perspectives follows changed social conditions so flexibly that it becomes meaningless even to think in terms of deeply rooted cultural values. If values are no more than constantly updated decision rules for dealing with life, then people are better thought of as rational calculators than as the bearers of culture.

The investigations presented in this book suggest that Eckstein is right to conclude that people are still cultural animals. Although rapid change in cultural values does occur, it happens only with a struggle. Cultural change is a contentious process of resolving rival claims of how we should think about each other, about our natural and social environments, and about the most pressing purposes of collective action. The civil rights, environmental, antiwar, consumer, and women's movements have challenged widely held beliefs about racial hierarchies, the freedom of individuals to use their property as they wish, America's role in the world, and the ineffaceable differences between men and women. Reaction to these movements has been heated, going well beyond the kind of debate generated by a mere clash of interests. If change in cultural values were a matter of clear-eyed calculations unweighted by the baggage of cherished beliefs, the entire nexus of critical communities, movements, and social and political audiences would not be needed to initiate change or to give it direction.

The focus of this book on the major transformative movements of American history may seem to carry the hidden message that cultural change is always a good thing. Looked at retrospectively, changes in cultural values are readily but misleadingly viewed as the abandonment of flawed beliefs for those that are more humane, or even "correct." As John Dewey wrote in 1929, it is easy to "confuse rapidity of change with advance, and to take certain gains in our own comfort and ease as signs that cosmic forces were working inevitably to improve the whole state of human affairs" (cited in Joas 1990: 184). But there is no reason to assume a priori that rapid cultural change is always adaptive to altered social conditions, or (contrary to the philosophes) that change necessarily contributes to the process of perfecting society. Which new ideas come to be accepted may depend more on the vigor of rival movement organizations and the receptivity of social and political institutions, than on the relative merits of competing value systems.

No one individual will agree that all cultural changes initiated in critical communities and movements over the past half century have been for the good. Remedies for one injustice commonly create other injustices. When some recently mobilized interests gain new privileges, other interests are harmed. Yet, if we cannot say that all cultural change is good, we can surely say that the absence of cultural change would be disastrous.

Observing social decay during the expansion of the Roman Empire, Livy lamented that "In our times we can neither endure our faults nor the means of correcting them." Our rather more complex and interdependent society leaves us no choice but to endure the means of correcting our faults. The twentieth-century development of a critical community-movement nexus has helped to embed in our culture the idea that change is eternal, powerful, and (taken in the aggregate) for the better. It remains for the inhabitants of the twenty-first century to put these tools to good use.

REFERENCES

Adam, Barry (1987) *The Rise of a Gay and Lesbian Movement* (Boston: Twayne).

Adams, Frank (1975) *Unearthing the Seed of Fire: The Idea of Highlander* (Charlotte, NC: John Blain).

Adams, John (1961) *The Diary and Autobiography of John Adams*, volume 4 (Cambridge, MA: Harvard University Press).

Alberoni, Francesco (1984) *Movement and Institution* (New York: Columbia University Press).

Alexander, Jeffrey, and Piotr Sztompka (eds.) (1990) *Rethinking Progress: Movements, Forces and Ideas at the End of the Twentieth Century* (Boston: Unwin Hyman).

Almond, Gabriel, and Sidney Verba (1963) *The Civic Culture* (Princeton, NJ: Princeton University Press).

Arrhenius, Svante (1896) "On the Influence of Carbonic Acid in the Air upon the Temperature on the Ground," *Philosophy Magazine* 41: 237.

Baker, Keith Michael (1990) *Inventing the French Revolution: Essays on French Political Culture in the Eighteenth Century* (New York: Cambridge University Press).

Ball, Terence (1976) "From Paradigms to Research Programs: Toward a Post-Kuhnian Political Science," *American Journal of Political Science* 20 (February): 151–177.

Ball, Terence, James Farr, and Russell Hanson (1989) *Political Innovation and Conceptual Change* (New York: Cambridge University Press).

Barkan, Stephan (1979) "Strategic, Tactical and Organizational Dilemmas of the Protest against Nuclear Power," *Sociological Problems* 27 (October): 19–37.

Barnes, Samuel, Max Kaase, et al. (1979) *Political Action* (Beverly Hills, CA: Sage).

Barrows, Susanna, and Robin Room (eds.) (1991) *Drinking: Behavior and Belief in Modern History* (Berkeley: University of California Press).

Baumgartner, Frank, and Bryan Jones (1993) *Agendas and Instability in American Politics* (Chicago: University of Chicago Press).

Behr, R. L., and Shanto Iyengar (1985) "Television News, Real-World Cues, and Changes in the Public Agenda," *Public Opinion Quarterly* 49 (Spring): 38–57.

Bennett, W. Lance, and Regina Lawrence (1994) "The Journalist's Tool Kit: News Icons and the Framing of Social Change." Paper presented at the meetings of the American Political Science Association, New York.

Bentley, Judith (1984) *The Nuclear Freeze Movement* (New York: Franklin and Watts).

Black, Cyril E. (1967) *The Dynamics of Modernization* (New York: Harper and Row).

Blumer, Herbert ([1939]1974) "Social Movements," reprinted on pages 4–20 of R. Serge Denisoff (ed.), *The Sociology of Dissent* (New York: Harcourt, Brace, Jovanovich).

Bobo, Lawrence, and Franklin Gilliam (1990) "Race, Sociopolitical Participation, and Black Empowerment," *American Political Science Review* 84 (June): 377–393.

Boles, Janet (1991) "Form Follows Function: The Evolution of Feminist Strategies," *Annals of the American Academy of Political and Social Sciences* 515 (May): 38–49.

Bosso, Christopher (1987) *Pesticides and Politics* (Pittsburgh: University of Pittsburgh Press).

Bourdieu, Pierre (1991) *Language and Symbolic Power* (Cambridge: Polity Press).

Boynton, G. R. (1982) "On Getting from Here to There," pages 29–68 in Elinor Ostrom (ed.), *Strategies of Political Inquiry* (Beverly Hills, CA: Sage).

Bradford, Neil (1994) "Ideas, Institutions and Innovation: Economic Policy in Canada and Sweden," pages 83–103 in Stephen Brooks and Alain-G. Gagnon (eds.), *The Political Influence of Ideas: Policy Communities and the Social Sciences* (Westport, CT: Praeger).

Brady, Henry, Sidney Verba, and Kay Schlozman (1995) "Beyond SES: A Resource Model of Political Participation," *American Political Science Review* 89 (June): 271–294.

Brand, Karl-Werner (1990), "Cyclical Aspects of New Social Movements," pages 23–42 in Russell Dalton and Manfred Kuechler (eds.), *Challenging the Political Order* (New York: Oxford University Press).

Braungart, Margaret, and Richard Braungart (1991) "The Effects of the 1960s Political Generation on Former Left-and Right-Wing Youth Activist Leaders," *Social Problems* 38 (August): 297–315.

Brewer, Marilynn (1979) "In-Group Bias in the Minimal Intergroup Situation: A Cognitive-Motivational Analysis," *Psychological Bulletin* 86 (March): 307–324.

Briggs, Asa (1960) "The Language of Class," pages 43–73 in Asa Briggs and John Saville (eds.), *Essays in Labour History in Memory of G. D. H. Cole* (London: Macmillan).

Brinton, Crane (1952) *The Anatomy of Revolution* (New York: Prentice-Hall).

Brooks, Stephen and Alain-G. Gagnon (eds.) (1994) *The Political Influence of Ideas: Policy Communities and the Social Sciences* (Westport, CT: Praeger).

Bryner, Gary (1993) *Blue Skies, Green Politics* (Washington, DC: Congressional Quarterly Press).

Buckley, William F., Jr. (1993) *Happy Days Were Here Again* (New York: Random House).

Burstein, Paul (1985) *Discrimination, Jobs and Politics* (Chicago: University of Chicago Press).

Burstein, Paul (1991) "Legal Mobilization as a Social Movement Tactic," *American Journal of Sociology* 96 (March): 1201–1225.

Calhoun, Craig (1995) "'New Social Movements' of the Early Nineteenth Century," pages 175–215 in Mark Traugott (ed.), *Repertoires and Cycles of Collective Action* (Durham, NC: Duke University Press).

Carmichael, Stokely, and Charles Hamilton (1967) *Black Power* (New York: Vintage).

Carmines, Edward, and James Stimson (1989) *Issue Evolution: Race and the Transformation of American Politics* (Princeton, NJ: Princeton University Press).

Chartier, Roger (1991) *The Cultural Origins of the French Revolution* (Durham, NC: Duke University Press).

Chidester, David (1988) *Salvation and Suicide* (Bloomington: Indiana University Press).

Chong, Dennis (1991) *Collective Action and the Civil Rights Movement* (Chicago: University of Chicago Press).

Cigler, Allan, and John Mark Hansen (1983) "Group Formation through Protest: The American Agriculture Movement," pages 84–109 in Allan Cigler and Burdett Loomis (eds.), *Interest Group Politics* (Washington, DC: Congressional Quarterly Press).

Clark, Janet (1991) "Getting There: Women in Political Office," *Annals of the American Academy of Political and Social Science* 515 (May): 63–76.

Cleaver, Eldridge (1968) *Soul on Ice* (New York: Dell).

Cole, Elsa Kircher (1986) "Recent Legal Developments in Sexual Harassment," *Journal of College and University Law* 13 (Winter): 267–284.

Collins, Barbara, and Mary Whalen (1989) "The Rape Crisis Movement: Radical or Reformist?" *Social Work* 34 (January): 61–63.

Conover, Pamela (1988) "The Role of Social Groups in Political Thinking," *British Journal of Political Science* 18 (January): 51–76.

Converse, Philip (1976) *The Dynamics of Party Support* (Beverly Hills, CA: Sage).

Costain, Anne (1992) *Inviting Women's Rebellion: A Political Process Interpretation of the Women's Movement* (Baltimore: Johns Hopkins University Press).

Costain, Anne, and Douglas Costain (1985) "Movements and Gatekeepers: Congressional Response to Women's Movement Issues, 1900–1982," *Congress and the Presidency* 12 (Spring): 21–42.

Costain, Anne, and Steven Majstorovic (1994) "Congress, Social Movements and Public Opinion: Multiple Origins of Women's Rights Legislation," *Political Research Quarterly* 47 (March): 111–135.

Coulter, Jim, Susan Miller, and Martin Walker (1984) *State of Siege: Politics and Policing of the Coalfields* (London: Canary Press).

Crane, Diana (1972) *Invisible Colleges: Diffusion of Knowledge in Scientific Communities* (Chicago: University of Chicago Press).

Cross, William E., Jr. (1971) "The Negro-to-Black Conversion Experience," *Black World* (July): 13–27.

Dalton, Russell (1988) *Citizen Politics in Western Democracies* (Chatham, NJ: Chatham House).

Dalton, Russell (1994) *The Green Rainbow* (New Haven: Yale University Press).

Dalton, Russell, Manfred Kuechler, and Wilhelm Bürklin (1990) "The Challenge of New Movements," pages 3–20 in Russell Dalton and Manfred Kuechler (eds.), *Challenging the Political Order: New Social and Political Movements in Western Democracies* (New York: Oxford University Press).

Darnton, Robert (1984) *The Great Cat Massacre* (New York: Basic Books).

Davis, Flora (1991) *Moving the Mountain: The Women's Movement in America since 1960* (New York: Simon and Schuster).

DeLong, Marilyn, and Elizabeth Bye (1990) "Apparel for the Senses: The Use and Meaning of Fragrances," *Journal of Popular Culture* 24 (Winter): 81–88.

Denzau, Arthur, and Douglass North (1994) "Shared Mental Models: Ideologies and Institutions," *Kyklos* 47 (1): 3–31.

Deutsch, Karl (1961) "Social Mobilization and Political Development," *American Political Science Review* 55 (September): 493–502.

Deutsch, Karl (1963) *The Nerves of Government* (Glencoe, IL: Free Press)

Diani, Mario (1992) "The Concept of Social Movement," *Sociological Review* 40 (February): 1–25.

Diani, Mario (1995) *Green Networks* (Edinburgh: Edinburgh University Press).

Dillon, Merton (1974) *The Abolitionists* (DeKalb: Northern Illinois University Press).

Downey, Gary (1986) "Ideology and the Clamshell Identity: Organizational Dilemmas in the Anti-Nuclear Power Movement," *Social Problems* 33 (June): 357–373.

Downs, Anthony (1957) *An Economic Theory of Democracy* (New York: Harper and Row).

Downs, Anthony (1972) "Up and Down with Ecology: The Issue Attention Cycle," *Public Interest* 28 (Summer): 38–50.

Eckstein, Harry (1988) "A Culturalist Theory of Political Change," *American Political Science Review* 82 (September): 789–804.

Edelman, Murray (1964) *The Symbolic Uses of Politics* (Urbana: University of Illinois Press).

Eisinger, Peter (1973) "Conditions of Protest," *American Political Science Review* 67 (March): 11–28.

Eldersveld, Samuel (1956) "Experimental Propaganda Techniques and Voting Behavior," *American Political Science Review* 50 (March): 154–165.

Elster, Jon (1989) *Nuts and Bolts for the Social Sciences* (New York: Cambridge University Press).

Entman, Robert, and Andrew Rojecki (1993) "Freezing Out the Public: Elite and Media Framing of the U.S. Anti-nuclear Movement," *Political Communication* 10 (April–June): 155–173.

Epstein, Barbara (1991) *Political Protest and Cultural Revolution: Nonviolent Direct Action in the 1970s and 1980s* (Berkeley: University of California Press).

Estrich, Susan (1987) *Real Rape* (Cambridge, MA: Harvard University Press).

Euchner, Charles (1996) *Extraordinary Politics: How Protest and Dissent Are Changing American Democracy* (Boulder, CO: Westview).

Evans, Sara (1979) *Personal Politics* (New York: Alfred Knopf).

Evans, Sara, and Harry Boyte (1986) *Free Spaces: The Sources of Democratic Change in America* (New York: Harper and Row).

Ewen, Stuart (1976) *Captains of Consciousness* (New York: McGraw-Hill).

Eyerman, Ron (1990) "Intellectuals and Progress: The Origins, Decline and Revival of a Critical Group," pages 91–105 in Jeffrey Alexander and Piotr Sztompka (eds.), *Rethinking Progress: Movements, Forces and Ideas at the End of the Twentieth Century* (Boston: Unwin Hyman).

Eyerman, Ron, and Andrew Jamison (1991) *Social Movements: A Cognitive Approach* (University Park: Pennsylvania State University Press).

Eyerman, Ron, Lennart Svensson, and Thomas Söderqvist (eds.) (1987) *Intellectuals, Universities and the State in Western Modern Societies* (Berkeley: University of California Press).

Fantasia, Rick (1988) *Cultures of Solidarity: Consciousness, Action, and Contemporary American Workers* (Berkeley: University of California Press).

Farley, Lin (1978) *Sexual Shakedown: The Sexual Harassment of Women on the Job* (New York: McGraw-Hill).

Farmer, James (1985) *Lay Bare the Heart: An Autobiography of the Civil Rights Movement* (New York: New American Library).

Feighan, Edward (1983) "The Freeze in Congress," pages 29–55 in Paul Cole and William Taylor (eds.), *The Nuclear Freeze Debate* (Boulder, CO: Westview).

Fendrich, James (1977) "Keeping the Faith or Pursuing the Good Life: A Study of the Consequences of Participation in the Civil Rights Movement," *American Sociological Review* 42 (February): 144–157.

Fendrich, James, and Robert Turner (1989) "The Transition from Student to Adult Politics," *Social Forces* 67 (June): 1049–1057.

Ferree, Myra Marx (1974) "A Woman for President? Changing Responses 1958–1972," *Public Opinion Quarterly* 38 (Fall): 390–399.

Ferree, Myra Marx (1987) "Equality and Autonomy: Feminist Politics in the United States and West Germany," pages 172–195 in Mary Katzenstein and Carole Mueller (eds.), *The Women's Movements of the United States and Western Europe* (Philadelphia: Temple University Press).

Ferree, Myra Marx (1992) "The Political Context of Rationality: Rational Choice Theory and Resource Mobilization," pages 29–52 in Aldon Morris and Carol Mueller (eds.), *Frontiers in Social Movement Theory* (New Haven, CT: Yale University Press).

Ferree, Myra Marx and Beth B. Hess (1985) *Controversy and Coalition: The New Feminist Movement* (Boston: Twayne).

Ferree, Myra Marx and Frederick Miller (1985) "Mobilization and Meaning: Toward an Integration of Social Psychology and Resource Perspectives on Social Movements," *Social Inquiry* 55 (Winter): 38–61.

Filler, Louis (1960) *The Crusade against Slavery, 1830–1860* (New York: Harper Brothers).

Fink, Leon (1983) *Workingmen's Democracy: The Knights of Labor and American Politics* (Urbana: University of Illinois Press).

Finkel, Steven, Edward Muller, and Karl-Dieter Opp (1989) "Personal Influence, Collective Rationality and Mass Political Action," *American Political Science Review* 83 (September): 885–903.

Firebaugh, Glenn, and Kenneth Davis (1988) "Trends in Antiblack Prejudice, 1972–1984: Region and Cohort Effects," *American Journal of Sociology* 94 (September): 251–272.

Fireman, Bruce, and William Gamson (1979) "Utilitarian Logic in the Resource Mobilization Perspective," pages 8–44 in Mayer Zald and John McCarthy (eds.), *The Dynamics of Collective Action* (Cambridge, MA: Winthrop).

Fishman, Jacob, and Fredric Solomon (1970) "Youth and Social Action: Perspectives on the Student Sit-in Movement," pages 143–156 in Richard Young (ed.), *The Roots of Rebellion* (New York: Harper and Row).

Flacks, Richard (1967) "The Liberated Generation: An Explanation of the Roots of Student Protest," *Journal of Social Issues* 23 (July): 52–75.

Fredrickson, George (1971) *The Black Image in the White Mind: The Debate on Afro-American Character and Destiny, 1817–1914* (New York: Harper and Row).

Freeman, Jo (1975) *The Politics of Women's Liberation* (New York: Longman).

Gallup, George H. (1972) *The Gallup Poll—Public Opinion, 1935–1971*, volume 2: *1949–1959* (New York: Random House).

Gallup, George, Jr. (various years) *The Gallup Poll—Public Opinion* (Wilmington, DE: Scholarly Resources).

Gamson, Josh (1989) "Silence, Death and the Invisible Enemy: AIDS Activism and Social Movement 'Newness,'" *Social Problems* 36 (October): 351–367.

Gamson, William (1988) "Political Discourse and Collective Action," pages 219–244 in Bert Klandermans, Hanspeter Kriesi, and Sidney Tarrow (eds.), *From Structure to Action: International Social Movement Research*, volume 1 (Greenwich, CT: JAI Press).

Gamson, William (1990) *The Strategy of Social Protest*, 2nd edition (Belmont, CA: Wadsworth).

Gamson, William (1991) "Commitment and Agency in Social Movements," *Sociological Forum* 6 (March): 27–50.

Gamson, William (1992) "The Social Psychology of Collective Action," pages 53–76 in Aldon Morris and Carol Mueller (eds.), *Frontiers in Social Movement Theory* (New Haven, CT: Yale University Press).

Gamson, William, and David Meyer (1996) "Framing Political Opportunity," pages 275–290 in Doug McAdam, John McCarthy, and Mayer Zald (eds.), *Comparative Perspectives on Social Movements* (New York: Cambridge University Press).

Gamson, William, and Andre Modigliani (1989) "Media Discourse and Public Opinion on Nuclear Power: A Constructionist Approach," *American Journal of Sociology* 95 (July): 1–37.

Gamson, William, and David Stuart (1992) "Media Discourse as a Symbolic Contest: The Bomb in Political Cartoons," *Sociological Forum* 7 (1): 55–86.

Gamson, William, and Gadi Wolfsfeld (1993) "Movements and Media as Interacting Systems," *Annals of the American Academy of Social and Political Science* 528 (July): 114–125.

Gans, H. J. (1979) *Deciding What's News* (New York: Vintage).

Garfinkle, Adam (1984) *The Politics of the Nuclear Freeze* (Philadelphia: Foreign Policy Research Institute).

Geer, John (1991) "The Electorate's Partisan Evaluations: Evidence of a Continuing Democratic Edge," *Public Opinion Quarterly* 55 (Summer): 218–231.

Geer, John (1996) *From Tea Leaves to Opinion Polls: A Theory of Democratic Leadership* (New York: Columbia University Press).

Gelb, Joyce (1989) *Feminism and Politics* (Berkeley: University of California Press).

Gelb, Joyce (1990) "Feminism and Political Action," pages 137–155 in Russell Dalton and Manfred Kuechler (eds.), *Challenging the Political Order: New Social and Political Movements in Western Democracies* (New York: Oxford University Press).

Gimpel, James, and Robin Wolpert (1996) "Opinion-holding and Public Attitudes toward Controversial Supreme Court Nominees," *Political Research Quarterly* 49 (March): 163–176.

Ginsberg, Benjamin (1986) *The Captive Public: How Mass Opinion Promotes State Power* (New York: Basic Books).

Gitlin, Todd (1980) *The Whole World Is Watching: Mass Media in the Making and Unmaking of the New Left* (Berkeley: University of California Press).

Glover, David, and Cora Kaplan (1972) "Guns in the House of Culture? Crime Fiction and the Politics of the Popular," pages 213–223 in Lawrence Grossberg, Cary Nelson, and Paula Teichler (eds.), *Cultural Studies* (New York: Routledge).

Goldenberg, Edie (1975) *Making the Papers: The Access of Resource-Poor Groups to the Metropolitan Press* (Lexington, MA: Heath).

Goldie, Mark (1989) "Ideology," pages 266–291 in Terence Ball, James Farr, and Russell Hanson (eds.), *Political Innovation and Conceptual Change* (New York: Cambridge University Press).

Goldstone, Jack A. (1980) "The Weakness of Organization: A New Look at Gamson's *The Strategy of Social Protest*," *American Journal of Sociology* 85 (March): 1017–1042.

Goodwyn, Lawrence (1978) *The Populist Moment* (New York: Oxford University Press).

Gormley, William, Jr. (1989) *Taming the Bureaucracy: Muscles, Prayers and Other Strategies* (Princeton, NJ: Princeton University Press).

Gossett, Thomas (1963) *Race: The History of an Idea in America* (Dallas: Southern Methodist University Press).

Gould, Stephen Jay (1981) *The Mismeasure of Man* (New York: Norton).

Graber, Doris (1984) *The Mass Media and American Politics*, 2nd edition (Washington, DC: Congressional Quarterly Press).

Graber, Doris (1988) *Processing the News*, 2nd edition (New York: Longman).

Gusfield, Joseph (1970) *Symbolic Crusade: Status Politics and the American Temperance Movement* (Champaign: University of Illinois Press).

Gusfield, Joseph (1981) "Social Movements and Social Change: Perspectives of Linearity and Fluidity," pages 317–339 in Louis Kriesberg (ed.), *Research in Social Movements, Conflict and Change*, volume 4. (Greenwich, CT: JAI Press).

Gusfield, Joseph (1982) "Prevention: Rise, Decline and Renaissance," pages 402–425 in Edith Gomberg, Helene White, and John Carpenter (eds.), *Alcohol, Science and Society Revisited* (Ann Arbor, MI, and New Brunswick, NJ: University of Michigan Press and Rutgers Center of Alcohol Studies).

Gutierrez, Armando, and Herbert Hirsch (1973) "The Militant Challenge to the American Ethos: 'Chicanos' and 'Mexican-Americans,'" *Social Science Quarterly* 53 (March): 830–845.

Haas, Peter (1992) "Introduction: Epistemic Communities and International Policy Coordination," *International Organization* 46 (Winter): 1–35.

Habermas, Jürgen (1979) *Communication and the Evolution of Society* (Boston: Beacon).

Habermas, Jürgen (1984) *Theory of Communicative Action*, volume 1 (Boston: Beacon).

Hahn, Robert (1994) "United States Environmental Policy: Past, Present and Future," *Natural Resources Journal* 34 (Spring): 305–348.

Hamilton, Charles (1972) *The Black Preacher in America* (New York: William Morrow).

Harford, Barbara, and Sarah Hopkins (1984) *Greenham Common: Women at the Wire* (London: Women's Press).

Hawkins, Robert, and Suzanne Pingree (1981) "Using Television to Construct Social Reality," *Journal of Broadcasting* 25 (Fall): 347–364.

Hersh, Blanche Glassman (1978) *The Slavery of Sex: Feminist-Abolitionists in America* (Urbana: University of Illinois Press).

Hicks, John (1961) *The Populist Revolt* (Lincoln: University of Nebraska Press).

Hilgartner, Stephen, and Charles Bosk (1988) "The Rise and Fall of Social Problems: A Public Arena Model," *American Journal of Sociology* 94 (July): 53–78.

Hirsch, Eric (1986) "The Creation of Political Solidarity in Social Movement Organizations," *Sociological Quarterly* 27 (September): 373–387.

Hirsch, Eric (1990) "Sacrifice for the Cause," *American Sociological Review* 55 (April): 243–254.

Hirschman, Albert (1982) *Shifting Involvements: Private Interest and Public Action* (Princeton, NJ: Princeton University Press).

Hochschild, Jennifer (1984) *The New American Dilemma: Liberal Democracy and School Desegregation* (New Haven, CT: Yale University Press).

Hoff, Joan (1994) *Nixon Reconsidered* (New York: Basic Books).

Hoffer, Eric (1951) *The True Believer* (New York: New American Library).

Hoge, Dean, and Teresa Ankney (1982) "Occupations and Attitudes of Former Student Activists Ten Years Later," *Journal of Youth and Adolescence* 11 (October): 355–371.

Humphrey, Ronald, and Howard Schuman (1984) "The Portrayal of Blacks in Magazine Advertisements: 1950–1982," *Public Opinion Quarterly* 48 (Fall): 551–563.

Huntington, Samuel (1971) "The Change to Change: Modernization, Development and Politics," *Comparative Politics* 3 (April): 283–322.

Imig, Douglas (1992) "Mobilization of the Hunger Lobby: Issue Attention, Collective Action and Institutional Response." Paper presented at the annual meeting of the American Political Science Association, Chicago.

Inglehart, Ronald (1990) "Values, Ideology, and Cognitive Mobilization in New Social Movements" pages 43–66 in Russell Dalton and Manfred Kuechler (eds.), *Challenging the Political Order* (New York: Oxford University Press).

Inkeles, Alex (1969) "Participant Citizenship in Six Developing Countries," *American Political Science Review* 63 (December): 1120–1141.

Iyengar, Shanto, and Donald Kinder (1987) *News That Matters* (Chicago: University of Chicago Press).

Iyengar, Shanto, Mark Peters, and Donald Kinder (1982) "Experimental Demonstrations of the 'Not-so-Minimal' Consequences of Television News Programs," *American Political Science Review* 76 (December): 848–858.

Jackman, Mary (1978) "General and Applied Tolerance: Does Eduction Increase Commitment to Racial Integration?" *American Journal of Political Science* 22 (May): 302–324.

Jacobs, James (1989) *Drunk Driving: An American Dilemma* (Chicago: University of Chicago Press).

James, Hunter (1993) *They Didn't Put That on the Huntley-Brinkley!* (Athens: University of Georgia Press).

Jefferson, Thomas (1984) *Thomas Jefferson: Writings* (New York: Library of America).

Jenkins, J. Craig (1985) *The Politics of Insurgency: The Farm Worker's Movement in the 1960s* (New York: Columbia University Press).

Jenkins, J. Craig (1989) "Social Movement Philanthropy and American Democracy," pages 292–314 in Richard Magat (ed.), *Philanthropic Giving* (New York: Oxford University Press).

Jennings, M. Kent (1987) "Residues of a Movement," *American Political Science Review* 81 (June): 367–382.

Jennings, M. Kent and Richard Niemi (1981) *Generations and Politics* (Princeton, NJ: Princeton University Press).

Joas, Hans (1990) "The Democratization of Differentiation: On the Creativity of Collective Action," pages 182–201 in Jeffrey Alexander and Piotr Sztompka (eds.), *Rethinking Progress: Movements, Forces and Ideas at the End of the Twentieth Century* (Boston: Unwin Hyman).

Johnson, Donald, and Kirk Porter (1973) *National Party Platforms, 1840–1972*, 5th edition (Champaign: University of Illinois Press).

Jones, Charles O. (1995) "A Way of Life and Law," *American Political Science Review* 89 (March): 1–9.

Joseph, Paul (1993) *Peace Politics* (Philadelphia: Temple University Press).

Kanter, Rosbeth (1972) "Commitment and the Internal Organization of Millennial Movements," *American Behavioral Scientist* 16 (November–December): 219–243.

Katz, Milton (1986) *Ban the Bomb: A History of SANE, the Committee for a Sane Nuclear Policy* (New York: Praeger).

Keller, Mark (1982) "On Defining Alcoholism," pages 119–133 in Edith Gomberg, Helene White, and John Carpenter (eds.), *Alcohol, Science and Society Revisited* (Ann Arbor, MI, and New Brunswick, NJ: University of Michigan Press and Rutgers Center of Alcohol Studies).

Kempton, Willett, James Boster, and Jennifer Hartley (1995) *Environmental Values in American Culture* (Cambridge, MA: MIT Press).

Kielbowicz, Richard, and Clifford Scherer (1986) "The Role of the Press in the Dynamics of Social Movements," pages 71–96 in Kurt Lang and Gladys Engel Lang (eds.), *Research in Social Movements, Conflict and Change*, volume 9 (Greenwich, CT: JAI Press).

Kilpatrick, James (1962) *The Southern Case for School Segregation* (n.p.: Crowell-Collier).

Kinder, Donald, and David Sears (1981) "Prejudice and Politics: Symbolic Racism versus Threats to the Good Life," *Journal of Personality and Social Psychology* 40 (March): 414–431.

Kingdon, John (1984) *Agendas, Alternatives and Public Policies* (Boston: Little, Brown).

Kitschelt, Herbert (1986) "Political Opportunity Structures and Political Protest: Antinuclear Movements in Four Democracies," *British Journal of Political Science* 16 (January): 57–85.

Klandermans, Bert (1984) "Mobilization and Participation: Social-Psychological Expansions of Resource Mobilization Theory," *American Sociological Review* 49 (October): 583–600.

Klandermans, Bert (1988) "The Formation and Mobilization of Consensus," pages 173–196 in Bert Klandermans, Hanspeter Kriesi, and Sidney Tarrow (eds.), *From Structure to Action: International Social Movement Research*, volume 1 (Greenwich, CT: JAI Press).

Klandermans, Bert (1992) "The Social Construction of Protest and Multiorganizational Fields," pages 77–103 in Aldon Morris and Carol Mueller (eds.), *Frontiers in Social Movement Theory* (New Haven, CT: Yale University Press).

Klein, Ethel (1984) *Gender Politics* (Cambridge, MA: Harvard University Press).

Knafla, Leonore, and Christine Kulke (1987) "15 Jahre neue Frauenbewegung," pages 89–108 in Roland Roth and Dieter Rucht (eds.), *Neue soziale Bewegungen in der Bundesrepublik Deutschland* (Frankfurt: Campus).

Knopf, Jeff (1997) "The Nuclear Freeze Movements' Effect on Policy," in Thomas Rochon and David Meyer (eds.), *Coalitions and Political Movements: The Lessons of the Nuclear Freeze* (Boulder, CO: Lynne Rienner).

Kornhauser, William (1958) *The Politics of Mass Society* (Glencoe, IL: Free Press).

Kunen, James Simon (1968) *The Strawberry Statement: Notes of a College Revolutionary* (New York: Random House).

Kyvig, David (1979) *Repealing National Prohibition* (Chicago: University of Chicago Press).

Laitin, David (1988) "Political Culture and Political Preferences," *American Political Science Review* 82 (June): 589–593.

Lazerow, Jama (1993) "Spokesmen for the Working Class: Protestant Clergy and the Labor Movement in Antebellum New England," *Journal of the Early Republic* 13 (Fall): 323–354.

Lee, Shu-Ching (1970) "Group Cohesion and the Hutterian Colony," pages 165–178 in Tamotsu Shibutani (ed.), *Human Nature and Collective Behavior* (Englewood Cliffs, NJ: Prentice-Hall).

Lee, Taeku (1996) "'Dear Mr. President . . .' Constituency Mail on the Civil Rights Movement as Public Opinion, 1948–1965." Paper presented at the meetings of the American Political Science Association, San Francisco.

Levine, Harry Gene (1978) "The Discovery of Addiction: Changing Conceptions of Habitual Drunkenness in America" *Journal of Studies on Alcohol* 39 (1): 143–173.

Lewis, Jay (1982) "The Federal Role in Alcoholism Research, Treatment and Prevention," pages 385–401 in Edith Gomberg, Helene White, and John Carpenter (eds.), *Alcohol, Science and Society Revisited* (Ann Arbor, MI, and New Brunswick, NJ: University of Michigan Press and Rutgers Center of Alcohol Studies).

Lijphart, Arend (1984) *Democracies: Patterns of Majoritarian and Consensus Government in Twenty-one Countries* (New Haven, CT: Yale University Press).

Lindblom, Charles (1990) *Inquiry and Change: The Troubled Attempt to Understand and Shape Society* (New Haven, CT: Yale University Press).

Lipsky, Michael (1968) "Protest as a Political Resource," *American Political Science Review* 62 (December): 1144–1158.

Lo, Clarence (1992) "Communities of Challengers in Social Movement Theory," pages 224–247 in Aldon Morris and Carol Mueller (eds.), *Frontiers in Social Movement Theory* (New Haven, CT: Yale University Press).

Lough, John (1960) *An Introduction to Eighteenth Century France* (London: Longmans).

Lough, John (1982) *The Philosophes and Post-Revolutionary France* (New York: Oxford University Press).

Lough, John (1987) *France on the Eve of the Revolution: British Travellers' Observations, 1763–1788* (Chicago: Dorsey).

MacKinnon, Catherine (1979) *Sexual Harassment of Working Women* (New Haven, CT: Yale University Press).

MacKuen, Michael, and Steven Coombs (1981) *More Than News: Media Power in Public Affairs* (Beverly Hills, CA: Sage).

Magat, Richard (1979) *The Ford Foundation at Work* (New York: Plenum Press).

Magdol, Edward (1986) *The Antislavery Rank and File* (New York: Greenwood Press).

Mansbridge, Jane (1986) *Why We Lost the ERA* (Chicago: University of Chicago Press).

Marshall, Anna-Maria (1996) "The Political Dimensions of Rights Consciousness: Women Confronting Sexual Harassment." Paper presented at the annual meeting of the Law and Society Association.

Marwell, Gerald, Michael Aiken, and N. J. Demerath III (1987) "The Persistence of Political Attitudes among 1960s Civil Rights Activists," *Public Opinion Quarterly* 51 (Fall): 359–375.

Marwell, Gerald and Pamela Oliver (1993) *The Critical Mass in Collective Action* (New York: Cambridge University Press).

Marx, Karl, and Friedrich Engels (1848) *The Communist Manifesto*. Reprinted on pages 469–500 in Robert C. Tucker (1978), *The Marx-Engels Reader*, 2nd edition (New York: Norton).

Mathews, Donald, and Jane De Hart (1990) *Sex, Gender, and the Politics of the ERA* (New York: Oxford University Press).

Matthews, Donald, and James Prothro (1966) *Negroes and the New Southern Politics* (New York: Harcourt, Brace and World).

Mayer, William (1992) *The Changing American Mind: How and Why American Public Opinion Changed between 1960 and 1988* (Ann Arbor: University of Michigan Press).

Mayhew, David (1991) *Divided We Govern* (New Haven, CT: Yale University Press).

McAdam, Doug (1982) *Political Process and the Development of Black Insurgency, 1930–1970* (Chicago: University of Chicago Press).

McAdam, Doug (1986) "Recruitment to High-Risk Activism: The Case of Freedom Summer," *American Journal of Sociology* 92 (July): 64–90.

McAdam, Doug (1989) "The Biographical Consequences of Activism," *American Sociological Review* 54 (October): 744–760.

McAdam, Doug (1994) "Culture and Social Movements," pages 36–57 in Enrique Laraña, Hank Johnston, and Joseph Gusfield (eds.), *New Social Movements: From Ideology to Identity* (Philadelphia: Temple University Press).

McAdam, Doug (1995) "Initiator and Spin-off Movements: Diffusion Processes in Protest Cycles," pages 217–239 in Mark Traugott (ed.), *Repertoires and Cycles of Collective Action* (Durham, NC: Duke University Press).

McCarthy, John, Clark McPhail, and Jackie Smith (1996) "Images of Protest: Dimensions of Selection Bias in Media Coverage of Washington Demonstrations, 1982 and 1991," *American Sociological Review* 61 (June): 478–499.

McCarthy, John, and Mark Wolfson (1992) "Consensus Movements, Conflict Movements, and the Cooptation of Civic and State Infrastructures," pages 273–297 in Aldon Morris and Carol Mueller (eds.), *Frontiers in Social Movement Theory* (New Haven, CT: Yale University Press).

McCombs, Maxwell and Donald Shaw (1972) "The Agenda-Setting Function of the Mass Media," *Public Opinion Quarterly* 36 (Summer): 176–187.

McCrea, Frances, and Gerald Markle (1989) *Minutes to Midnight* (Newbury Park, CA: Sage).

McKean, Margaret (1980) "Political Socialization through Citizen's Movements," pages 228–272 in Kurt Steiner, Ellis Krauss, and Scott Flanagan (eds.), *Political Opposition and Local Politics in Japan* (Princeton, NJ: Princeton University Press).

McKivigan, John (1984) *The War against Proslavery Religion: Abolitionism and the Northern Churches, 1830–1865* (Ithaca, NY: Cornell University Press).

McMath, Robert, Jr. (1993) *Populism: A Social History, 1877–1898* (New York: Hill and Wang).

McPherson, James (1975) *The Abolitionist Legacy: From Reconstruction to the NAACP* (Princeton, NJ: Princeton University Press).

Melucci, Alberto (1995) "The Process of Collective Identity," pages 41–63 in Hank Johnston and Bert Klandermans (eds.), *Social Movements and Culture* (Minneapolis: University of Minnesota Press).

Meyer, David (1990) *A Winter of Discontent: The Nuclear Freeze and American Politics* (New York: Praeger).

Meyer, David (1995) "Framing National Security: Elite Public Discourse on Nuclear Weapons during the Cold War," *Political Communication* 12 (June): 173–192.

Meyer, David, and Nancy Whittier (1994) "Social Movement Spillover," *Social Problems* 41 (May): 277–298.

Milburn, Michael, Paul Watanabe, and Bernard Kramer (1986) "The Nature and Sources of Attitudes toward a Nuclear Freeze," *Political Psychology* 7 (4): 661–674.

Miller, Arthur, Patricia Gurin, Gerald Gurin, and Oksana Malanchuk (1981) "Group Consciousness and Political Participation," *American Journal of Political Science* 25 (August): 494–511.

Molander, Earl, and Roger Molander (1990) "A Threshhold Analysis of the Antinuclear War Movement," pages 37–52 in Sam Marullo and John Lofland (eds.), *Peace Action in the Eighties* (New Brunswick, NJ: Rutgers University Press).

Montagu, Ashley (1942) *Man's Most Dangerous Myth: The Fallacy of Race* (New York: Columbia University Press).

Moore, Mark (1988) "What Sort of Ideas Become Public Ideas?" pages 55–83 in Robert Reich (ed.), *The Power of Public Ideas* (Cambridge, MA: Ballinger).

Morris, Aldon (1984) *The Origins of the Civil Rights Movement* (New York: Free Press).

Morris, Aldon, and Carol Mueller (eds.) (1992) *Frontiers in Social Movement Theory* (New Haven, CT: Yale University Press).

Nagai, Althea, Robert Lerner, and Stanley Rothman (1994) *Giving for Social Change* (Westport, CT: Praeger).

Navarro, Armando (1995) *Mexican American Youth Organization: Avant-Garde of the Chicano Movement in Texas* (Austin: University of Texas Press).

Nelson, Barbara (1984) *Making an Issue of Child Abuse* (Chicago: University of Chicago Press).

Neuman, W. Russell (1990) "The Threshhold of Public Attention," *Public Opinion Quarterly* 54 (Summer): 159–176.

Neuman, W. Russell, Marion Just, and Ann Crigler (1992) *Common Knowledge: News and the Construction of Political Meaning* (Chicago: University of Chicago Press).

Newby, I. A. (1965) *Jim Crow's Defense: Anti-Negro Thought in America, 1900–1930* (Baton Rouge: Louisiana State University Press).

Newby, I. A. (ed.) (1968) *The Development of Segregationist Thought* (Homewood, IL: Dorsey).

Nixon, David, and Randy Glean (1994) "The Clarence Thomas Hearings and Reception of Political Information." Paper presented at the meetings of the American Political Science Association, New York, September 1–4.

Nolen, Claude (1967) *The Negro's Image in the South* (Lexington: University of Kentucky Press).

Oliver, Pamela, and Gerald Marwell (1992) "Mobilizing Technologies for Collective Action," pages 251–272 in Aldon Morris and Carol Mueller (eds.), *Frontiers in Social Movement Theory* (New Haven, CT: Yale University Press).

Olson, Mancur (1965) *The Logic of Collective Action* (New York: Schocken).

Opp, Karl-Dieter (1988) "Grievances and Participation in Social Movements," *American Political Science Review* 53 (December): 853–864.

Opp, Karl-Dieter (1989) *The Rationality of Political Protest* (Boulder, CO: Westview).

Oppenheimer, Martin (1989) *The Sit-In Movement of 1960* (New York: Carlson).

Oppenheimer, Michael, and Robert Boyle (1990) *Dead Heat: The Race against the Greenhouse Effect* (New York: Basic Books).

Oskamp, Stuart (1991) *Attitudes and Opinions*, 2nd edition (Englewood Cliffs, NJ: Prentice-Hall).

Owen, Oliver, and Daniel Chiras (1995) *Natural Resource Conservation* (Englewood Cliffs, NJ: Prentice-Hall).

Page, Benjamin, and Robert Shapiro (1983) "Effects of Public Opinion on Foreign Policy," *American Political Science Review* 77 (March): 175–190.

Paul, Ellen Frankel (1991) "Bared Buttocks and Federal Cases," *Society* 28 (4): 4–7.

Peters, B. Guy, and Brian Hogwood (1985) "In Search of the Issue Attention Cycle," *Journal of Politics* 47 (February): 239–253.

Phillips, Susan (1994) "New Social Movements and Routes to Representation: Science versus Politics," pages 57–81 in Stephen Brooks and Alain-G. Gagnon (eds.), *The Political Influence of Ideas: Policy Communities and the Social Sciences* (Westport, CT: Praeger).

Piore, Michael, and Charles Sabel (1984) *The Second Industrial Divide: Possibilities for Prosperity* (New York: Basic Books).

Plater, Zygmunt, Robert Adams, and William Goldfarb (1992) *Environmental Law and Policy* (St. Paul, MN: West Publishing).

Polsby, Nelson (1984) *Political Innovation in America* (New Haven, CT: Yale University Press).

Press, Daniel (1994) *Democratic Dilemmas in the Age of Ecology: Trees and Toxics in the American West* (Durham, NC: Duke University Press).

Rabinowitz, Alan (1990) *Social Change Philanthropy in America* (New York: Quorum).

Regens, James, and Robert Rycroft (1988) *The Acid Rain Controversy* (Pittsburgh: University of Pittsburgh Press).

Reinarman, Craig (1988) "The Social Construction of an Alcohol Problem," *Theory and Society* 17 (January): 91–120.

Ricci, David (1993) *The Transformation of American Politics* (New Haven, CT: Yale University Press).

Ricoeur, Paul (1971) "The Model of the Text: Meaningful Action Considered as a Text," *Social Research* 38 (Autumn): 529–562.

Riger, Stephanie (1991) "Gender Dilemmas in Sexual Harassment Policies and Procedures," *American Psychologist* 46 (May): 497–505.

Riker, William (1986) *The Art of Political Manipulation* (New Haven, CT: Yale University Press).

Rochon, Thomas (1988) *Mobilizing for Peace* (Princeton, NJ: Princeton University Press).

Rochon, Thomas (1997) "Three Faces of the Freeze," in Thomas Rochon and David Meyer (eds.), *Coalitions and Political Movements: The Lessons of the Nuclear Freeze* (Boulder, CO: Lynne Rienner).

Rochon, Thomas, and Ikuo Kabashima (1998) "Movement and Aftermath: Mobilization of the African American Electorate" in John G. Geer (ed.), *New Perspectives on Party Politics* (Baltimore: Johns Hopkins University Press).

Rochon, Thomas, and Stephen Wood (1997) "Yodelling in the Echo Chamber: Public Opinion and the Nuclear Freeze," in Thomas Rochon and David Meyer (eds.), *Coalitions and Political Movements: The Lessons of the Nuclear Freeze* (Boulder, CO: Lynne Rienner).

Rodgers, Daniel (1987) *Contested Truths: Keywords in American Politics since Independence* (New York: Basic Books).

Rojecki, Andrew (1997) "Elite and Mass Media Coverage of the Nuclear Freeze," in Thomas Rochon and David Meyer (eds.), *Coalitions and Political Movements: The Lessons of the Nuclear Freeze* (Boulder, CO: Lynne Rienner).

Room, Robin (1982) "Alcohol, Science and Social Control," pages 371–384 in Edith Gomberg, Helene Raskin White, and John Carpenter (eds.), *Alcohol, Science and Society Revisited* (Ann Arbor: University of Michigan Press).

Rosenberg, Gerald (1991) *The Hollow Hope* (Chicago: University of Chicago Press).

Rubin, Charles (1994) *The Green Crusade: Rethinking the Roots of Environmentalism* (New York: Free Press).

Rubin, Jay (1979) "Shifting Perspectives on the Alcoholism Treatment Movement," *Journal of Studies on Alcohol* 40 (5): 376–386.

Rucht, Dieter (1990) "The Strategies and Action Repertoires of New Movements," pages 156–175 in Russell Dalton and Manfred Kuechler (eds.), *Challenging the Political Order: New Social and Political Movements in Western Democracies* (New York: Oxford University Press).

Rucht, Dieter (1996) "The Impact of National Contexts on Social Movement Structures: A Cross-Movement and Cross-National Comparison," pages 185–204 in Doug McAdam, John McCarthy, and Mayer Zald (eds.), *Comparative Perspectives on Social Movements* (New York: Cambridge University Press).

Rudé, George (1964) *The Crowd in History, 1730–1848* (New York: John Wiley and Sons).

Sabatier, Paul (1988) "An Advocacy Coalition Framework of Policy Change and the Role of Policy-Oriented Learning Therein," *Policy Sciences* 21 (2): 129–168.

Sabatier, Paul, and Hank Jenkins-Smith (eds.) (1993) *Policy Change and Learning: An Advocacy Coalition Approach* (Boulder, CO: Westview).

Sabel, Charles (1982) *Work and Politics* (Ithaca, NY: Cornell University Press).

Sale, Kirkpatrick (1973) *SDS* (New York: Random House).

Sale, Kirkpatrick (1993) *The Green Revolution: The Environmental Movement, 1962– 1992* (New York: Hill and Wang).

Scheppele, Kim Lane (1995) "Sex in der Öffentlichkeit," *Sozialwissenschaftliche Informationen* 24 (1): 58–65.

Scheppele, Kim Lane, and Jack Walker Jr. (1991) "The Litigation Strategies of Interest Groups," pages 157–183 in Jack Walker Jr., *Mobilizing Interest Groups in America: Patrons, Professions and Social Movements* (Ann Arbor: University of Michigan Press).

Schindler, Peter (ed.) (1994) *Datenhandbuch zur Geschichte des deutschen Bundestages, 1983 bis 1991* (Baden Baden: Nomos).

Schlesinger, Arthur, Jr. (1986) *The Cycles of American History* (Boston: Houghton-Mifflin).

Schneider, Anne, and Helen Ingram (1993) "Social Construction of Target Populations," *American Political Science Review* 87 (June): 334–347.

Schuman, Howard, Charlotte Steeh, and Lawrence Bobo (1985) *Racial Attitudes in America* (Cambridge, MA: Harvard University Press).

Schwantes, Carlos (1985) *Coxey's Army: An American Odyssey* (Lincoln: University of Nebraska Press).

Scott, Hilda (1982) *Sweden's Right to Be Human* (London: Allison and Busby).

Sears, David, Carl Hensler, and Leslie Speer (1979) "Whites' Opposition to Busing: Self-Interest or Symbolic Politics?" *American Political Science Review* 73 (June): 369–384.

Shabecoff, Philip (1993) *A Fierce Green Fire: The American Environmental Movement* (New York: Hill and Wang).

Shingles, Richard (1981) "Black Consciousness and Political Participation: The Missing Link" *American Political Science Review* 75 (March): 76–91.

Shufeldt, R. W. (1907) *The Negro: A Menace to American Civilization* (Boston: Gorham Press).

Sigal, Leon (1973) *Reporters and Officials* (Lexington, MA: D. C. Heath).

Sitkoff, Harvard (1978) *A New Deal for Blacks*, volume 1: *The Depression Decade* (New York: Oxford University Press).

Sitkoff, Harvard (1981) *The Struggle for Black Equality, 1954–1980* (New York: Hill and Wang).

Skinner, Quentin (1978) *The Foundations of Modern Political Thought*, volume 2 (New York: Cambridge University Press).

Sniderman, Paul, Richard Brody, and James Kuklinski (1984) "Policy Reasoning and Political Values: The Problem of Racial Equality," *American Journal of Political Science* 28 (February): 74–94.

Sniderman, Paul, Richard Brody, and Philip Tetlock (1991) *Reasoning and Choice: Explorations in Political Psychology* (New York: Cambridge University Press).

Snow, David, and Robert Benford (1988) "Ideology, Frame Resonance, and Participant Mobilization," pages 197–218 in Bert Klandermans, Hanspeter Kriesi, and

Sidney Tarrow (eds.), *From Structure to Action: International Social Movement Research*, volume 1 (Greenwich, CT: JAI Press).

Snow, David, and Robert Benford (1992) "Master Frames and Cycles of Protest," pages 133–155 in Aldon Morris and Carol Mueller (eds.), *Frontiers in Social Movement Theory* (New Haven, CT: Yale University Press).

Snow, David, Louis Zurcher, and Sheldon Ekland-Olson (1980) "Social Networks and Social Movements," *American Sociological Review* 45 (October): 787–801.

Social Policy (1991) Special Issue: "Myles Horton and the Highlander Folk School." 21 (Winter).

Solo, Pam (1988) *From Protest to Policy* (Cambridge, MA: Ballinger).

Staggenborg, Suzanne (1991) *The Pro-choice Movement: Organization and Activism in the Abortion Conflict* (New York: Oxford University Press).

Stange, Douglas (1977) *Patterns of Antislavery among American Unitarians, 1831– 1860* (Cranbury, NJ: Associated University Presses).

Stokes, Donald (1992) "Valence Politics," pages 141–164 in Dennis Kavanagh (ed.), *Electoral Politics* (Oxford: Clarendon Press).

Stone, Deborah (1989) "Causal Stories and the Formation of Policy Agendas," *Political Science Quarterly* 104 (Summer): 281–300.

Strodthoff, Glenn, Robert Hawkins, and A. Clay Schoenfeld (1985) "Media Roles in a Social Movement," *Journal of Communication* 35 (Spring): 134–153.

Sundquist, James (1968) *Politics and Policy: The Eisenhower, Kennedy and Johnson Years* (Washington, DC: Brookings).

Swidler, Ann (1986) "Culture in Action: Symbols and Strategies," *American Sociological Review* 51 (April): 273–286.

Sztompka, Piotr (1990) "Agency and Progress: The Idea of Progress and Changing Theories of Change," pages 247–263 in Jeffrey Alexander and Piotr Sztompka (eds.), *Rethinking Progress: Movements, Forces and Ideas at the End of the Twentieth Century* (Boston: Unwin Hyman).

Tajfel, Henri (1974) "Social Identity and Intergroup Behavior," *Social Science Information* 13 (April): 65–93.

Tarrow, Sidney (1988) "National Politics and Collective Action," *American Review of Sociology* (14): 421–440.

Tarrow, Sidney (1989) *Struggle, Politics, and Reform: Collective Action, Social Movements and Cycles of Protest*, Western Societies Paper no. 21 (Ithaca, NY: Cornell University).

Tarrow, Sidney (1990) "The Phantom at the Opera," pages 251–273 in Russell Dalton and Manfred Kuechler (eds.), *Challenging the Political Order* (New York: Oxford University Press).

Tarrow, Sidney (1992) "Mentalities, Political Cultures, and Collective Action Frames," pages 174–202 in Aldon Morris and Carole Mueller (eds.), *Frontiers in Social Movement Theory* (New Haven, CT: Yale University Press).

Tarrow, Sidney (1994) *Power in Movement* (New York: Cambridge University Press).

Tarrow, Sidney (1995) "Cycles of Collective Action: Between Moments of Madness and the Repertoire of Contention," pages 89–115 in Mark Traugott (ed.), *Repertoires and Cycles of Collective Action* (Durham, NC: Duke University Press).

Tarrow, Sidney (1996) "States and Opportunities: The Political Structuring of Social Movements," pages 41–61 in Doug McAdam, John McCarthy, and Mayer Zald (eds.), *Comparative Perspectives on Social Movements* (New York: Cambridge University Press).

Tate, Katherine (1991) "Black Political Participation in the 1984 and 1988 Presidential Elections," *American Political Science Review* 85 (December): 1159–1176.

Taylor, Charles (1971) "Interpretation and the Sciences of Man," *Review of Metaphysics* 25 (September): 3–52.

Taylor, Verta, and Nancy Whittier (1995) "Analytical Approaches to Social Movement Culture: The Culture of the Women's Movement," pages 163–187 in Hank Johnston and Bert Klandermans (eds.), *Social Movements and Culture* (Minneapolis: University of Minnesota Press).

Tesh, Sylvia (1993) "New Social Movements and New Ideas." Paper presented at the meetings of the American Political Science Association, Washington, DC.

Thompson, E. P. (1967) "Time, Work-Discipline, and Industrial Capitalism," *Past and Present* 38 (December): 56–97.

Tilly, Charles (1964) *The Vendée* (Cambridge, MA: Harvard University Press).

Tilly, Charles (1985) "Models and Realities of Popular Collective Action," *Social Research* 52 (Winter): 717–747.

Timberlake, James (1963) *Prohibition and the Progressive Movement, 1900–1920* (Cambridge, MA: Harvard University Press).

Tuana, Nancy (1992) "Sexual Harassment in Academe: Issues of Power and Coercion," pages 49–60 in Edmund Wall (ed.), *Sexual Harassment: Confrontations and Decisions* (Buffalo, NY: Prometheus).

Tuchman, Gaye (1973) "Making News by Doing Work: Routinizing the Unexpected," *American Journal of Sociology* 79 (July): 110–131.

Tuchman, Gaye (1974) *The TV Establishment* (Englewood Cliffs, NJ: Prentice-Hall).

Tuchman, Gaye (1978) *Making News: A Study in the Construction of Reality* (New York: Free Press).

Tucker, Robert C. (1978) *The Marx-Engels Reader*, 2nd edition (New York: Norton).

Useem, Michael (1972) "Ideology and Interpersonal Change in the Radical Protest Movement," *Social Problems* 19 (Spring): 451–469.

Useem, Michael (1973) *Conscription, Protest, and Social Conflict: The Life and Death of a Draft Resistance Movement* (New York: John Wiley and Sons).

Useem, Bert, and Mayer Zald (1982) "From Pressure Group to Social Movement: Efforts to Promote Use of Nuclear Power," *Social Problems* 30 (December): 144–156.

Verba, Sidney, and Norman Nie (1972) *Participation in America* (Chicago: University of Chicago Press).

Verba, Sidney, Kay Schlozman, and Henry Brady (1995) *Voice and Equality: Civic Volunteerism in American Politics* (Cambridge, MA: Harvard University Press).

Verba, Sidney, Kay Schlozman, Henry Brady, and Norman Nie (1993) "Race, Ethnicity and Political Resources: Participation in the United States," *British Journal of Political Science* 23 (October): 453–497.

Vickers, George (1975) *The Formation of the New Left* (Lexington, KY: D. C. Heath).

Vogler, Roger, and Wayne Bartz (1982) *The Better Way to Drink* (New York: Simon and Schuster).

Wagner, David, and Marcia Cohen (1991) "The Power of the People: Homeless Protesters in the Aftermath of Social Movement Participation," *Social Problems* 38 (November): 543–561.

Walker, Jack (1963) "The Functions of Disunity: Negro Leadership in a Southern City," *Journal of Negro Education* 32 (Summer): 227–236.

Walker, Jack (1991) *Mobilizing Interest Groups in America: Patrons, Professions and Social Movements* (Ann Arbor: University of Michigan Press).

Wall, Edmund (1991) "The Definition of Sexual Harassment," *Public Affairs Quarterly* 5 (4): 371–385.

Waller, Douglas (1987) *Congress and the Nuclear Freeze* (Amherst: University of Massachusetts Press).

Walsh, Edward (1988) *Democracy in the Shadows* (New York: Greenwood).

Walsh, Edward, and Rex Warland (1983) "Social Movement Involvement in the Wake of a Nuclear Accident," *American Sociological Review* 48 (December): 764–780.

Walters, Ronald (1976) *The Antislavery Appeal: Abolitionism after 1830* (Baltimore: Johns Hopkins University Press).

Wattenberg, Martin (1991) *The Rise of Candidate-Centered Politics: Presidential Elections of the 1980s* (Cambridge, MA: Harvard University Press).

Wattenberg, Martin (1994) *The Decline of American Political Parties, 1952–1992* (Cambridge, MA: Harvard University Press).

Weaver, David, and Swanzy Elliot (1985) "Who Sets the Agenda for the Media?" *Journalism Quarterly* 65 (Spring): 87–94.

Weir, Margaret (1989) "Ideas and Politics: The Acceptance of Keynesianism in Britain and the United States," pages 53–86 in Peter Hall (ed.), *The Political Power of Economic Ideas* (Princeton, NJ: Princeton University Press).

Weiss, Carol (1992) *Organizations for Policy Analysis: Helping Government Think* (Newbury Park, CA: Sage).

West, Cornel (1990) "The Religious Foundations of the Thought of Martin Luther King Jr.," pages 113–129 in Peter Albert and Ronald Hoffman (eds.), *We Shall Overcome: Martin Luther King Jr. and the Black Freedom Struggle* (New York: Pantheon).

Whalen, Jack, and Richard Flacks (1989) *Beyond the Barricades: The Sixties Generation Grows Up* (Philadelphia: Temple University Press).

White, Helene Raskin (1982) "Sociological Theories of the Etiology of Alcoholism," pages 205–232 in Edith Gomberg, Helene White, and John Carpenter (eds.), *Alcohol, Science and Society Revisited* (Ann Arbor, MI, and New Brunswick, NJ: University of Michigan Press and Rutgers Center of Alcohol Studies).

Wiener, Carolyn (1981) *The Politics of Alcoholism* (New Brunswick, NJ: Transaction Books).

Wilson, Frank (1993) "Political Demonstrations in France: Protest Politics or the Politics of Ritual?" Paper presented at the meetings of the American Political Science Association, Washington DC.

Winter, James, and Chaim Eyal (1981) "Agenda Setting for the Civil Rights Issue," *Public Opinion Quarterly* 45 (Fall): 376–383.

Woodward, C. Vann (1955) *The Strange Career of Jim Crow* (New York: Oxford University Press).

Yale University (1945) *Alcohol, Science and Society* (New Haven: Quarterly Journal of Studies on Alcohol).

Zaller, John (1992) *The Nature and Origins of Mass Opinion* (New York: Cambridge University Press).

Zolberg, Aristide (1972) "Moments of Madness," *Politics and Society* 2 (Winter): 183–207.

INDEX

About the Author

THOMAS R. ROCHON is Director of the School for Politics and Economics at Claremont Graduate University. He is the author of *Mobilizing for Peace: The Antinuclear Movement in Western Europe.*